D1069175

JESUIT SPIRIT
IN A
TIME OF CHANGE

JESUIT SPIRIT
IN A
TIME OF CHANGE

Edited by

Raymond A. Schroth, S. J.

James P. Jurich, S. J.   Patrick H. Samway, S. J.

Robert C. Collins, S. J.   Richard A. Blake, S. J.

NEWMAN PRESS

Westminster, Md.   New York, N. Y.   Glen Rock, N. J.

Amsterdam   Toronto   Montreal

IMPRIMI POTEST:
Edward J. Sponga, S.J.
Provincial, Maryland Province

NIHIL OBSTAT:
Joseph F. Donahue, S.J., S.T.L.
Censor Deputatus

IMPRIMATUR:
✠ Bernard J. Flanagan, D.D.
Bishop of Worcester

November 24, 1967

The Nihil Obstat and Imprimatur are official declarations that a book or pamphlet is free of doctrinal or moral error. No implication is contained therein that those who have granted the Nihil Obstat and Imprimatur agree with the contents, opinions or statements expressed.

Library of Congress
Catalog Card Number: 68–16673

Published by Newman Press
Editorial Office: 304 W. 58th St., N.Y., N.Y. 10019
Business Office: Westminster, Maryland 21157

Printed and bound in the
United States of America

Contents

General Introduction

Each man arrives at his vision of his vocation through a long, and sometimes excruciating, analysis of his own experience. A person with a sense of history or one attuned to the religious and political currents of his own time will most likely formulate his philosophy in relation to a broader historical trend and in the context of a religious system. Any Christian, for example, who feels called by grace to a life of holiness—either in the religious life or in married life—will search the Scriptures to discover the heart and spirit of Christ and try to incorporate the life-experience of Christ into his own. A member of a religious order will view his commitment in the broad context of a Christian tradition, but he will also see the world at least partly through the eyes of the founder of his institution. Still, to live realistically in a contemporary situation, an institution must constantly re-examine its founder's thought to make sure his unique spirit is not lost, and to re-adapt it to meet the needs of a civilization in constant flux.

We have collected these essays, nearly all of which have appeared in WOODSTOCK LETTERS during the past few years, because we believe that the experience and vision of St. Ignatius of Loyola offer every Christian a particular way of looking at the world. The book appears at a time when the whole post-Vatican II Church, in its various diocesan structures, in its great variety of religious congregations—many of which are founded on an Ignatian spirituality—in its missionary and intellectual apostolates and in the daily lives of individual Christians, is asking itself how it can retain the essence of its tradition and still speak relevantly to this industrialized and computerized age.

Conflicting obligations make God's will seem more inscrutable. Both the older and younger generations face a new crisis of faith. The value of some older fundamentals of religious asceticism, such as long mental prayer, long courses of training, and "blind" obedience

1

are being called into question. The inexorable surge of freedom and democracy are weakening the customary respect for authority. Form Criticism in recent Scripture studies has undermined our old excessively literal concept of the historicity of the gospels. The faithful are demanding a liturgy that meets their intellectual and emotional needs, and the poor of the world are crying for a social revolution that the Church—if it is to be true to the spirit of its Founder—must inspire.

St. Ignatius' life was, basically, the discovery, through prayer and action, of the person of Jesus Christ and the decision to continue the work that Jesus began by serving the Church in the company of his friends. In 16th-century terminology, he was fighting for his Lord to spread his kingdom over all the earth. But Ignatius' organization was flexible and highly mobile, and throughout history Jesuits have had to adapt their talents, their rites, their language and their lives to the courts of Cathay, the jungles of Paraguay, the slave quarters of Cartagena, the theological debates of Trent and Vatican II, the concentration camps of World War II, the educational needs and ambitions of the American Catholic middle class, the competition of academic research, the worker-priest movement of Europe, and, recently, the demonstrations for civil rights and world peace. It would not be difficult to find critics who maintain that sometimes Jesuits have adapted themselves to their environments either too slowly or too well. Nevertheless, the truest Ignatians have been driven both by the desire to serve the world and by the ability, founded in the Spiritual Exercises of St. Ignatius, to find God in all things.

WOODSTOCK LETTERS is a quarterly journal founded in 1872 to record the lives of the men and the histories of the houses of the Society of Jesus in the United States. It has printed letters from missionaries, documents from Rome, obituaries, book reviews and news reports, thus providing a valuable historical record and binding together a band of men spread all over the world. In recent years however, WOODSTOCK LETTERS has concentrated on more scholarly articles examining the contemporary Jesuit's progressive involvement with the world, his prayer, his formation for professional service, his living history. Many of the essays included here were influential at the recent General Congregation of the Society in Rome and they are now made available to a wider audience—with the hope that they will be helpful to priests and religious men and women who are adapting their spirituality and their institutions to current needs—to historians of religion, to every person who could profit from St. Ignatius' insights as he tries to find God's will.

RAYMOND A. SCHROTH, S.J.

PART I

Christian Life

Introduction

The essays in Part I of our collection deal with the call of the Spirit within each one of us, inviting us to a fuller Christian life. Parts II and III deal with another channel through which the Spirit communicates to us—the history of an institution founded under his inspiration and continued under his guidance to a greater or lesser degree. Part IV deals with the perennial sources of all Christian spirituality, of whatever school—Scripture and the liturgy. Part V reminds us that wherever we may hear the Spirit most clearly speaking to us—our own interior experience, religious institutions, Scripture, liturgy—the fruits of that Spirit's presence with us remain what they were for the first Christians: zeal to spread the message of salvation to all men, the preaching of the Good News to the poor, continuing struggle, reform and growth.

The third essay in Part I describes the situation of the contemporary Christian who, even as he believes, is unsure of himself, the institutions which should be mediating the presence of God to his world, and other men who claim to be the authentic voice of God for him despite their quarrels with one another. The essay is entitled "The Faith of the Priest Today," but, as Rahner himself points out, the priest's faith is no different from that of any other Christian, or at least it ought not to be different if it is to be true to today's world. God's self-revelation to us, as Rahner never tires of reminding us, is historical and incarnate. If we are going to find God anywhere at all, we must find him in the world of today. And since each "today" is unique despite its ties with the past, and since each man is unique, it is the task of each of us to seek God through the signs he gives us today. Yesterday's signs were for yesterday's men. In any age this search is a demanding task, and few succeed well enough at it to earn the title "saint," but in our day it is more difficult than ever. For if the chief of God's signs to us is the Church, we in this post-Vatican II era are trying to change the sign even as we look to it for revelation. The result is that there is no place for serenity or complacency in the faith today.

7

And how are we to search? Fortunately, Fr. Rahner is never content with a subject until he has at least sketched out the shape a theological doctrine might take on in the daily life of a Christian. He has dealt in a number of essays with the problem of the discernment of spirits and the methods of making an election (the traditional terms in the Ignatian tradition for searching out the signs of God's presence and personal call to each of us—a search to which our Christian vocation obliges us all).

Fr. Dulles has gathered the main points of these essays into two articles of his own which form the opening pair of Part I, providing us with an accurate summary of Rahner's spiritual theology and a helpful critique of its merits and inadequacies. The first essay deals with the specific problem of discerning God's will in a situation where a concrete choice is to be made. The second describes Rahner's spiritual theology as a whole, showing its roots in Rahner's philosophy of man, his views on the experience of grace, and his understanding of Ignatian spirituality in general.

According to Rahner's essay, "Ignatian Spirituality and the Devotion to the Sacred Heart," three characteristics of Ignatian spirituality are indifference, a kind of existentialist concern for the individual person, and a strong Church-consciousness. All three are virtues needed by the true reformer; but if left to grow wild, they can produce a man of rationalistic mind, calculating eye, and frozen heart —in short, a "jesuitical" man. Without love, indifference becomes unconcern, individualism becomes opportunism, Church-consciousness becomes collective egoism. But with love—the burning, enthusiastic, bold, divine-human love which is the center of authentic devotion to the Sacred Heart—the contemporary Christian can become what Vatican II urges him to be: a loving critic of himself, his Church and his world.

ROBERT C. COLLINS, S.J.

Finding God's Will

Avery Dulles, S.J.

In his analysis of the complexity of making moral decisions, Fr. Dulles explores the three times St. Ignatius discusses the election in the *Spiritual Exercises*. If the *Exercises* center around finding God's will for the individual by making an election concerning the vocation of the exercitant "by virtue of his positive individuality," then the second election seems the most significant. The correct election leaves the individual in a state of consolation; thus, the discernment of spirits is intrinsically linked with deciding one's vocation. Fr. Dulles stresses the individual's uniqueness in times of decision-making and sees Fr. Rahner's position in this matter as being overly philosophical and not emphasizing enough the Christological dimensions of the election.

In his famous lecture, *Existentialism as a Humanism*,[1] Jean-Paul Sartre undertakes to expose the inadequacy of Christian ethics. As an illustration he proposes the case of a pupil of his who, during the Nazi occupation, was anxious to decide whether he ought to leave and join the Free French Forces or stay home with his mother, who depended very much on his presence. Christian doctrine, Sartre remarks, could say nothing to this young man, torn as he was between the conflicting demands of filial devotion and patriotic generosity. No priest could settle the problem, for everything depended on which priest he consulted. In the last analysis, the student would be responsible for the choice of his own counselor, and the counselor's answer would be as arbitrary as the student's own. "I had but one reply to make," says Sartre. "You are free, therefore choose —that is to say, invent. No rule of general morality can show you what you ought to do: no signs are vouchsafed in this world. . . . We ourselves decide our being." [2]

[1] Translated in Walter Kaufmann (ed.), *Existentialism from Dostoevsky to Sartre* (New York: Meridian Books, 1963), pp. 287–311.
[2] *Ibid.*, pp. 297f.

9

Sartre here expresses a growing feeling among Christians and non-Christians that in many of the truly vital decisions of actual life, universal moral norms, whatever their abstract validity and binding force may be, afford no adequate guidance. Reliance on the advice of others, moreover, cannot relieve the individual of ultimate responsibility for his own actions. It is, after all, he who decides whether to follow the directions of others, and whose directions he shall follow.

The problem of moral decision, always difficult, has become enormously more complex for men of our time. In previous ages man lived comparatively close to nature, in a relatively homogeneous cultural environment. His field of choice was consequently narrow, and even within that field custom and tradition often played a determining role. But modern technology has to a great extent mastered the forces of nature and environment. Man lives in a culturally pluralistic society, in which a bewildering number of world views and ethical systems compete for his allegiance. Social structures are in rapid flux; venerable precedent no longer holds unquestioned sway. Modern man is anxiously groping for a method and a logic which can help him find the course of action which is right for him as a particular person in a particular and rapidly changing situation. This need is felt with special urgency by earnest Christians in the spiritually momentous decisions of their lives. How can they be assured of finding the will of God?

Karl Rahner, who makes it his business to explore the most pressing theological and religious questions of the hour, has recently turned his attention to this very question.[3] Instead of beginning with an original treatment, however, he has preferred to cast his discussion in the form of a commentary on the methods of election set forth in the *Spiritual Exercises* of St. Ignatius. The art of finding God's will for the individual exercitant is, according to Rahner, the very heart of the *Exercises*. And St. Ignatius, wrestling with this problem, fashioned a completely new technique, far in advance of his times. His very precocity, according to Rahner, has tended to obscure his actual thinking. For the commentators on the *Exercises,* unable to rise to their master's level, impoverished and deformed his thought.

---

[3] "The Logic of Concrete Individual Knowledge in Ignatius Loyola," in *The Dynamic Element in the Church* (trans. W. J. O'Hara; Quaestiones Disputatae 12; New York: Herder & Herder, 1964), pp. 84–170.

Rahner's own study, which intends to rectify this situation, is sure to arouse keen interest among all students of Jesuit spirituality. Because his argument is lengthy and involved, and at some points difficult to follow, a rather full summary and analysis may prove useful.

As a background for his own interpretation of the election, Rahner presupposes what he has elsewhere maintained regarding the individual dimension of ethical decisions.[4] He insists that there are objectively valid ethical norms discoverable by human reason and knowable to the Christian through the teaching of the Church. But it would be a mistake to imagine that all man's ethical decisions could be reached by logical inference from the general principles of natural and supernatural morality, as applied to concrete situations. The fact that my action at the moment is not determinable by general laws, Rahner insists, by no means implies that I am morally free to do as I please. This contention Rahner founds on two premises. In the first place, the living God remains free vis-à-vis his creatures, and can at any moment manifest his good pleasure in a binding manner. Secondly, the human person is not a mere instance of the species to which he belongs; he has his own positive, though ineffable, individuality. "Insofar as the same man subsists in his own spirituality, his actions are also always more than mere applications of the universal law to the *casus* in space and time; they have a substantial positive property and uniqueness which can no longer be translated into a universal idea and norm expressible in propositions constructed of universal notions." [5]

The Three "Times"

In the light of these previously developed positions, Rahner gives a strikingly new interpretation to the three "times" (or "occasions," as we might call them today) of election which hold such a crucial position in the *Spiritual Exercises*. The first time of election, as explained by Ignatius, occurs "when God our Lord so moves and attracts the will that a devout soul without hesitation, or the possibility of hesitation, follows what has been manifested to it" (n. 175). The second time is identified as one in which "much light and understanding are derived through experience of desolations and consola-

---

[4] "On the Question of a Formal Existential Ethics," *Theological Investigations* II (Baltimore: Helicon, 1963), pp. 217–34.

[5] *Ibid.*, p. 226.

tions and the discernment of diverse spirits" (n. 176). The third time is "a time of tranquillity, that is, a time when the soul is not agitated by different spirits, and has free and peaceful use of its natural powers" (n. 177).

Reflecting on these three times, Rahner maintains that they are specifically distinct, insofar as each has its own proper object. In the first time, the object to be known is a free decree of God which cannot be fathomed except through a special disclosure whereby God makes known his mind. This disclosure, in practice, comes down to a private revelation, such as we read of in the lives of certain saints—e.g., when St. Catherine of Siena, St. Margaret Mary, and others were divinely called to various tasks which they could not have discovered independently of revelation. In his discussion of the election Rahner says little about this type of knowledge, for he maintains that it is mentioned in the *Exercises* simply as a limit case, in order to show forth more clearly the proper sphere of the second time. Ignatius himself alludes only briefly to the first time, presupposing that if it is given it will be infallibly recognized, and that in any case it lies beyond the control of all methods. Rahner has given his views on the criteria and value of private revelations in a separate work.[6]

The third time of election, as Rahner interprets it, is that of Christian rationality. This time obtains, per se, when the moral goal can be recognized by reference to the principles of abstract ethics and the general moral imperatives of the Gospel and of the Church, as applied to a particular situation through normal discursive thinking. Rahner's exposition of the process by which such a prudential judgment is reached is very sketchy. His most enlightening comments on the third time come in connection with his discussion of the second, which chiefly interests him.

The per se object of the second time, Rahner maintains, cannot be identical with that of the first or the third. Thus it is not a free decree of God, spontaneously restricting the range of what is morally eligible for a given individual (first time). Nor is it the general will of God as communicated by the objective order of creation viewed in the light of faith and reason (third time). But what is left? The only remaining possibility, Rahner contends, is for the second-time

---

[6] *Visions and Prophecies* (Quaestiones Disputatae 10. New York: Herder & Herder, 1963).

election to bear on the unique vocation of the concrete person by virtue of his positive individuality. This call, which God utters by making the individual naturally and supernaturally the person he alone is, must necessarily be grasped through a perception of one's own spiritual orientations.

Before justifying in detail this identification of the second-time election with the sphere of individual ethical decisions, Rahner argues very convincingly that the second time is the usual one, at least for persons making the *Spiritual Exercises*. Since the first time is plainly extraordinary, the debate can be only between the second and the third. But Ignatius himself tells us that the third-time methods are to be used only in the event that the first or second time is not given (n. 178). This time occurs when the soul is not moved by various spirits (n. 177), a fact which is itself an unfavorable sign (n. 6). Finally, the typical theme of the Ignatian election—the choice of a state of life according to the evangelical counsels—is a highly individual matter, not deducible from the general invitation for all Christians to pursue sanctity.

In this connection, Rahner has some interesting remarks on the priestly and religious vocation. He is evidently dissatisfied with the tendency of many Catholic authors, especially since Canon Lahitton,[7] to give primary weight to objective and universal norms, subject only to the decisions of ecclesiastical authority. While Lahitton's criteria can in a certain sense be defended, Rahner wants to make it clear that no man is apt for the religious life unless he as an individual is suited to it, called thereto by the grace of God. Such a call (of which Ignatius speaks in n. 98) cannot be simply equated with good health, intelligence, and moral character; still less can it be ascertained by objective psychological questionnaires. The individual vocation can scarcely be discerned except through a process analogous to the second-time election, even though the Ignatian directives are not consciously followed. In these days of widespread—and no doubt quite necessary—vocational testing, Rahner's insistence on the personal and subjective dimension of the divine call is very welcome.

As further confirmation of his views on the primary importance of the second time, Rahner points out that even the third-time election, as Ignatius conceives it, is never arrived at by purely objective con-

[7] J. Lahitton, *La vocation sacerdotale* (Nouvelle éd. Paris: Beauchesne, 1913).

siderations. For all its rationality, it contains elements which properly belong to the other two times, especially to the second. Thus the exercitant is directed to pray in advance that God will "bring to my mind what I ought to do" (n. 180). He should choose in response to a pure love of God "descending from above" (n. 184). After making up his mind, he is to offer his decision to God, "that the Divine Majesty may deign to accept and confirm it for His greater service and praise" (n. 183). The form which such confirmation is expected to take is indicated by n. 213, where Ignatius speaks of "lights, consolations, and divine inspirations." The third time, therefore, is governed by an inner movement of the Holy Spirit, which is at work in the soul even while it is discursively taken up with objective considerations. Thus the third time is in practice a *modus deficiens* of the second.

Rahner's view that the second-time election is the ordinary one is, I think, convincing, even though some very distinguished authorities on the *Spiritual Exercises* are of the opinion that Ignatius himself preferred the third time.[8] But perhaps Rahner, in his zeal to find distinct formal objects for the three times, overemphasizes the objectivity of the third time, taken in itself. If it were a matter of mechanically applying evident precepts of the natural or positive law, there would hardly be room for an election at all. But if the application depends on a more or less delicate prudential judgment, the third time, in its own right, contains an element of subjectivity. Connaturality and discretion belong to it per se, and not merely, as Rahner contends, insofar as it participates in the second time. Rahner, having defined the third time almost rationalistically, is then forced to add that Ignatius fails to apply it in its purity.

Discernment of Spirits

A very important feature of Rahner's study, to which we may now turn our attention, is his explanation of the role of discernment of spirits in the second-time election. As is well known, Ignatius took over from the patristic and medieval tradition the idea that God, angels, and demons more or less regularly invade the human con-

[8] For example, Erich Przywara, S.J., holds that Ignatius preferred the third time as being more humble. *Deus Semper Maior,* II (Freiburg i. B.: Herder, 1939), p. 189.

sciousness, producing virtuous or sinful inclinations.[9] In order to identify the source of these impulses, discernment is needed. St. Ignatius, building on this received doctrine, applied the techniques of discernment to the election. This was his proper contribution.

But the whole enterprise of *discretio spirituum* strikes the modern man as highly dubious. Modern science attributes to physical and psychic causes most of the impulses formerly ascribed to these supernatural agencies. The modern reader is compelled to "demythologize" the Ignatian doctrine, at least to some extent. Can the essential still be salvaged? Rahner is convinced that it can.

On the basis of his own philosophical anthropology, Rahner assumes that the human person, while endowed with positive individuality, cannot know himself in his uniqueness by express conceptual knowledge. But in considering the world about him he obtains an implicit, concomitant knowledge of himself as a spiritual subject. This self-perception affords a point of insertion for the call of God, which reaches each man as an individual through the graces given to him.

Rahner vigorously maintains that grace, as a spiritual reality, is experienced as an element in consciousness. But it is not so clearly experienced as to enable us, by simple introspection, to identify it as such. How then can we single out the impulses which are truly from God, in order to follow them? This is the crux of the problem in the second-time election.

By careful study of the Ignatian texts Rahner thinks it possible to find a privileged type of consolation which is incontrovertibly divine in origin, which can then be applied as a criterion and prototype of all other movements of grace. This Rahner discovers in the second and eighth rules of discernment for the second week (nos. 330, 336). Such self-validating consolation is described in terms of two attributes, the one negative, the other positive. On the negative side, Ignatius calls it *"sine causa praecedente,"* i.e., "without any previous perception or knowledge of any subject by which the soul might be led to such a consolation through its own acts of intellect and will" (n. 330). On the positive side, the soul finds itself "wholly drawn to the love of His Divine Majesty" (*ibid.*).

[9] On the earlier history of the discernment of spirits see particularly: Hugo Rahner, S.J., " 'Werdet kundige Geldwechsler'—Zur Geschichte der Lehre des heiligen Ignatius von der Unterscheidung der Geister," in Friedrich Wulf, S.J. (ed.), *Ignatius von Loyola* (Würzburg, 1956), pp. 301–41. Also the article "Discernement des esprits" in *Dictionnaire de spiritualité* 3, cols. 1222–91.

But these attributes themselves give rise to difficulties. The expression *"sine causa praecedente,"* as Rahner recognizes, has been traditionally expounded as a sudden experience whose divine origin is clear inasmuch as God alone can act immediately on the will. Modern depth psychology, however, knows of apparently sudden experiences which have been under preparation for a considerable time in the subconscious. Mere suddenness and unexpectedness, then, can hardly afford solid evidence of a special intervention of God.[10] Against the majority of commentators, therefore, Rahner proposes an original interpretation of this self-validating type of consolation, which he thinks more consonant with the mind of Ignatius himself. The main feature, in this theory, would be the positive one, scil., that the soul finds itself wholly drawn to the love of God. This experience, according to Rahner, is the same as that described in Ignatius' famous letter to Sister Teresa Rejadella: "The Lord himself moves our soul and constrains us as it were to this or that action by making our soul wide open. That is to say, he begins to speak within us without any sound of words, he draws up the soul wholly to his love and gives us a sense of himself, so that even if we wished, we could not resist. . . ." In this description no mention is made of suddenness or surprise. When Ignatius says "without words," he must certainly mean without any concept which could be an occasion for this divine attraction.

From all this Rahner concludes that the phrase "without preceding cause" in the rules of the second week means, in effect, without conceptual object. If one asks with Suarez, *"Si enim nihil obiectum est, quid amabitur aut de quo laetabimur?"* Rahner replies, in line with his own existential epistemology, that God is non-objectively present in consciousness, somewhat in the same fashion as we are interiorly present to ourselves. According to Rahner man has in all his conscious acts an indistinct awareness of God as transcendent horizon, but this awareness does not ordinarily emerge into express consciousness.

[10] In confirmation of Rahner's observations on this point one may cite the remarks of W. W. Meissner, S.J., who has recently scrutinized the rules for discernment in the light of contemporary psychoanalytic ego-psychology. The view that "consolation without any preceding cause" is an effect of grace, he points out, is "at least questionable since the effect could be attributed to purely natural causes working through unconscious motivation." "Psychological Notes on the Spiritual Exercises—III," *Woodstock Letters* 93 (1964) 180; reprint edition, p. 70.

Pure consolation arises when this consciousness becomes express. The soul at such moments "is inflamed with love for its Creator and Lord, and, as a consequence, can love no creature on the face of the earth for its own sake, but only in the Creator of them all" (n. 316). Even this consolation, however, can be realized in various degrees. Short of the level of properly mystical experience, it can happen that finite objects present in consciousness become, as it were, transparent, and practically fade out before the transcendence of God. In such an experience no deception is possible. The content is immediately given. Since nothing finite can make itself present as infinite, the divine origin of the consolation is indubitable.

Further Questions

Here again, as at so many points in this essay, the reader is amazed at the success with which Rahner can use his own existential Thomism to illuminate problems that arise out of the Ignatian texts. It may be conceded that if we are in truth immediately conscious of the divine, then God himself is really present within us. But if anything is to follow as regards the election, it seems necessary to show that this experience is a free and gracious self-communication of God, rather than a Promethean act whereby man consciously confronts the divine ground of his own being. Is there such a thing as natural mysticism, and would it sufficiently explain the type of consolation here described? If the answers to these questions are affirmative, it would seem that indulgence in such consolation might at times be actually contrary to the will of God.

Rahner in this essay does not answer these difficulties with all clarity. But in another brief article, thus far available only in German, he has some very helpful things to say.[11] He points out that the Christian experience of transcendent joy is wont to come at moments of self-renunciation and that it attracts the soul to poverty, humility, suffering and even martyrdom. God is apprehended as a nameless and ineffable blessedness, almost as a non-entity. To find fullness in emptiness, life in death, and delight in sharing the chalice of Christ is not given to man, at least in the long run, apart from the free commitment of faith. The attraction is so patently from above that the believer can only acknowledge it with deepest gratitude. At such mo-

---

[11] "Über die Erfahrung der Gnade," *Geist und Leben* 27 (1954), 460–62; reprinted in *Schriften zur Theologie* 3 (4th ed., Einsiedeln, 1961), pp. 105–10.

ments we Christians know that the Holy Spirit himself is at work; we experience the hour of grace.

But once we have granted that this "uncaused" consolation is self-validating as the gift of God, there still remains the task of applying it to the election. How are we to establish a positive connection between the proposed course of action and the transcendent God in whom the soul finds its blessedness?

A full discussion of this question would involve a detailed treatment of the various rules of consolation and desolation for the first and second weeks, which Rahner does not attempt within the limits of this study. He is content to set forth the fundamental idea which underlies the second-time election. This he finds to consist in a basic affinity between the person, as gratuitously drawn in pure openness to God, and the possible object of his choice. The right decision for a particular individual will be that which leaves intact the consolation of pure union, and even intensifies it, rather than one which weakens or destroys it.

The ultimate decision in a second time—and to some extent in the third time, insofar as this participates in the second—depends upon the perdurance of the effects of pure consolation when the mind is focussed on the matter of the election. This perdurance is discovered by a process of prolonged experimentation, examples of which may be found in the *Spiritual Diary* of Ignatius. Often enough the compatibility of the object of choice with the soul in its total self-donation will best appear from a kind of "play-acting" in which the exercitant imaginatively places himself within the situation which he is thinking of entering (cf. nn. 186–87). By a concrete logic of this kind the subject can eventually judge whether the prospective choice so harmonizes with his own inner religious orientation that he experiences "peace, tranquillity, and quiet" (n. 333).

The method of discernment of spirits is thus closely related to what Rahner calls the "fundamental formula of Ignatian spirituality" —the finding God in all things. This, in Rahner's view, is simply "the persistent putting into practice of that supernatural concrete logic of discovering the will of God through the experimental test of consolation." The affective logic of the second-time election, therefore, is inseparably connected with the characteristically Ignatian synthesis of contemplation and action which has always been a mark of Jesuit spirituality.

At the close of his essay Rahner raises the question whether an individual who is not a suitable candidate for the second week of the *Exercises* has any means of discovering what is for him the existential will of God. Must he be content to follow the general prescriptions of the moral law as applied to the situations in which he is placed? Rahner replies, quite convincingly, that just as many persons speak prose without knowing what prose is, and engage in syllogistic reasoning without having studied formal logic, so too they may apply the concrete logic of the existential choice without being able to grasp its principles in the abstract. The pious but unsophisticated Christian, when confronted with an important religious decision of a personal nature, normally ponders it for some time. At the end he opts for what inwardly satisfies him; he selects a calling which satisfies what he vaguely feels to be his own higher impulses; he embraces a state in which he would feel spiritually at home. The standard is therefore one of congruence with a man's deepest religious attitudes. Thus the methods of election in the *Spiritual Exercises* are only an explicit and technical statement of what the normal conscientious Christian instinctively applies in cruder form.

All in all, Rahner's exposition of the Ignatian existential logic is a most impressive contribution to the literature on the election. His entire treatment is governed by a lively sense of the concerns and presuppositions of contemporary man. His argument proceeds through a series of systematic "reductions" which are startling in their illuminative power. Having first reduced the *Spiritual Exercises* to the election, he then proceeds to reduce the election to the "second time," and the second-time election to the rules of discernment for the second week. Finally he shows that these rules themselves can be reduced to the "first principle" of pure consolation, which is self-validating. A further remarkable feature of Rahner's discussion is his ability to clear up a whole series of problems by appealing to his own philosophical anthropology, including his metaphysic of knowledge and his existential ethic. Rahner's answers will be convincing to those who accept his fundamental philosophical and theological positions. To those as yet uncommitted, the fact that he can apply his philosophical theses so successfully to the Ignatian logic of the election will seem to tell strongly in favor of the theses themselves.

Program for Future Work

As so often happens in Rahner's writings, this essay, notwithstanding its length and density, is not so much a completed piece as a sketch of an immense program of future work. It leaves abundant scope for other spiritual theologians who may wish to delve into questions which Rahner treats insufficiently.

For one thing, Rahner is content to move in a very rarified atmosphere of theory. He is interested in constructing a theoretical apologia for the Ignatian logic of discernment but leaves the problem of its concrete application almost untouched. In applying the logic, I would suggest, the exercitant rarely needs to verify that he has experienced the pure and self-authenticating consolation which forms the heart of Rahner's theory.[12] By following the "rules of thumb" given in Ignatius' numerous directions, one can often obtain very satisfactory results. A man quite incapable of justifying the rules on the theoretical plane may be a master in applying them in practice— and the converse is also true.

In connection with the application of the Ignatian rules, it seems worthwhile to mention a rather obvious point too often overlooked, namely, that a prudent decision presupposes accurate information about what the decision involves in the actual order. If I am convinced, for instance, that the Black Franciscans do what the Carthusians do in fact, my decision to join the former order, though otherwise thoroughly in accord with the rules of election, might well be a disaster. The technique of discernment, in its affective aspects, reveals only the harmony between my personal religious orientations and my *idea* of the object under consideration. To overlook this limitation in the method of consolations and desolations would be to risk discrediting the method itself by demanding too much from it. Too often people imagine that the method dispenses a man from ferreting out the facts.

[12] M. A. Fiorito, S.J. ["Apuntes Para una Teologia del Discernimento de Espiritus," *Ciencia y Fe* 19 (July–Dec., 1963) 401–15] remarks on the danger that Rahner's theory could in practice limit the use of the rules of election to persons sufficiently advanced in the spiritual life to recognize the non-objective experience which Rahner describes. He rightly calls attention to the importance of supplementing Rahner's theoretical analysis by a detailed study of the *praxis* of the election. For a major contribution to this field see Gaston Fessard, S. J., *La Dialectique des Exercices Spirituels de S. Ignace de Loyola* (Paris: Aubier, 1956), chap. 4.

In his theoretical analysis of the Ignatian doctrine, Rahner's contribution is mainly on the philosophical side. But there are a number of points which seem to call for a more strictly theological treatment lest the thought of Ignatius should be deformed. Even though it be true that pure transcendence is self-authenticating, I should doubt that a philosophical maxim of this kind is the true key to the Ignatian doctrine of consolation. He takes his stand simply and surely on the ground of faith. He knows that God calls us to eternal happiness, and he finds in the inner experience of spiritual joy an unmistakable foretaste of this blessedness. A theology of Christian joy—has anyone undertaken to write such a thing?—would doubtless show that grace, as the *primitiae gloriae,* tends by its very nature to refresh the soul with peace. Rahner's philosophical insights could no doubt be confirmed and deepened by a more theological approach to the phenomenon of consolation.

A final area where Rahner's essay seems deficient is its failure to accentuate the Christological dimension of the Ignatian election. The method described in the *Exercises* requires that the decision be made in the course of a series of meditations on the life of Christ. In such an atmosphere the exercitant will be secure against making a choice simply on the basis of what suits his natural temperament. Viewing his own existence with the eyes of faith in relation to Christ as his leader and exemplar, a man will feel most powerfully the dynamisms imparted from on high. In the light of Christ he will be able to sense most surely whether God is calling him to work out his holiness by developing his natural talents or perhaps by sacrificing certain natural possibilities in order to be more perfectly conformed to his crucified Lord.

The role of Christ in the *Exercises,* as August Brunner has remarked,[13] is not simply to provide a superlative example of the virtues which we seek. He constitutes a concrete, living, personal norm. As the absolute self-mediation of the divine, he comes to us embodying the love of God in visible form and evoking our own response of love. Communion with him, achieved through meditation on his attitudes and deeds, enkindles similar attitudes in us. At the moment of the election the exercitant should be able to say

[13] "Die Erkenntnis des Willens Gottes nach den Geistlichen Übungen des hl. Ignatius von Loyola," *Geist und Leben* 30 (1957) 199–222. The following few sentences are heavily influenced by the last section of this incisive article.

with Paul, "It is no longer I that live, but Christ lives in me" (Gal. 2:20). This spiritual companionship with Christ actuates our highest spiritual potentialities and prepares us to give new historical realization to Christ's own life of obedience, worship, and service. The discernment of spirits, then, is not simply a matter of viewing the object of the election in the light of my own spiritual inclinations; even more importantly, it demands reference to Christ as the living concrete norm. The right decision is the one which will best enable me to reenact Christ's own decisions within his body, which is the Church.

Rahner's brilliant essay on the Ignatian logic, with its heavily philosophical emphasis, seems to demand completion through greater attention to these theological points. Such a development, I believe, would not contradict the principal conclusions of this essay. It could advantageously incorporate much that Rahner himself has said in other articles concerning the mysteries of the life of Jesus and the ecclesial dimension of all authentic spirituality. Even as it stands, in all its incompleteness, Rahner's study of the Ignatian election is a major breakthrough in the theology of the *Spiritual Exercises*.

The Ignatian Experience as Reflected in the Spiritual Theology of Karl Rahner

Avery Dulles, S.J.

Rahner's theology, intimately linked with religious experience and the spiritual life, has its deep roots in Christ and is exemplified by the saints who responded to Christ in their own way. Rahner seeks to unite all the elements of theology—the created and the uncreated, the sacramental and the personal, the ecclesial and the individual, the sacred and the secular, the institutional and the charismatic—in order to see grace as opening up the person to God's love. The concept of the contemplative in action shows that the Ignatian orientation is an affirmation of human values and an attachment to what is helpful in attaining perfection. Ultimately, the focal point of the spiritual life is Christ on the cross who died and rose from the dead and thus gave life to mankind. (This article first appeared in *Philippine Studies*, 1965.)

Karl Rahner is famed primarily as a speculative theologian. On the assumption that doctrinal and spiritual theology are distinct disciplines, we might be inclined to think that his spirituality should be sought first of all in his popular devotional writings. A careful study of his volumes of sermons and prayers will surely repay the effort, but it would not be the best place to begin if one wished to grasp his conceptions of the spiritual life. For with Rahner theology and spirituality are not two separable quantities. He deliberately and on principle refuses to divide either from the other. "A theological statement," he maintains, "is a statement that carries one into mystery." [1]

---

[1] "Was ist eine dogmatische Aussage?", *Schriften zur Theologie* V (Einsiedeln: Benziger, 1962), p. 72.

In all genuinely theological or dogmatic discourse the conceptual content must point beyond itself to the incomprehensible reality of God himself—of God whose self-communication is the tremendous reality we call grace. Neither God nor his self-communication can be adequately represented in conceptual thought and statements. If the theologian is not to misrepresent the content of his speech, he must somehow manage to "conjure up the gracious experience of the absolute mystery itself." [2] This experiential component must be present not only in preaching but in the most academic study of theology. Even in the seminary, Rahner declares, the student must be made to see "that he will not have truly mastered his subject until his reflections become a genuine religious experience for him." [3] For Rahner, therefore, theology is intimately bound up with religious experience and with the spiritual life.

To provide a framework for the precise questions which will concern us in this paper, it seems best to begin with some general features of Rahner's spiritual doctrine. Like his theology as a whole, it is multidimensional. It is integrally human, Christian, and Catholic—as vast and diversified, one might almost say, as the reality of God's encounter with man.

From one point of view Rahner's spirituality might be called theocentric, for it has its beginning and end in the ineffable God who dwells in light inaccessible, who is infinitely greater than all our words and ideas about him. At the same time it is Christocentric because Christ, in Rahner's view, is the one unrepeatable and unsurpassable realization of the deepest obediential potency by which human nature is defined—the potency to be raised to personal union with the godhead. All spiritual life is for Rahner a partial re-enactment, on a lower plane, of what happened once and for all in Jesus as the Incarnate Word. All authentic piety is therefore an *imitatio Christi:* not in a mechanical or servile way but in a free and original way proportioned to one's authentic self and situation. The mysteries of the life of Christ—not simply (Rahner insists) his cross and resurrection but all the constitutive acts of his earthly existence—have inexhaustible value as exemplary and efficacious causes of our redemption.

The white light of Christ's redeeming activity is broken down for

---

[2] *Ibid.,* p. 74.
[3] "Über die theoretische Ausbildung künftiger Priester heute," *Stimmen der Zeit* 175 (1964–65) 192–93.

us and applied in various historical contexts in the lives of the saints. They serve to mediate to us something of the exemplary power of the redemption, and point the way to new and creative realizations of Christian sanctity. The saint is one who follows faithfully and yet in a profoundly original way, under the leading of the Holy Spirit, the path marked out by Christ. What is here said of the saints in general applies most of all to the Blessed Mother, in whom Rahner sees "the most perfect instance of what it means to be a Christian," the "type or figure that manifests completely the meaning of the Church, and grace, and redemption, and God's salvation." [4] Rahner's spirituality therefore has a strongly Marian ingredient.

On the basis of his anthropology, which emphasizes the corporeal, social, and historical aspects of human nature, we could assign still other labels to Rahner's spiritual theology. We could say that it is incarnational; for the grace of Christ, as Rahner sees it, never comes to us *"senkrecht von oben,"* like a bolt from the blue; it is channeled to us through very concrete historical situations. There is also a strongly social or communitarian dimension. The Word became flesh, Rahner reminds us, in order to unite to himself a holy people. But this cannot be by a merely interior communion of souls invisibly linked together by grace. Granted the spatio-temporal quality of human life, the communion of saints must realize itself as a corporate, socially organized body. Grace always has an ecclesial as well as a Christic dimension. It comes to us through the people whom God has fashioned and tends to incorporate the recipient ever more deeply into that people.

For much the same reason, all grace is in some sense sacramental. "The seven sacraments are the seven basic embodiments of the occurrence and appropriation of grace." [5] In them the Christian's encounter with God achieves its most perfect and tangible form. But the sacraments must never be separated from the rest of life. "The 'Mass of life' is a necessary condition for the 'Mass of the Church' ";[6] and our liturgical life positively demands that we should carry its fruits into our conduct in the world.

For all his esteem of Church, society, and sacraments, Rahner

---

[4] *Mary, Mother of the Lord* (New York: Herder & Herder, 1963), p. 37.
[5] "Personal and Sacramental Piety," *Theological Investigations* II (Baltimore: Helicon, 1963), p. 126.
[6] *The Christian Commitment* (New York: Sheed & Ward, 1963), p. 148.

never neglects the value of freedom and spontaneity. The only central point of the spiritual life, he declares, is God; and that center is everywhere.[7] If we are obliged to turn toward certain focal institutions, God's grace is not restricted by these. We must be on our guard against elevating any particular devotion—were it even the Sacred Heart, the Mass, or the Blessed Mother—into an absolute of the religious life. No one method can be imposed upon all. Each individual man or woman, Rahner observes, as a unique and unrepeatable term of God's creative love, must find his path to God in a way proper to himself. The saints were strikingly unsystematic people because they were aware of the overriding greatness of God. Countless are the ways in which God may call a man to serve him in the Church or in the world. Even the most humble layman in the Church has his own special gift to make, provided he responds to the particular gifts which the Holy Spirit confers on him.

In the vast dialectic of Rahnerian theology, all these orientations are dynamically conjoined—the uncreated and the created, the Christic and the Marian, the sacramental and the personal, the ecclesial and the individual, the sacred and the secular, the institutional and the charismatic. Unless we keep in mind the breadth of Rahner's perspectives, we shall be in danger of misunderstanding the import of his particular statements about specific problems.

In the following pages no effort will be made to present a full survey of Rahner's spiritual theology. We shall confine our attention to a problem of central interest in our times, that of religious experience. After some discussion of Rahner's general doctrine on this point, we shall examine more concretely the Ignatian quality of the Christian experience as Rahner portrays it.

1. Experience in the Spiritual Life

As the opening paragraphs of this study have shown, Rahner avoids attaching primary importance to abstract concepts and propositional formulas. However valid and necessary these may be, they are, in Rahner's view, derivative and therefore secondary. They are signs which embody and to some extent communicate what has its origin in a preconceptual grasp of the real, which may in some sort be

[7] *Ibid.,* p. 140.

called experiential. Rahner's notion of experience is rich and involved, utterly removed from any shallow empiricism.[8]

In the primary act of consciousness, he maintains—that is to say, in the root experience (*Urerfahrung*) which occurs as often as one returns to the wellsprings of his mental life—man apprehends himself as such. He perceives himself as a being oriented to things and to the world, as the subject and ground of his own thinking and activity. Experience therefore includes more than what is directly presented to us as object. It transcends even the superficial consciousness of our own mental acts—that which we can clearly grasp by simple introspection. In its plentitude experience reaches also to the half-acknowledged depths of consciousness—to the indistinct, the implicit, the obscure.

On the basis of this wide notion of experience, Rahner does not hesitate to speak of an immediate experience of God. God is perceived before us or within us as an object, as a being alongside of others. He is not, strictly speaking, one of the data of experience. But in every act of knowledge God is always present as transcendent horizon, as underlying ground, as that which gives reality and intelligibility to all that is seen and known. "Conceptual statements about God, necessary as they are, live off the non-objective experience of transcendence as such." [9] This marginal experience of God— Rahner calls it a *Grenzerfahrung* (boundary experience)—is the point of departure and indispensable foundation of all religious experience in the strict sense.

But it is only a foundation. For genuinely religious experience Rahner requires something more than this tangential awareness of the infinite horizon against which all the objects of our knowledge are etched. God is experienced in a properly religious way when he draws near to man in grace—and this, not simply in the objective occurrences of salvation history, nor in the outward hearing of the Gospel or the material reception of the sacraments, but over and above all these, inwardly, in the recesses of the spirit. "Together with the word of revelation," Rahner declares, there must come "the communication by grace of an inner, conscious, non-objective dynamism"

[8] Cf. article "Erfahrung" in K. Rahner and H. Vorgrimler, *Kleines Theologisches Wörterbuch* (Freiburg i. B.: Herder, 1961), pp. 94–95.
[9] "Über den Begriff des Geheimnisses," *Schriften* IV (Einsiedeln: Benziger, 1960), p. 70.

toward the God who saves and beatifies.[10] For man to read aright the signs of God's presence in history or to accept the tidings of the Gospel, God must himself prepare our souls; he must by his inward touch elevate and divinize the absolute horizons of the human spirit. Man's initial contact with God in grace, therefore, takes the form of an immediate but non-objective experience of which we are not distinctly aware.[11]

To the question whether grace is experienced, Rahner answers with an unequivocal "yes." The idea of a purely ontic or entitative elevation, which would leave no mark on a man's conscious life, would be repugnant in Rahner's theological system. Man, he maintains, is essentially spirit—albeit "spirit in the world" (*Geist in Welt*)—and spirit is defined in terms of conscious self-possession. Grace must affect man in his spiritual existence, and therefore any bestowal of grace implies a modification of man's conscious life.

This principle Rahner boldly applies to his theology of justification and of spiritual progress. When the sinner is restored to grace, he must actively orient himself to God through repentance and charity. Sacramental justification should not be depicted as a cheaper and easier way—as a kind of shortcut which dispenses us from personal activity, or even diminishes its importance. Rather, sacraments are the visible gestures of Christ in his Church which elicit as their only appropriate response a more intense activity on our part. When a sacrament is properly received our own dispositions do change, and the inner intensity of our religious life is stepped up.

It would be a merely superficial empiricism to try to deny this statement by appealing to a contrary "experience" on the occasion of a pious reception of the sacraments. One would in that case confound certain verifiable feelings of consolation, uplift, etc., which are accessible to direct internal experience, with more profound spiritual-supernatural acts which can become more interior, personal and "existential" without this fact being necessarily verifiable by ordinary internal experience.[12]

As Rahner emphasizes in his essay on "priestly existence," this

[10] "Was ist eine dogmatische Aussage?", *Schriften* V, p. 84.
[11] "Warum und wie können wir die Heiligen verehren?", *Geist und Leben* 37 (1964) 335, 337.
[12] "Personal and Sacramental Piety" (supra, note 5), p. 131.

analysis holds also for sacraments which confer a permanent state. Ordination transforms a man and makes a total claim on his existence, imparting an inner dynamism to do priestly work.[13]

In a highly original discussion of the degrees of Christian perfection, Rahner applies this personal-existential norm to the question of spiritual progress. He refuses to admit that progress can be adequately measured in terms of habits acquired by repeated actions. Such tendencies to act in determinate patterns, he objects, can be produced or destroyed by purely mechanical means. And even the best habits have a certain ambivalence about them. They can deprive our religious actions of spontaneity and real commitment. If habits have a value, Rahner concludes, it is primarily because they liberate a man from lesser concerns so that he can devote his energies more fully to acts of greater moment.

By good habits we gradually overcome to some extent the drag of concupiscence, the moral sluggishness that ordinarily prevents us from putting our full selves into our deliberate actions. The highest perfection consists in acts of love of God and neighbor performed with the maximum degree of personal engagement. For more traditional delineations of the paths of spiritual progress—such as the purgative, illuminative, and unitive ways—Rahner proposes to substitute what he calls "the law of the existential deepening of our acts." [14] Insofar as we perceive the intensity of our own acts, growth in perfection is, in some sense, a matter of experience. But the man who is truly progressing does not count his "merits"; he is totally taken up with the love of God and neighbor.[15]

All other virtuous activities are preparations for, or expressions of, love. And love, Rahner adds, is not just an obligation alongside of others, as if it were permissible or even possible to love simply because it is commanded. Personal love is man's primary act, the fulfillment of his very being. In communion with his fellow men, who constitute this normal spiritual environment—and in no other way, —man can find both God and himself. Reversing Sartre's famous

---

[13] "Priesterliche Existenz," *Schriften* III (4th ed., Einsiedeln, 1961), pp. 285–312.

[14] "Über das Problem des Stufenweges zur christlichen Vollendung," *Schriften* III, p. 34.

[15] "Trost der Zeit," *Schriften* III, pp. 171–72.

dictum, "hell is other men," Rahner proclaims: "heaven is the other as beloved." [16]

In vain would one object: the love of God is higher than the love of neighbor. The two are inseparable. If a man *thinks* that he loves God and does not *really* love his neighbor, he deceives himself. And a committed love of the other as an absolutely accepted "thou" is already, inclusively, love of God. Traditional theology, Rahner reminds us, teaches that charity toward neighbor is itself a theological virtue—which means that it has God as its *obiectum formale*. For this reason the last judgment can be described in Mt. 25 as if rendered on the basis of "atheistic" norms.[17] "As long as you did it for one of these, the least of my brethren, you did it to me." To many seemingly pious Christians, Rahner would apparently wish to say: the godless humanitarians—"anonymous Christians"—go into heaven before you.

But must we not distinguish between natural and supernatural charity? Rahner of course does make this distinction, but he refuses to turn it into a separation. The actual world in which man lives is shot through with the supernatural. The concrete nature with which we are born is ordained by God to the beatific vision; it is a nature touched and radically sanctified by the incarnation of the Word of God. God's universal salvific will surrounds us on every side and fills the very air we breathe. Elevating grace, then, as Rahner conceives it, is not just an occasional sally of God's saving power into the created order; rather it is a permanent offer—an *"existential"*—always given and yet freely given. Because of this thesis regarding the constant presence of God's grace, Rahner inclines strongly to the opinion of Ripalda, that every naturally good act is in point of fact supernaturally elevated.

In our incessant dialogue with God as he comes to us through our human environment, we continually experience supernatural grace.

Life, as such, in the concrete, everyday life, has an inward openness towards God through that grace which is constantly being offered to it, grace which desires to become living and fruitful in the very concreteness of this life. Joy, seriousness, responsibility, daring, commitment to an unforeseeable future, love, birth, the burden of work and thousands of other aspects of life which everyone experiences have an undercurrent which comes from grace and leads into it, if they are rightly interpreted and really accepted in their true, undiluted being.[18]

But in the ordinary business of daily living the visitations of the Holy Spirit are bound up with natural and earthly values. We do not directly encounter God in his transcendence. Even in our restlessness toward God, which refuses to be appeased by any lesser good or any created reflection of him, we cannot clearly distinguish, by mere introspection, between that which is due to the limitless natural openness of the human spirit as such and that which is due to the gratuitously superadded call of God.

There are privileged moments, however, in which we find ourselves related directly to God, not simply as the crowning perfection of the world, but as a free, personal being, immeasurably above it. When we act out of pure generosity, obey out of pure submission to God's will, and sacrifice without any feeling of inner satisfaction, we begin to apprehend in all earnestness that the true meaning of life does not consist in anything this world can offer. Rahner writes eloquently of this privileged experience of the immediacy of divine grace:

. . . when we yield ourselves to this experience of the Spirit, when everything that can be grasped, named, or tasted fades away, when everything resounds with a deathly silence, when all things take on the taste of death and doom, or when everything vanishes, so to speak, into a nameless, white, colorless, and intangible blessedness, then we can be sure that not only the spirit, but the Holy Spirit, is at work in us. Then is the hour of grace. Then the apparently uncanny fathomlessness of our existence, which we experience, is really the unfathomableness of God, who is communicating himself to us; it is the first approach of his infinity, in which there are no paths to be found, and which tastes like nothing, because it is Infinity. When we have yielded ourselves and no longer hear our own voices, when we have denied ourselves and no longer control our own lives, when all things including our very being are torn from us and flung into the distance, then we begin to live in the world of God, the God of grace and of eternal life. At first this may seem strange and unfamiliar. Ever and again we shall be tempted to flee back into the accustomed and the near; indeed we shall be compelled and permitted to do so. But we must seek to acquire a taste for the pure wine of the Spirit, that which is charged with the Holy Spirit. Or at least we must come to the point of not putting the chalice away when His providence reaches it to us.

[18] *The Christian Commitment,* p. 104.

The chalice of the Holy Spirit in this life is identical with the chalice of Christ. He alone will drink it who has accustomed himself by degrees to find fullness in emptiness, success in failure, life in death, riches in renunciation. He who has learned this is capable of experiencing the Spirit, the pure Spirit, and in so doing experiences the Holy Spirit of grace. For such a spiritual liberation is not normally granted, at least in the long run, unless one accepts in faith the grace of Christ. And when a soul is liberated in this way, it is set free by supernatural grace to plunge into the very life of God.[19]

In summary, then, we may conclude that the experience of grace is for Rahner the beginning, middle, and consummation of the spiritual life. Even though we can never apprehend divine grace as an object or verify it by inspection, the supernatural experience illumines all our paths. Ordinarily we find God in and through our dealings with other men in the world. The immediacy of God is normally mediated to us through the human persons we encounter and to whom we respond in love. But God who comes to us through the circumstances of life, through our fellow men, and especially through the humanity of Jesus, surpasses all the creatures through whom he manifests himself. And therefore we can still experience his presence at moments when all worldly supports and comforts fail. When our entire being is filled with unalloyed delight, with an unmixed joy such as no creature is capable of arousing, then we can be assured that it is God who communicates himself. But these moments are never at our command. When they are graciously vouchsafed to us, and especially then, we are made painfully aware of how unprepared we are to receive the purity of God's gift. We shrink in terror from his love, and learn as Elijah did, *grandis nobis restat via.* But since the way lies open before us, let us then come and taste the sweetness of the Lord: *"Venite et gustate, quam suavis sit Dominus."* [20]

2. The Ignatian Experience

It is difficult to draw a line between Rahner's own spiritual theology, of which we have been speaking, and his interpretation of the Ignatian experience, which it remains for us to describe. Rahner makes the ideas of St. Ignatius so completely his own, and interprets Ignatius so much according to his personal theology, that the two almost

---

[19] Über die Erfahrung der Gnade," *Schriften* III, pp. 108–109.
[20] *Ibid.,* p. 109.

merge. He consciously makes use of the *Spiritual Exercises* as a theological source. He is convinced that the Holy Spirit has raised up in St. Ignatius an original, creative reinterpretation of the Christian life, which should enrich our understanding of revelation. For what follows I shall rely primarily on the articles in which Rahner is discussing such matters as: Ignatian mysticism, Ignatian piety, Jesuit obedience, and the logic of the election in the *Spiritual Exercises*.

The mysticism of St. Ignatius, as Rahner analyzes it,[21] is compounded of an absorbing preoccupation with God's utter transcendence and an astonishing ability to find him in the actual situations of life, in the here and now. How can this God, whom Ignatius knows to be immeasurably exalted above all finite things, be encountered in the busy market places of the world?

One answer might be because the world is a mirror of its divine creator. This is, of course, true enough, but it does not suffice to ground any authentic worship, let alone a Christian and Ignatian mysticism. In the absence of revelation, Rahner maintains, man incessantly tends to reduce God to a kind of *anima mundi,* with the result that piety degenerates into a form of devotion to creatures. In such a system God is shoved into the position of an idle spectator, a horizon for the divinity of the world itself.

Ignatius is far removed from such idolatrous pantheism. He knows no such smiling harmony between the cosmos and its creator, between time and eternity. His ability to encounter God in the daily affairs of life rests on a very different principle. The God of St. Ignatius, dwelling in inscrutable mystery, is free with respect to all he has created. Since God, as master of all things, can show himself at any point in history, the world loses its autonomy. It cannot be the final norm and determinant of human actions. It is necessarily subject to God, who can call man to serve him as he chooses.

God's sovereignty over all creation provides the doctrinal foundation of the principle of indifference which Rahner calls "the primary characteristic of Ignatian piety." [22] In its negative aspect this involves an acute sense of the provisional and expendable character of everything that is not God, and hence a certain "last reserve" toward all created things. Since nothing outside of God is to be sought except it,

---

[21] "Die ignatianische Mystik der Weltfreudigkeit," *Schriften* III, pp. 329–48.
[22] "Ignatianische Frömmigkeit und Herz-Jesu-Verehrung," *Sendung und Gnade* (Innsbruck: Tyrolia Verlag, 1959), p. 520.

because, and as long as God pleases, this negative indifference, unless balanced by other principles, can lead to a cold, calculating and almost cynical relativism with regard to persons and institutions. But on the positive side indifference involves a readiness of service and a positive attachment to all that God loves and desires. Ignatian piety characteristically involves a deep loyalty to the humanity of Christ and to all that represents him in the world—to Church, hierarchy, and pope. In the devotion to the Sacred Heart Rahner finds a providential antitoxin for the hardness and functionalism which might otherwise invade the Jesuit spirit. In the broken heart of the Savior, the source of that divine-human charity which animates the people of God, Rahner finds the symbol which can effectively lend warmth and generosity to the Ignatian form of service in the Church.

Indifference always looks to the future. It can never take for granted that what has been must continue to be. It respects the liberty of God and is ever ready to adapt to new situations and take up new causes as circumstances may indicate. Man lives in dialogue with God. Success in the spiritual life depends entirely on hearing his summons and responding promptly and generously. We must find ourselves and our calling in inspirations from above, and thereby find at the same time the love of the "ever greater God." [23]

How does God manifest his will to the individual? The Ignatian theology of vocations (in the widest sense of that word) is treated at length in Rahner's article on the epistemology of the election.[24] A study of this essay is central to any understanding of the role of religious experience in Rahner's vision of the spiritual life.

Needless to say, Ignatius, and Rahner with him, presuppose and explicitly declare that God's call can come to the individual only within the framework of what is permitted by the natural law and by the commands of legitimate authority. This being granted, the individual is still faced by many choices of spiritual moment. In the absence of a private revelation—something obviously rare and not

---

[23] *Ibid.*, p. 538.

[24] "The Logic of Concrete Individual Knowledge in Ignatius Loyola," in *The Dynamic Element in the Church. Quaestiones Disputatae* 12 (New York: Herder and Herder, 1964), pp. 84–170. This essay presupposes, and builds on, principles set forth in Rahner's "On the Question of a Formal Existential Ethics, *Theological Investigations* II, pp. 217–34. Cf. my previous article in this volume, "Finding God's Will," pp. 9–22.

lightly to be admitted[25]—a man may very well have to chart his course by the light of general moral principles, making a prudent assessment of the probable consequences of his acts. But there is still a third possibility: the type of choice Ignatius considers in his so-called "second-time" election. In this case the choice is made according to what is seen to be suitable for a particular individual with his unique role to fulfill.

One of the major contributions which Ignatius, according to Rahner, made to the growth of spiritual theology was his keen awareness that the personal vocation of the individual is in part constituted by his positive individuality. He must choose that which is connatural to himself with his own particular spiritual capacities and endowments. This connaturality, moreover, is to be discerned by a concrete, affective logic which Ignatius discovered and applied in his own life. This is his famous calculus of consolations and desolations.

The cardinal principle of this process of discernment is what Rahner identifies as pure consolation. This occurs, Ignatius tells us, when the soul is "inflamed with love for its Creator and Lord, and as a consequence can love no creature on the face of the earth for its own sake, but only in the Creator of them all." [26] In such privileged moments, Ignatius writes in another context, God "makes our soul wide open . . . He begins to speak to us without any sound of words." [27] Rahner maintains that what Ignatius here describes is nothing other than what we have already shown to be Rahner's own interpretation of the privileged, non-objective experience of grace.

But how is this related to the election? In the religiously correct choice, Rahner maintains, something of this pure and untarnished joy normally shines through. Since the state to which God is calling me must be one which harmonizes with my own religious make-up, including my own fundamental spiritual orientations, it will not interfere with, but rather intensify, the experience of union with God. The choice may then be made by a lengthy process of experimentation (one we find described not only in the book of the *Exercises* but in

---

[25] On the criteria of private revelations see Rahner's *Visions and Prophecies,* reprinted in *Inquiries* (New York: Herder & Herder, 1964), pp. 88–188.

[26] *The Spiritual Exercises,* trans. by Louis J. Puhl, S.J. (Westminster: Newman Press, 1951), no. 316; cf. nos. 330, 336.

[27] *The Dynamic Element* (supra, note 24), p. 152. Cf. *Mon. Ign.* I, 105.

the letters and *Spiritual Diary* of Ignatius). Through a process of "play-acting" we imaginatively place ourselves in the situation we are on the point of choosing, attempting to measure whether it is translucent to pure consolation. Such inner joy is not the same as ease or comfort; it can survive in the midst of pain, bewilderment, difficulties, privations of all sorts. By this affective logic, Rahner maintains, Ignatius made a permanently valid contribution of vast significance for the future of spiritual theology. Thanks to this germinal insight, Ignatius is in step with the most advanced personalistic thinking of our times.

Closely related to this method of discernment through religious experience is the famous Ignatian formula of "finding God in all things," which Rahner calls a "fundamental formula of Ignatian spirituality." [28] In view of the divine sovereignty, all the situations in which the individual finds himself are pregnant with spiritual possibilities. They are occasions for discovering God as he draws near to us. The Lord of History has been pleased to come to us in Christ—and in the whole human race insofar as it is, in one way or another, in solidarity with Christ. Recognizing Christ in my neighbor, I can find God in all my dealings with others. More generally, the omnipresence of the saving God implies that his grace may be expected anywhere. As Rahner expresses it in prayer inspired by both Ignatius and Ruysbroeck:

If You have given me no single place to which I can flee and be sure of finding You, if anything I do can mean the loss of You, then I must be able to find You in every place, in each and every thing I do. Otherwise I couldn't find You at all, and this cannot be, since I can't possibly exist without You. Thus I must seek You in all things. If every day is "everyday," then every day is *Your* day, and every hour is the hour of Your grace.[29]

Ignatius, with his profoundly positive evaluation of the contingencies of history, stands at the head of a new spiritual tradition. The Jesuit outlook has been characterized by what Rahner calls *Weltfreudigkeit*—an affirmation of the world and its values, a disposition to accept the achievements of culture, to esteem humanism, to adapt

---

[28] *Ibid.*, p. 155.
[29] *Encounters with Silence* (Westminster: Newman Press, 1960), p. 50.

oneself to human progress and to the demands of varying situations.[30] Since God is at work in history and present in the world, there is no need to retire to the desert in order to find him. Ignatius boldly severed the essence of the religious life from the observance of strict monastic forms. He became, in Nadal's famous phrase, *in actione contemplativus*. He may even be said to have laid the groundwork for a lay theology, in which Christian perfection is to be sought precisely through devotion to the world and its values. In his own writings on the lay state, Rahner boldly develops this facet of Ignatian piety. He stresses that the Christian should not hesitate to devote himself to worthy secular goals; to make himself almost "faceless" by doing what the pagans also do.[31] In faithfulness to the Ignatian tradition, Rahner does not hesitate to approve a type of lay Christianity which bears definite resemblances to Teilhard de Chardin, if not even to Dietrich Bonhoeffer and J. A. T. Robinson.

But this is only one phase of the dialectic. For Ignatius, as Rahner interprets him, was never primarily concerned with this world and its values. We have seen already how the principle of indifference involves a certain ultimate reserve toward all created goods. This reserve becomes, through the so-called "third degree of humility," a higher love. Ignatius assimilated into his spiritual doctrine the ascetical tradition of the old religious orders. With his companions, he bound himself to God by vows of poverty, chastity and obedience. While remaining physically in the city, he practiced a genuine flight from the world; he lived spiritually in the desert. If Ignatius held that God can be encountered through creatures, he also saw quite clearly that God has no need of creaturely service. He is greater than all the means by which we think to serve him. His grace is never obtained by our efforts alone; it remains always his free gift.

The lesson of the cross, to which Ignatius incessantly returns, is that where creatures fail, God's grace can still triumph. His power is made perfect in infirmity. The cross is the annihilation of created goodness, the squandering of human resources, the foundering of human hopes, the ultimate in terms of suffering and dereliction. Christ in his nakedness is reduced to creaturely impotence. And it is here, precisely here, that man's redemption is achieved.

Behind the apparent worldliness of Jesuit piety, there must always

[30] "Die ignatianische Mystik," (supra note 21), pp. 344–45.
[31] Über die evangelische Rate," *Geist und Leben* 37 (1964) 37.

lurk a secret devotion to the cross. In the passion Ignatius finds the supreme victory of grace. His deepest longing is to be with Christ, to wear the garments in which he was clad, to suffer and be called a fool for his sake.[32] A spirituality which spoke only of self-fulfillment, of efficiency and success, even in the apostolate, would be profoundly un-Ignatian.

Thus the piety of Ignatius, as Rahner depicts it, is in its deepest inspiration a *fuga saeculi*. No less than the desert monks, he wills to put on the dying of Jesus. He flees into the night of the senses and of the spirit in order to drink from the chalice of pure grace. The heart of the religious life consists in renunciation. The religious state is a sign of contradiction; like the cross itself, it is a scandal and folly to the children of this world. The three vows are so many ways of placarding before the world the Christian's faith in the power of the cross. By surrendering the goods of this world and the normal means by which God wills to be served, the religious makes it clear that he is not seeking, titanically, to manipulate the gifts of God. By this empty gesture of an empty heart, says Rahner, he proclaims to the world that man's highest goal lies beyond this world. He opens up a void for God to fill by the outpouring of his love and his grace.[33]

In pondering the Ignatian mystique of the cross we are by no means abandoning our theme of Christian experience. The cross is something we daily take up and daily experience. Baptism, the very doorstep of the Christian life, is already a plunging of self into the death of Jesus, sustained by the faith that it will lead to a share in the glory of his risen life. The religious may be described as one who, through devotion to the cross, deliberately undertakes to become crucified to self and to the world. He wills to be without family, without possessions, and without the option to follow his own individual will. Any such renunciation of the normal means which God has provided for human development would be, ordinarily speaking, forbidden in a purely natural order. There is no strictly rational justification for the religious state. If it is even licit, this can only be because Christ has made the cross a way of salvation, and because the Church has recognized that religious orders are "a true and practical expression of a divinely oriented existence."[34] And even so, no one can enter upon

---

[32] "Die ignatianische Mystik," pp. 335–36.
[33] "Zur Theologie der Entsagung" *Schriften* III, pp. 70–71.
[34] Cf. *infra*, "A Basic Ignatian Concept: Some Reflections on Obedience."

this path without an individual vocation from God—discovered, normally, through the discernment of spirits. But once all these conditions are verified, the life of the vows becomes a valid and fruitful expression of faith and love. "Perhaps the truly obedient man," writes Rahner, "is simply the lover, for whom the sacrifice of self-surrender is a sweet and blessed delight." [35]

Rahner's theology of the cross and of the religious life ultimately converge in his theology of death.[36] With no less right than Heidegger he can proclaim that man's life is *"zum Tode sein"* (being unto death). Each of us must die daily to himself, and with the advancing years the ratio of passivity, suffering, and renunciation may be expected to increase in our lives. As man's powers decline and his failures accumulate, the capacity to suffer becomes continually more important. As Christians we have no right to look upon privation as pure loss. Rather we should constantly tend toward it by discreet, but energetic, self-denial. Christian asceticism is an initiation into the passion of Christ, to be practiced by each according to the measure of God's grace. It is an anticipation of the ultimate self-denial which will be required of each of us, when our very existence will be engulfed in the apparently total annihilation of death.

By holy dying the Christian can at length experience, in his last and finest act, the coming of the Lord. The dialectic of affirmation and denial is crowned by a total surrender in which the Christian, freely relinquishing all, is entitled to expect that the God who waits beyond death will give him all in return. God, who lacks every definable determination, comes in the form of nothingness because he is the reality of all that is. To die is to let the world pass away—Rahner quotes from the *Didache*—in order that grace may come.[37]

Rahner's theology of the religious state takes on its full significance in the light of his theology of death. To live in religion is to remind the world that grace is not a product of worldly striving but a free gift of God, that all Christians, including those who labor to improve the world, are pilgrims; that the true center of our existence lies beyond this mortal life. Under one aspect the religious life is a prolonged rehearsal for the supreme moment which will come to all:

[35] *Ibid.,* p. 374.
[36] *On the Theology of Death.* Quaestiones Disputatae 2. New York: Herder & Herder, 1961.
[37] "Passion und Askese," *Schriften* III, p. 97.

As for ultimate obedience, which demands and silently takes everything, it will be exacted by God alone. It is the command to die the death which overshadows every minute of our life, and more and more detaches us from ourselves. This command to move on and leave all, to allow ourselves in faith to be absorbed in the great silence of God, no longer to resist the all-embracing nameless destiny which rules over us—this command comes to all men. The question whether man obediently accepts it, is decisive for time and for eternity.[38]

Rahner's particular interpretation of the Ignatian experience, and the spiritual theology which he develops from it, stand out very clearly when we compare him with another great Jesuit spiritual thinker of the twentieth century, Teilhard de Chardin. Each of them looks on the Christian life in cosmic terms. Both are convinced that human existence, and the physical universe itself, have been radically transformed by the touch of the redeeming God. For both of them God can and must be found in charity toward other men. Christianity is the religion of love, a pure human love which is by that very fact divine. Both of them have a deep devotion to the Church as the people which God is gathering to himself. They are alike sustained by the Ignatian synthesis of contemplation and action. And they perceive in the unfolding of history the stages by which God is leading mankind along paths as yet unexplored.

And yet I am not sure that the views of these two great spiritual thinkers coalesce into a single coherent synthesis. They differ radically by temperament, by training, experience, and preoccupation. The French paleontologist is thrilled by the spectacle of human progress. He is convinced that evolution must succeed; only if the phylum of love triumphs can the ultimate fulfillment come. Only the fully developed society will be capable of receiving Christ in his fullness, as he will appear at the *parousia*. Rahner, as I understand him, would not say this. He sees God as utterly free to intervene as he pleases in history or at the end of history. He can use or dispense with the service which we seek to render. Our task is to labor while it is day, for soon the night comes in which no man can labor.

To Christianity and the Church her Founder promised not only that they would endure until the end of time but, just as clearly, that his work would always be a sign of contradiction and persecution, of dire and (in secular terms) desperate combat; that love would grow

[38] Cf. *infra*, "A Basic Ignatian Concept: Some Reflections on Obedience."

cold; that he, in his disciples, would be persecuted in the name of God; that the struggle would narrow down to an ever more critical point; that the victory of Christianity would not be the fruit of immanent development and widening and a steady, progressive leavening of the world but would come as the act of God coming in judgment to gather up world history into its wholly unpredictable and unexpected end.[39]

If our efforts fail, if there are woes and defections, if we are thwarted in our obedient striving to spread the Gospel of Christ, our hearts need not be troubled. We neither have nor seek a lasting city here on earth. God is greater than either our success or our failures. He, the *Deus semper maior,* is our only lasting hope.

[39] *The Christian Commitment,* pp. 18–19.

The Faith of the Priest Today

Karl Rahner, S.J.

The faith, like God is ever old,
ever new; its timeless truth must
find contemporary expressions.

In an age of scientism and skepticism, a priest finds doubt in the confessional, in the parlor, and at professional meetings. A major challenge for the priest today is to believe in God, in himself, and in the people about him. As a theologian, a priest is unable to amass all the subtle areas of knowledge needed to alleviate the fears and doubts of the modern world. Still, he has the task of communicating God: when he sees his own limitations in communicating, he can then learn to appreciate the difficulties others experience. Fr. Rahner sees the level of palpable experience as the area where man will test God's grace. When all men, priests included, open themselves to the mystery, the grace, and the love of the trinity, then they can begin to see Christ as the root of their existence. The dynamic experience of faith should not hide behind routine formulas.

Christian faith has by its very nature a new historical form in any given age. God himself is changeless, but his call to men has a history. Therefore, it makes sense to speak of and ask about the faith *today*. Each age and each individual must realize the faith anew, and in many respects differently than it was done in previous ages. Likewise, within a given age, there are many different situations in which men live—the European and the African realize the same faith in a different form, as do the peasant and the scientist. There-

Note: This translation, by Fr. William Dych, S.J., is based on Fr. Rahner's "Der Glaube Des Priesters Heute," in *Orientierung*, nos. 19 and 20 (1962).

43

fore, we must not only believe, but we must let our faith express itself in the form that is called for by the situation in which we live. We shall single out four characteristics that should be present in our faith today.

Fraternal Faith

The faith that is called for in today's world is a faith which is deeply conscious of our relations to others who are brothers—the laity, and even unbelievers. This relation should be a dimension in our faith itself. It is of the nature of faith that it presupposes and creates a community. This relation is not to abstract man, nor to man as he should be or we would like him to be, but to man as he is today—our faith involves us with this man. But priests are in constant danger of seeing themselves as different in their faith than the laity, as having some kind of a different faith. We are God's ministers, yes, but first we are believers just as the laity are believers, with all the difficulties, risks, darkness and temptations that their faith entails. We tend to see ourselves as the administrators of God's love in his government of the world, as God's specialists and experts; we act as though we knew God's plans through and through, and that others would do well to listen to us whenever there is question of heavenly things. This attitude blinds us to our fundamental situation as believers, and prevents us from entering into dialogue with other men. Therefore, fraternal faith is the faith of the priest who is aware that he is fundamentally a member of the community of believers, that he believes with these others, and not in some superior and privileged fashion.

This calls for humility in the priest. Our faith cannot be that of the *beati possidentes,* but that of one who is constantly searching to discover what the formulas of his faith really mean, what the significance of his faith is for the fulfillment of his existence and that of his brothers. We cannot let the faith become or be suspected of being a mere traditional superstructure from another age erected over today's reality in which it has no roots.

This means that we must make our faith really worthy of belief —we must propose nothing to others which we do not live or try to live ourselves. We must be engaged in a daily battle against the routine of theological words and formulas, against moral recipes which we learned without really understanding. All theological clarity and accuracy is secondary in comparison with the strength of spirit and heart with which the final questions of life must be faced, and in which we priests have no advantage over the laity.

We must see ourselves and be seen by the laity as constantly praying: "Lord, I believe; help Thou my unbelief." There is no place for serenity or complacency in the faith today—we must be searching, seeking, striving for God, and not present ourselves as those who have found him, and with him the answers to everything. It is by entering into the world of today, and being with men in their difficulties, their anxieties and doubts, that we can bring this world to faith, and not by posing as somehow different. Our obligation and grace as priests is to come to faith from whatever situation in which the men of our world are, because that is where they have to come to faith from, i.e., the world of science, of technology, of skepticism and disillusionment. Our faith must be such that even the unbeliever cannot deny that here a man believes who is like himself, a man of today, on whose lips the word God does not come easily and cheaply, who doesn't think he has mastered everything, and in spite of all this, rather because of all this, he believes.

For Christianity is not a formula which makes everything clear, but the radical submission of myself to an incomprehensible Mystery who has revealed himself as ineffable love. If we have such fraternal faith, the unbeliever could not so easily suspect that what we are so earnestly defending is ourselves and the established order in which we find ourselves, being interested in him.

Imperiled Faith

Every age has its own task before God; the task of today's world is to believe. For today it is not this or that belief, this or that article of the faith which is called into doubt, but faith itself, man's capacity to believe, man's ability to commit himself completely to a single, unambiguous, demanding conviction. He finds himself in a world changing more rapidly than he can keep up with, a world in which new discoveries are constantly upsetting the worldview he has grown used to. Psychology has discovered unknown depths within him and astronomy has shown him the vast, limitless reaches of the universe outside of him. What new discoveries, what new world he shall find himself in tomorrow he doesn't know. All this is a threat, a challenge, a danger to faith, to man's very capacity to believe.

And this is the world in which our own faith must manifest itself; our faith is imperiled, unless we close our eyes to the world in which we are living. We must see and accept this danger if the men of today's world are to come to faith in such a situation. It is a sobering thought for any priest to realize that no single priest, no single theologian is in a position to bring forward a proof for the reasonableness of faith in today's world, for no single theologian can master all the various sciences and disciplines that would have to be mastered if answers were to be given to all the difficulties which arise from so many different quarters. What we need in fundamental theology is a global proof of the reasonableness of faith, showing that in spite of the fact that no individual can answer all the difficulties, man can and must believe.

The danger is that we shall not relate our faith to this situation, that we shall substitute theological formulas and pastoral routine for real faith, that we shall erect a thin ideological superstructure over an existence that is radically profane and secular. We must accept the fact that it is not theology, but God who protects our faith, that our weakness, even the weakness of our faith, is God's strength. We must admit the inadequacy of our formulas to express the reality we believe in. We must admit our vulnerability, we must confess the threatening emptiness of life, of everything human, including ourselves and our ideas, and we must admit this more radically than the most radical skeptic, more disillusioned than the strictest positivist. When we thus admit the dangers to our faith, we have entered into the ground on which alone the faith today can stand and from which men today must come to believe. Only this will show the world that what we believe in is not ourselves or our ideas or our capacities, but in God. This will show that man and the world are not God, that only God is God—incomprehensible mystery to which man must give himself without understanding, but in faith and hope and love. This is the beginning and the end of Christianity. Man must experience the bottomless abyss of his own existence before he can experience the nearness of the mystery that is God.

Integrated Faith

It is no longer adequate for us to present the content of our faith as a gigantic collection of propositions which together and individually are certified only from without, by the authority of the revealing

God, the fact of revelation itself being treated only abstractly and formally. This dogmatic positivism, this formal, abstract, extrinsic understanding of revelation cannot be accepted by the men of today, whose notion of God is of one who is too transcendent, too absolute, too incomprehensible for him to be imagined as having given us an arbitrary collection of propositions, alongside of which any number of others are equally conceivable. This collection of sentences man is supposed to accept without seeing that they are the fulfillment of his own existence.

Faith today will be accepted only if it is presented as the one, single, total answer of God to the one, single, total question that man in his existence poses and is. This does not in any way compromise the factual and historical nature of God's revelation, nor does it mean eliminating or ignoring any of the truths, in which we believe. We are not calling for a reduction of the faith, but a simplification and unification in which everything will be related to the central mystery, and this central mystery to the existential situation of contemporary men.

We can say that there are three fundamental mysteries in Christianity—trinity, incarnation, and grace—and these three are themselves intrinsically related to each other. We would have to bring out that in the functional trinity the immanent trinity is already given, since in Christ is given the absolute *self*-communication of God. We would have to understand man as being in the depths of his existence an openness to the mystery of God, which mystery in revelation presents itself as a forgiving and loving self-giving to men, without ceasing to be a mystery. We must develop a meta-physical, *a priori* Christology to be added to the *a posteriori* Christology of Jesus of Nazareth, the former being developed from a metaphysical anthropology, making it intelligible that the definitive self-expression of God implies the God-Man in a divinized humanity, that the absolute giving of salvation and the definitive acceptance of such self-communication of God through humanity means the God-Man of the Chalcedon dogma.

We must show that the essence of Christianity, with all its contingency and historicity, is the most self-evident of truths, for in a correct understanding of man the most self-evident thing is the absolute mystery of God in the depths of man's own existence—and the easiest and most difficult fact of our existence is to accept the self-evident mystery in its ineffable, loving and forgiving nearness. This is the essence of Christianity, for the whole of the history of salvation and the history of revelation is the divinely ordered history of man's coming-to-himself, which is a reception of the divine self-communication, having its unsurpassable highpoint (subjectively and objectively) in the person of Jesus Christ. In this way Christianity can be shown to be not just another religion alongside of many others, but the fulfillment of all religions, and only thus will the man of today in his concrete reality and thinking be existentially and psychologically in a position to accept God's revelation in Jesus Christ.

We are in constant danger in our life of faith, in our prayer and meditation, and in our preaching, of missing the forest for the trees, of not letting our faith become existential, rooted in, and an expression of, the depths of our own existence. Such an existential deepening of our faith means necessarily a concentration and simplifying of the content of our faith, not in the sense of rejection and exclusion, but in the sense of integration and putting in perspective.

We must show the man of today that he has had experiences of supernatural, divine grace, that he again and again and necessarily has had these experiences, and it is on this level, not that of conceptualization of the experience, that he first comes into contact with Christianity. This of course presupposes that we ourselves are open to these experiences, and do not remain on the level of conceptualization alone. This will show that Christianity is not essentially a system to be taught, a system whose blasé ideology evaporates before the brute facts of everyday living. This is necessary today in a special way because Christianity no longer has the support of tradition and sociological factors which it had when Europe was Catholic.

Transcendent Faith

In our philosophical and theological theism we know that God is infinitely beyond whatever else is or can be thought, that no similarity between him and creatures can be thought which does not involve a greater dissimilarity in the very similarity, that we have no knowledge whatsoever of God's essence, that God is the completely incomprehensible mystery. Is this always evident in our thinking and speaking about God? Does it make itself felt in every step we take in our theological work; or do we lose sight of the mystery of God in our preoccupation with problems about God? Are we as aware as we should be of the transcendence of God, the godness of God, the silence and the mystery of God?

We must never allow ourselves to make God one element among many others in the life of man. He is not an element in anything. He is and must remain the Absolute. God in revealing himself did not cease being ineffable mystery. We can well ask ourselves whether, when contemporary man rejects God, he is really rejecting God or simply rejecting the God that we present to him? Does his search for a transcendent God lead him to reject the God that we seem to have fitted nicely into our concepts and formulas? Is he atheist only in regard to the God who is one element in, the highest point of, and the final piece in *our* explanation of the universe? We often speak as though we knew the plans of God, were in on his councils, rather than of him to whose absolute will all is subject, who is the transcendent ground of being in all reality, nature and history, who is responsible for all that happens and is himself responsible to no one. The question, then, is whether in our speaking about God (in the overtones, not in the dogmas themselves) we are too primitive, too categorical, too univocally tied to worldly conceptions in our formulations. We must so speak that it is clear that our speaking brings not concepts and propositions, but the effective Word of the Gospel—the communication and the acceptance of God.

Presence of God in the World

If, then, "God" does not mean one element in the world and in experience alongside of many other elements, only more powerful than they, but rather the incomprehensible ground and horizon of all things, then God is that towards which our spirit tends in its confrontation with all realities: God does not enter into our horizon as an object coming from without, but as the utterly transcendent goal of our spirit. Given this transcendence of God, and the supernaturally elevated transcendence of man (granted the fact of an historical revelation and the possibility and necessity of expressing it in concepts), then our preaching always meets a man who, whether he knows it or not, whether he wants it or not, is an anonymous Christian—a man to whom grace is offered, a grace which is the self-communication of the trinitarian God in that expression of God we call the hypostatic union.

This means, and we should be conscious of this, that we do not live among pagans with no experience of grace, whose first contact with Christianity comes from without and through our concepts, but with men who are living in a supernatural context, the depths of whose existence has already been touched with grace, but who as yet have not come to discover their true identity. This consciousness should have its influence on our own faith, and be an important moment in its transcendental form. It should make our faith broad, confident, patient: the people of God live not in the midst of wolves, but among sheep who are still straying.

Such faith sees all men are brothers, whether they be believers or unbelievers, in the depths of whose being grace is working and coming to meet us when we approach from without to announce the historical message. Our obligation is to present the message in such a way that they can recognize it as the answer to the longings of their own hearts, as the fulfillment of their existence.

Such faith allows that God is bigger than our spirit, our heart, our word, our faith, our Church; it is the faith of the Church that God is greater than all else, even greater than the Church. He is greater in that he is more powerful, he is more victorious, he can enter where we cannot. Our faith, then, can always be confident, even today: God wants his victory to be not ours, to be enjoyed by us, but the victory of God, the God who wants us to believe in his victory even in our weakness and defeat. It will be a faith that is aware of the infinite difference between our words and the reality they seek to express, a reality that can be expressed only by the divine Logos speaking in the heart of man.

Thus when we speak the message and are not heard, we are defeated, but we must change this defeat into an increase of our own faith, a faith that knows that God can conquer in the defeat of his messengers; that we need God, but God does not need us. To such faith the future is secure; it is in God's hands.

Let us, then, say to ourselves and to others in our faith that God is—God, the eternal mystery that demands our worship, who while remaining mystery, gives himself to us in the most radical immediacy, corporally and historically in the person of Jesus Christ, and through his Holy Spirit in the depths of our own existence, and let this faith, and this alone, be our strength in living and our confidence in dying.

Ignatian Spirituality and Devotion to the Sacred Heart

Karl Rahner, S.J.

Any discussion of spirituality, as Fr. Rahner suggests, can easily degenerate into the realm of semantics because the dynamic experience of love is difficult to articulate. In this chapter, Fr. Rahner attempts to show that any weakness in Ignatius' ideas on indifference, on existential man, and on a Church-orientated society are rectified by devotion to the Sacred Heart. Men who are indifferent to the world do not back off into a bleak existence, but stand poised to seek God's will as it is manifested to them: they are fully disposed towards God's love. Man's individuality is preserved only when he understands that divine love reveals a unique task for him and that it is the heart of Christ which satisfies his unlimited quest for love. Should a Church-orientated person lose the reason for his activity, devotion to the heart of Christ, while not a supernatural wonder drug, can return him to the source and power of his spirituality.

First Characteristic: Indifference

Indifference here is not restricted to the leading principle that a man must be ready to do the will of God and so must be prepared to tear his heart away from a thing that would hinder him because of a divine command or divinely appointed circumstances. Indifference here means more, or else it is not at all characteristic of Ignatian spirituality. Here indifference is a sharpened sensitivity to the rela-

Note: Translation of a conference given by Fr. Karl Rahner to the theologians at Innsbruck on the Feast of the Sacred Heart in 1955. A French translation has appeared. The present translation from the original German text is the work of three missionaries in India who endeavored to remain as faithful as possible to the German text.

tivity of all that is not God: to the changeableness, limitation, imperfection and ambiguity of everything different from him, including things religious—for these last no less than others are different from him. It is true that the basic act of total surrender to God must find expression in special practices and methods, in devotions, usages, experiences, attitudes; otherwise the surrender would vanish into a mist of unreality. Yet all these expressions come under the rigorous law that all which is not God is subject to recall and replacement. For all things are subject to the free disposition of God, which cannot unequivocally be known from the thing itself or even its permanent structure, but which can be today one thing and tomorrow another. Ignatian indifference can never identify God with any particular way to him or experience of him. Always he is greater than what we know of him, greater too than what he has willed into existence. Always his holy will as the absolute criterion remains the reference point, and it is ever truly distinct from what he has willed. Thus the thing which man embraces as the thing willed by God for him is always embraced with the implicit reservation—exclusive of nothing within it—"If, while, and as long as it is pleasing to God."

Such indifference is cold, calculating and, if you will, voluntaristic. This is the source of what has often been blamed as a pragmatic rationalism, as a shallow straining of the will, as a misjudging of the deeper reaches of human nature and of its imaginative and spontaneous powers. Undoubtedly in small-souled people (and this can include Jesuits) such all too human mistakes and shortcomings can masquerade as the Ignatian spirit. But where the spirit is genuine, the things that people find hard and menacing in Jesuits spring from a deep root: the root of indifference. This spirit stems from an enormous and definitely dangerous experience of how terribly relative everything is that is not God, who alone is unclassifiable, unutterable, completely beyond our tiny experience; before whom absolutely all is small and relative. So much so that it is only in a very abstract sense (important as that is) than any absolute and immutable hierarchy holds among things; in the concrete, everything changes. A little example is to the point here. Francis of Assisi refused to shelter himself from the divine gift of tears in order to save his eyes: "Why should I," he said, "when they are nothing more than what a fly has?" Ignatius valued such mystic tears most highly, yet checked himself by what might appear to be cold calculation and decision that really was an anguished perplexity as to God's most profound will in this matter. For it might be thought that with the smaller gift of human sight that seemed alternative to the tears, one could perhaps serve God better than by tears. He wanted to find God in all things. At any rate, it is clear Ignatius knew the vast difference between God and even the choicest of religious gifts. To give another example: his love of the cross—for it is that—in the *Exercises* is permeated with this same icy fire of indifference. One might call Ignatius the man of transcendent as opposed to world-immanent spirituality.

Second Characteristic: Existentialist

Let us designate it by the controversial term "existentialist." The indifferent man is not individualistic in the same way as the Renaissance man, who jealously guarded the highly unique treasure of his own personality and esteemed it as of tremendous, if not of the highest, worth. Ignatius really had little to do with the Renaissance as such, much as some have tried to read him in its light. He had his own understanding of the world, based on a mystical death which can see worth in all things, because nothing really has much worth; quite the opposite of the Renaissance man, who in his new love for the world tended to divinize it. Ignatius was an individualist because for him the two aspects regarding men and the good things of this world—i.e., the common and the particular aspects, their isolation and their relatedness—are equally remote from God. While willing both, he identifies himself with neither and can be fully found in neither. Ignatius is thus not the individualist of the personality but of the person: and, when circumstances demand it, of the poor person rather than the rich, of the matter-of-fact man who knows his place, the man who recognizes himself to be at the direct beck of the will of that God who as he chooses and sees best disposes this or that, revealing only a part of the way at a time, and desiring that man hold himself open to him who can reveal himself in emptiness as well as in fullness, in death as in life, in external and internal riches for the cultural and religious man quite as fully as in the most dire poverty. This Ignatian attitude is the source of the skeptical, the prosaic, the reserved, the calculating, the apparently deceptive, the adaptation and imitation and planning of alternatives which in prosperity or misfortune mark out the Jesuit. On the one side is this quietly skeptical, disabused attitude, with an instinct for the provisional and temporary, ready to press into service anything but the divine itself. On the other is the preparedness for the unique and novel situation with its ever new challenge, together with the uncommon fact that this attitude is not aimed at profit but at service, and is accepted as a responsibility before which one can neither take refuge in generalities nor pervert the creatures in question to the enhancement of one's own personality. All of this we have chosen to term the "existential" in Ignatian spirituality. It seems so typical of Ignatius that Ignatian spirituality may be said to be even ahead of our time, and it will come into its own in the new epoch which is now announcing itself. Those who consider themselves historically the disciples of Ignatius will have to prove themselves worthy representatives of this spirit in the future.

Third Characteristic: Church-Consciousness

In every age men have loved the Church and lived by her. But for Ignatius the Church was ever at the center of his attention: the Church militant to be served despite its obvious flaws, the Church of the popes, in short the tangible, palpable Church. No one will contest that this is essential to Ignatian spirituality; it is too obvious. One might speculate as to whether it is a quality as fundamental as the two previously mentioned or only a complement of them; perhaps on ultimate analysis it will be the one as well as the other. For the man who really has experienced God's absolute transcendence—not merely his sublime infinity—will humbly accept his own divinely willed limitation. He equally will accept in simplicity and humility the finite creatures and their relative variations that thereafter become for him, in a certain sense, absolute. From this arises Ignatius' unreserved love for the humanity of Christ and of his earthly career with all its limitations, of the Church, the hierarchy, the pope, and of the rules of thinking with the Church. Not as though all these things were by a utopian enthusiasm somehow identified with God. Ignatius, who could confess that every fibre of his body quaked at the election of Paul IV, was far from that. His Church-consciousness is that of the man who deifies neither himself nor his personal mystical contacts, and thus is prepared to accept the limitation which marks God's self-representation among his creatures. It is this quiet love of humility, service, and objective self-evaluation, from which grows the Ignatian Church-consciousness that is at once the result of a healthy, and the antidote for an unhealthy, existential indifference.[1]

An Intrinsic Compensating Factor

So far we have tried to mark out the originality of Ignatian spirituality. Before proceeding, we should recall to our minds that this spirituality identifies itself with other spiritualities in most respects, including the most essential; it differs from them only in a few elements of less importance. In order to bring out its originality, we have to stress the aspects by which Ignatian spirituality diverges from others, leaving aside the elements common to all. We must continually keep in mind that the particularities of which we treat are neither the whole of this spirituality nor its most important elements. The tendency to ignore this fact in practice makes these particularities appear most dangerous. Biology shows us how some characteristics can grow and become bizarre, finally destroying the structure itself. It is the same in the realm of the spiritual. The prophylactic against such spiritual self-destruction is humility; by it man keeps himself open to outside influences while ever remaining within the limits in which alone the limited spiritual being can indefinitely be perfected. With humility a sound, orthodox and sober spirituality is possible; one that keeps consciously to its proper bounds and builds up with little effort a new protective force, protective (oddly enough) against itself; so balancing its internal forces that the particular within it builds up and does not destroy.

In reflecting on the three characteristics already noted as belonging to Ignatian spirituality, it is not necessary to dwell at length on a positive exposition of the likelihood of such an individualistic menace. When not consciously restrained in the manner just remarked, they can make for an attitude that is rationalistic, cold, calculating and skeptical. Exaggerating the relativity of all that is not God, they may lead to an interior unconcern about things, and so once more lose sight of the true nature of earthly and even religious realities. Such an indifference degenerates into a deadening pragmatism that will try its hand at anything because nothing is beyond its competence and so accomplishes nothing. God becomes a hazy idea, a mere word;

---

[1] For our own edification we may add as a note to these three characteristics that they are worthless if they are left as mere considerations: they must be adapted to life and death or they come to nothing.

the force behind that word unconsciously comes to be vested in creatures themselves: in the organization, the authority of the Church, the system, the numbers of the faithful, etc. The existential ascetic becomes a man who has so much control over himself that he possesses everything except a heart that knows how to give itself over to the free dispositions of the divine will; a heart that would have enabled him to laugh and to cry according to the varying experiences of life and not just according to the dictates of his own will. (Indeed he will want to laugh and cry, since he is no stoic.) Finally, the risks of emphasizing Church-consciousness are familiar. The Church may be considered autonomous instead of a divine instrument; it may be identified with a certain ruling clique, school, or discipline. And so only those who agree with one's private opinion will be considered loyal to the Church.

Our point now is to show how the devotion to the Sacred Heart is an inherent and necessary preventive for Ignatian spirituality against its own dangers.[2] It will be doubly profitable to reflect on this fact, since its consideration will show us something more of the meaning of the devotion itself. We may prefix our development with the remark that the connection between Ignatian spirituality and the devotion was first shown by the simple fact that the Jesuits—more exactly, some Jesuits—were among the first of its promoters. No Catholic would dare to say that the development of this devotion within the Church is a matter of mere chance. Nor would it be valid to offer as an explanation of the extent of Jesuit involvement in it a mere coincidence: St. Margaret Mary had a Jesuit confessor, and visionaries have a predilection for designating their confessors and their confessors' orders as the instruments of their missions!

Indifference and the Heart of Jesus

Indifference implies a transformation that in many respects must be likened to death. Man has to die to the world, not only to the evil world with its malice. Indifference means a death that prevents man from loving inordinately the world, from falling in love with it, from putting it in the place of God. Such a death in which all things lose their splendor—like nature in winter—and fall back into in-

---

[2] Such dangers grow with progress in spiritual life; tepid souls are, to their own disadvantage, immune to them.

significance, may turn out to be different from the death intended by God. It can be a chilling of the heart, a spiritless leveling-down that no longer takes account of the differences God has put into creatures and which he wants taken note of. The death involved in indifference is only a life-giving death when it is motivated by love and dies into love. Indifference must never kill the heart. It must be the death only of the secret self-seeking that knots itself, refusing to share in God's unending freedom. Indifference *must* be love. Where there is a stoical apathy; where this is a fundamental cowardice that gives up because it doubts of victory; where there is stinginess of heart which does not perceive the grandeur of the world, there is no real indifference. The theoretical truth of this is clear. In practice, however, even the man who fights to gain true indifference is in danger of accepting these false appearances, since they are more easily and less painfully come by than the true. For this reason indifference must include a veritable cult of love—a burning, enthusiastic, bold love. So if at all possible, the devotee must be continually reminded that the center of the world and of truth is a heart: a burning heart, a heart that offered itself to all the ups and downs of fortune and endured them to the end without any fainthearted pretense that they were not real; a heart quite unlike the stoic's predeceased heart to which no more inspiring challenges can ever come. Indifference must be a readiness of heart to love all to the full extent of its power; not only this one or that, but all. A complete lack of concern about things created has nothing to do with true indifference. Real indifference is a quality of the heart that is "pierced" and yet alive and itself a fountain of life. Indifference means that the perfect heart is ultimately, a heart "pierced through," giving its last drop of blood; a heart that, if it finds no response to its love, will not in self-concern step back from the risks of love.

It is this quality of true love which should specify the death that is indifference. If such a love did not specify, it would be better to love at least one thing than to have an ashen heart cynically reducing all things to a common worthlessness, and then call that state indifference. Indifference is a great gift, but it acts otherwise than as a lethal poison only when it belongs to someone who is in love with love. Such a one knows what a heart is for. So it may happen that without ever having heard the words, "Sacred Heart of Jesus," he loves that heart, the symbol of limitless love.

Defense against Dangers

We have described this existentialism as the individuality of the person conscious of that uniqueness. This results in his entertaining no inordinate concern to advance himself or expand his potentialities. He allows himself to be consumed in service, since he does not think himself more than the limited creature he is; he bows to the law of indifference. The danger of such an attitude is that it exposes its possessor to a fatal lack of love, to a harshness and a—though perhaps hidden—cynicism: a kind of secret contempt for men which, being "aware of what is in man," loves neither self nor others, but at best manages to maintain a studied patience with man and his foibles. Such an existentialist is in danger of being isolated in a deadly sense; of becoming as it were shrivelled and expressionless, and in any case worn and burnt out in his heart, too knowing to be able to love. He feels in himself something of that total incapacity of enthusiastic love; like melancholic bachelors who imagine such an unconcern to be celibate virtue and are irritated when someone else is weak enough to love. Such an existentialism tends to esteem not losing oneself as solid virtue; whereas virtue is actually salvation by grace of what is continually exposed to danger. Such an existentialism, lonely and on its way to becoming cold, only becomes sound and good when joined in its humility by a heart that loves, and that loves a heart. Only he who has love can stand himself and others for any length of time without coming to despise both himself and others. Only he who loves can humbly accept himself and others at their true value, without being stopped short by the limitations he finds. "It is very difficult," says Bernanos, "not to hate oneself." It is impossible, unless one loves, unless one loves that unique heart which is the heart of Christ.

He who knows self and is pressed down beneath the heavy burden of that knowledge, must—if he wants to escape self—forget self. Yet plunged in his own being, as he is, how can he? To forget self he must get out of self, and that is impossible unless he loves. In other words, how can he be liberated from his own emptiness and instability by something that is outside self, unless this something be an object of his love? Otherwise, instead of attracting, this object would only intensify the torment felt by this existentialist at the sight of his own limitation and relativity. Now, that love[3] can be directed only there where infinite love has lovingly taken a conditioned thing to himself and identified it with himself absolutely. He has done just that by taking the limitation of the humanity of Christ as his own; by taking—through the hypostatic union—the limitation of a human reality so really, absolutely and unconditionally to himself that it has become his own forever. Without ceasing to be in itself limited, it actually participates in an unimaginable way in the divine absolute. And if a man should desire lovelessly to relegate to the relative this exalted reality, he would relegate the absolute as such to the relative! This means also that every genuine love of a limited thing that has regard for the aspect of illimitation within that thing is in the present order a love directed to the heart of Christ. For such love has an incarnational character insofar as it connotes faith in the incarnation. Such love is, therefore, a form of devotion to the Sacred Heart of Jesus.

A man who has sounded the depths of his own being is not likely to love so naïvely and unguardedly as another. He feels the need of a love reaching the unlimited: the limited by itself is for him a disillusionment, unbearable in its insignificance. But if such a love is not to be perverted into a proud delight at the immensity of its own insatiable demand for an "all or nothing," then it must be a love of that concrete immensity which sets love free to soar into the illimited. Simultaneously it gives place and rank to other limited creatures as being worthy of love. That immensity is and can only be the concrete heart of the infinite God, the heart of the God-Man. Take a man who is not content to remain naïvely at the level of generalities, and who really perceives what his existence is. Such a person will not stand aghast at the thought of death since he knows by firm faith and hope that he is loved by someone whose love cannot be reduced to a childish and passing illusion. For it is the love of God, the love of his heart.

Church-Consciousness

It is scarcely necessary to stress the fact that fundamental Church-consciousness is only befitting and healthy when it is found in a

---

[3] Such love must somehow be "delimitized"—if such a hard-seeming paradox of loving something limited unlimitedly can really exist.

heart motivated by love, in a heart that is *lovingly* Church-conscious. When the servant of the Church is devoid of love, his "Church" becomes a collective egoism which talks of the honor of God and the salvation of souls, but means more precisely the power and glory of the Church and of himself as a member. This service can never be justified except in lovers, who justify it by serving lovingly. In this context truth is luminous only when it glows with the fire of love. Men come to the sacraments only when they see that the sacraments have worked in the minister that which is their single purpose, "the charity of God is poured forth in hearts." (Rom. 5:5). Only lovers can really serve the Church; only they can make of her what she is meant to be, the humbly serving means of salvation for all. When we see the life of the Church primarily from the point of view of one or another party or tradition, when we join with others like ourselves in fruitless justification of favorite usages and customs that suit and flatter our pride and opinions, when we no longer dare earnestly to ask ourselves whether we are really ready to be all to all and to go zealously to others rather than sit back complacently till they come to us—when we are like this, then should we not ask ourselves whether we have prayed enough for the grace that will make us humble and selflessly loving, sacrificing personal privileges in order to bring privileges to others.

How can man pray better for such grace, where better learn the humility needed for love[4] than from the heart of the Lord who was not ashamed to love? Only those who are modest enough to discern their own limitations, not only those of others, will be able to avoid the danger of degrading, even though unconsciously, the rules for thinking with the Church into rules of a petty, narrow-minded fanaticism. Only men who really love will love the Church. While making her pilgrimage through time in poverty and fatigue, while ardently awaiting the marriage of the Lamb, this spouse of the Lord longs for love—for a love which cannot be given by one who identifies himself with her as a fanatic with his party. In the last analysis the fanatic does not love, he hates.

Love is a quality all true spiritualities hold in common. The originality of any spirituality must be looked for in other gifts. But always it must be remembered: "if I do not have charity, I am

---

[4] Love is humiliating and it inevitably seems foolish and unmanly to the aloof non-lover.

nothing" (1 Cor. 13:2). This is as true of Ignatian as of any other spirituality. The very fountain of love, however, is the heart of the Lord. Thus Ignatian spirituality is only holy when it loves this heart and loves together with it. Without love, the other qualities become the more deadly the more exalted they are.

Genuine Development

So far we have tried to study the characteristics of Ignatian spirituality. We have asked ourselves why the devotion to the Sacred Heart is a protection against the dangers naturally accompanying such a spirituality, just as they accompany any other human creation. All such characteristics are limited, and the removal of the limits from the limited is a drastic step. The intrinsic union of the devotion to the Sacred Heart with the spirituality of St. Ignatius, their inner relationship, is precisely what makes the former a protection. There is no question of a foreign influence neutralizing a menace from within. We must not and cannot see the effect of the devotion to the Sacred Heart on Ignatian spirituality in such a light, as though one were the saving element and the other of its nature a real danger. Rather, the characteristics of this spirituality truly spring whole and entire from that devotion and draw from that origin the protective influence in question. The opposition between them reveals itself on deeper analysis as an inner unity. This unity differentiates itself into the duality we have dealt with so far. We may now ask why and how the divine-human love, adoringly honored under the appropriate symbol of the heart of Jesus, produces of itself the characteristics of Ignatian spirituality and preserves them.

Divine Love and Indifference

Love is primarily a going out of self, always a miracle of transcending one's own narrowness. St. Thomas has explained the profound truth that knowledge is in a sense a transcendence that draws all to itself and is aware of being enriched with the whole of reality. In the drama of life, however, the second act of the spiritual, personal being is the greater wonder of the bestowal of self on someone else. What this signifies first and necessarily is a triumphant renunciation of self, an indifference to self, a trustful going-out-of-self. This act rules out the existential fear of finite being, ever anxious to preserve, and mortally afraid to lose, itself.

In this generous opening outward [5] that is identical with the spiritual being's love, the true lover is really concerned with all even though he seems to devote himself to one alone. He is free, he loves all. He loves not only a collection of individuals but also the source of individuality—God. This insatiable love that tends to embrace all in God makes the lover indifferent not only to self but also to other individuals as such. We say "as such," for it is not as though he did not truly love those other individuals. Rather, he loves them as included within that limitless movement in which everything is loved, praised and esteemed. This other and primary All permeates and surrounds the created all. In this way man can really love only to the extent that, explicitly or otherwise, he loves God who is within and yet ever beyond whatever creature or creatures are loved.

Indifference seen in this way is nothing else than the individual keeping himself open to the All that is God, in order to be able to love others truly. He thus avoids the death which both the lover and the object of his love would have to suffer due to their essential limitation, were they not open to the limitless Fullness, who has lovingly willed himself to limited creatures to be *their* fulness and limitlessness. Hence indifference is the loving, positive reference to (and by) God of all that is limited and individual. It does not unmask the finite to lay bare its pettiness; it does not see through it as if it were empty nothingness. It notes its limitations in order to recognize its relation to the Illimited and the position of security granted it by and in the love of that Illimited. Indifference "pierces" the heart of the lover and breaks open the rigid closing-in-upon-themselves of the objects loved. Indifference is so strong that it does not shrink from the death prerequisite to this opening-up. Rather it realizes that this is the only way it can liberate the finite, that it becomes unlimited only by being loved in the limitless love of the Unlimited. When someone is loved in the manner just noted, and when the love of God for the person in question is the communication of God himself to that limited being in grace and glory, then that being is loved by the indifferent man as one rendered unlimited by grace, because the person is loved within that same communicated

---

[5] This is much more than a mere temporary leaving of self in order to arrange a federation with others, which would be a kind of collective egoism rather than love.

love of God. Man can love in the true sense of the word only in God in as much as there alone each and every being has a common meeting ground and can bestow itself on others. In this manner and for this reason anything can be loved as if it were, at the same time, the only thing and everything that exists. And this is exactly what love desires. Love itself thus becomes indifference. Indifference is nothing else than the phase of upsurging love which is still in time and history with the world on the way to God, "who is all in all," in whom finally there will be only love and nothing else.

It must also be remembered in this regard that in the present order (after the fall), the creature's closing in upon itself to the exclusion of all others, its anxiety to affirm itself, is sin or stems from sin. Indifference, therefore, as the opening of the creature to the all-unifying Love has a special bleeding character which it shares with the pierced heart of Jesus.

Love and the Existential

There never was love which did not consider itself quite unique, and this conviction is not foolish imagination. On the contrary, it is actually so, whenever love is real: love frees the lover for the expression of his truly personal uniqueness. When one lives in the universal and all-embracing love, then and then alone there is no other who could take his place and duplicate his giving. What he is constitutes precisely a uniqueness which embraces all. This center from which all is acknowledged and embraced exists only once. Love is the birth of the true and completely determined individuality. Such an individuality is not cramped loneliness but an image of the unique individualities in God, each of whom possesses in his own way the whole of the divine nature by affirming and loving the other as he is.

Love and love alone is existential in yet another sense: it reveals one's own unique, personal vocation, task and mission. For man will not achieve his true self in mere static being nor in conceptual objectivity, but in action. This is so to a much greater extent for man than for angels, or even for God; because man progresses from being a mere member of a species to the personality of unique individuality by his free decisions. This unique line of action, which means much more than conforming to universal laws or fulfilment of the common nature of man, can miss the mark. Man can discover his personality in the uniqueness of his personal guilt. But if he is determined to avoid this failure, where does man hear the call that beyond all general norms will tell him what exactly he has to be? Where will he find his vocation, his mission, liberating him from deadly solitude and boredom? Will he discover it in the depths of his own being? Although man does find it in self, the discovery is not of self but of a gift. Yet being a gift from God, it is for this very reason that it constitutes ultimately his own personality. So man can find what is most personal only by contemplating the image of self as seen by God. God, so to say, holds this image before our inner eyes. The contemplation of this image humiliates us in our imperfections, but at the same time fills us with joy since we know simultaneously ourselves and God. In this image we are constantly making new discoveries, though never here below will it be completely unveiled to us. Pilgrims that we are, we know as in a mirror not only God but also ourselves; only hereafter shall we know ourselves as we are known. Nevertheless we already sense something of our uniqueness which is rooted in God's grace in that God bestows on each one this very personal quality rendering us worthy of eternal existence.

How are we to discover this vocation, this image, which comes from God? Although the answer may appear to be too simple, it is the correct one: in the union of love with God. In love alone do we understand God; in him alone do we comprehend what he expects of us. In love of God are we alone disposed to accept ourselves as conceived by him in his love of us. Outside this love all would ultimately lead to despair and revolt. This would be the consequence even with regard to our own self; finding our individuality we would face the strange abyss of our nothingness. Not by accident do the *Spiritual Exercises,* if well understood, consist in finding the love for the ever greater God, in Jesus Christ, and in that same discovery, finding our own individual image, our vocation. This discovery comes from inspiration, from above, and not from a technique of purely rational planning, from below. Divine inspiration—whose manifestations may be quite ordinary—is only discerned by a person moved by love. Only as a lover can a human being enter into a dialogue with God, in whom alone the uniqueness of one's existence can be discovered. This process excludes all self-seeking pleasure and implies dedicated selfless service in an identification with the object.

With regard to the love for Christ we must say still more. We must remember that our own individual existence is meant to be a veritable participation in the life of Christ, a following of the Lord and his fortunes in the sense that we really prolong his life, and not merely copy it for the thousandth time. For this reason our Christian vocation and individuality can only be found in love for Christ. For precisely and solely by that love do we come to share, as if by loan, in the existence his love for us bestows.

Genuine Love of the Church Springs from Devotion to the Sacred Heart

Little need be added about this point. The Church herself is born of this heart. "From a pierced heart, the Church, the spouse of Christ is born" is not merely a pretty saying. The Spirit without whom the Church would be no more than an organization, a synagogue, springs from the pierced heart of Christ; and it is the Spirit of lavish love. This further implies that a correct understanding of the essence of the Church must be the result of viewing her in relation to her origin. Then only can we truly love the Church as she ought to be loved; then only can we escape the danger of having in our mind quite a different reality when striving to discover and love the Church. If we see her as coming from the heart of Christ, if, helped by grace, we love her by sharing and imitating the love that brought her into being, we imitate the love of Christ for his spouse the Church as it is described by St. Paul and as the Fathers of the Church understood it. Out of his love for sinful, lost humanity, he constitutes the Church as his bride by freeing and cleansing it. Out of love he takes mankind, in spite of its adulterous infidelity to God, and makes it his bride. Out of love he first makes it holy and worthy of love. Christ's love oscillates, so to say, between sinful mankind—which, by the way, has its representatives within the empirical Church—and the really holy Church. If our love for the Church, then, is to be like Christ's, it means we must love men—sinful, lost, groping men— and love them truly. We must love a Church which needs to be continually renewed by these very men. We must be able to love a Church that is by no means straightway made into a pure and holy bride of Christ without spot or wrinkle (Eph. 5:27), but one who is to become what she ought to be only through this same patient, long-suffering, forbearing love. In fact it is with this same patience and humility that we must love even ourselves, who are so sinful and imperfect and ever contributing our part to the aspect of slave-girl and sinner in the Church (Gal. 4:22).

In a word, we must love a Church which will only be perfect when all that is ordained by God for salvation will have "come home" to her. There we will not merely share in the splendor of the Church; we will also bring along all that the home-comers have of spirit, grace, life, individual character, unique experience. Then only will the Church be in a full sense "home" when all her children will have thus returned home. Love for the Church from the heart of Christ is daring and keen-sighted, not a jealously defensive attitude but a furtherance of the Church's imitation of Christ by service. "For he came not to be served but to serve and to give his life as a ransom for the many" (Mk. 10:45). Such a love does not seek the honor of the Church as a party, but the salvation and honor of those who must find the Church. Further, it seeks the reason why so few do find her, seeking first not among outsiders but among ourselves. This is missionary love, not an old guard, defensive love. This love knows that the Church will ever be renewed precisely at that moment when "someone" with a pierced heart seems to fail utterly. It will not despair but rather will recognize this hellish situation as the hour of his love, of his love for men and for the Father.

In all the above considerations we have taken as a tacit basis a devotion to the Sacred Heart of Jesus that need not insist in every case on its being a devotion expressly and definitely limited by the word "heart." Otherwise, we should not have been able to connect this devotion so closely and absolutely with the fundamental matters of Christianity and Ignatian spirituality. However, the explicit devotion to the Sacred Heart will achieve very little in the end unless the spirit of love of which we have spoken, flowing from the pierced heart of Christ, does come into our own hearts in the ways we have discussed. When the grace is offered us to name explicitly that unnamed essential component of Christianity, it is a new responsibility we cannot ignore and is the promise of a blessing to fall on all alike. When it is bestowed, we shall understand how we die in indifference in order to live, how we come to our own individualities in order to find others and serve them in love, and how we love the Church in order to love all.

PART II

Historical Origins

Introduction

In its *Decree on the Renewal of Religious Life,* Vatican Council II describes the task of appropriate renewal in terms of two simultaneous processes: "(1) a continuous return to the sources of all Christian life and to the original inspiration behind a given institute, and (2) an adjustment of the community to the changed conditions of the times." The decree goes on to specify the first process in this way: "Therefore loyal recognition and safekeeping should be accorded to the spirit of founders, as also to all the particular goals and wholesome traditions that constitute the heritage of each community" (n. 2).

It is perhaps paradoxical to identify renewal with a return to the sources, with a movement back into the past. And yet this will be a proper direction if it is true that the special grace given to the founder of a religious community by the Holy Spirit was intended not merely for the period of the original foundation. Such a grace can still be the moving force for the members of a religious community centuries after the founder's death.

The Society of Jesus now seems to be in an excellent position to attempt a rediscovery of its original inspiration after four centuries of development and codification. For more than half a century, Jesuit historians have been editing and publishing the documentary history of the Society, beginning with the writings of St. Ignatius and his contemporaries. It may now be possible to distinguish much more clearly the Ignatian insights from later Jesuit traditions.

The two chapters that follow are examples of what can be learned from the present stage of research. Fr. Robert McNally investigates the prayer-life of the early Society of Jesus, tracing its originality from the spiritual experience and apostolic concern of Ignatius himself. Fr. Anthony Ruhan turns our attention to the origin and early development of the tertianship, the final period in the training of a Jesuit. Both authors attempt to show how the more highly developed legal structures of succeeding generations tended to obscure the aims ex-

71

pressed by St. Ignatius, those aims which form part of the original inspiration of the Society of Jesus. Both illustrate the significant role that historical understanding can play in present-day ascetical doctrine.

JAMES P. JURICH, S.J.

St. Ignatius, Prayer and the Early Society of Jesus

Robert McNally, S.J.

From the early days of the Society of Jesus, Ignatius desired Jesuits to serve God and mankind in the manner most beneficial to both. Accordingly, the prayer life of the Society was so formulated as not to hinder the Jesuit from his apostolic work by singing the canonical hours or by one fixed method of prayer. Beginning with his experiences at Manresa, Ignatius gradually realized that prayer should be a balance between spiritual and bodily health and that the discovery of God each day should be regulated by the individual Jesuit. Throughout the centuries, several Jesuit General Congregations have added legislation concerning the prayer life of the Society to such an extent that Fr. McNally finds it difficult today to discern the original Ignatian freedom of spirit and flexibility.

It is well known that St. Ignatius Loyola occupies a distinguished place in the history of Catholic spirituality. In point of time the first of the great Spanish mystics of the sixteenth century,[1] he stood out as a saint of gigantic proportions in an age of heroes. His life-span (ca. 1491–1556), reaching from the medieval to the modern world, embraced years of grave crisis and decision in Western history. In the difficult period of transition, when the old order was passing and the new had not yet emerged, it was the good fortune of the Church to have had at its disposal the rare talents of this holy man who was to devise brilliant ways and means to meet the pressing demands of the changing world.

The character of the total achievement of Ignatius, to be appreci-

---

[1] Cf. E. A. Peters, *Studies of the Spanish Mystics* 1 (London 1951) 3.

ated in its fullness, must be measured not only by his personal sanctity, but also by his valuable contribution to the doctrinal and institutional development of the Church. For within the broad cadre of ecclesiastical history his greatness rests indeed on outstanding holiness as a testimonial to grace; but it also rests on the *Exercitia spiritualia,* as spiritual document, and on the Society of Jesus, as an original institution. In both the personal and doctrinal aspects of the Saint's life the distinctive character of his spirituality is evident; but it is especially evident in the institutional aspect, in the foundation of the Society of Jesus, in the basic religious thought and motivation which underlie its constitutional structure and fiber.

The *Spiritual Exercises* are the fruit of St. Ignatius' personal encounter with God in the opening years of his conversion. Conceived as early as 1522 in the mystical context of the Manresa-experience, they reached their full, definitive form only twenty years later, in 1542.[2] They are a compendium of very carefully planned meditations and contemplations, rules, insights and considerations which form a systematic spiritual method of self-reform in terms of Christian perfection. There is nothing arbitrary or capricious in either the purpose, the content or the structure of this little book. What Ignatius personally experienced at the hands of the Spirit—"things which he observed in his own soul and found useful to himself"—he analyzed, systematically ordered and set down with the conviction that these decisive moments of his religious life might prove helpful to others.[3] The result is a document which is theologically and psychologically sound. That its tenor is more practical than theoretical is not surprising in view of the fact that at the time of its first conception Ignatius was neither theologian nor scholar, but a simple, unlearned layman, "not knowing how to read and write except in Spanish." This intellectual deficiency served from an early date as a pedantic reproach against the spiritual doctrine which the Saint had embodied in his book of *Exercises.*[4]

Without answering the delicate question of the ultimate nature and purpose of the *Exercises,* it can be said that "the service of God" is their leitmotiv. By prayer and the action of the Spirit the exercitant is

---

[2] Cf. on the genesis of the *Exercises* H. Pinard de la Boullaye, S.J., *Les étapes de rédaction des Exercises de S. Ignace* (Paris 1955).

[3] *Acta P. Ignatii* 11, 99, *Fontes narrativi de S. Ignatio de Loyola* 1, *Monumenta Ignatiana* 1, ser. 4 (2 ed., Rome 1943) 504–505.

[4] *Acta P. Ignatii* 6, 62, p. 451. Cf. P. Nadal, *Apologia pro Exercitiis S. P. Ignatii, Epist.* 4 (Madrid 1905) 826.

led to discover the divine will; and in embracing it, he is committed to serve "the eternal Lord of all things." From the opening consideration of the *Exercises* to their conclusion the question of God's service remains central. It is the teaching of the *Principle and Foundation* that man is created "to praise, reverence and serve God." The meditation on the *Triple Sin* poses the challenging questions: "What have I done for Christ? What am I doing for Christ? What ought I do for Christ?" The *Election* declares that the "first aim should be to seek to serve God"; and in the *Contemplatio ad amorem* the exercitant is reminded in clear terms that "love is shown more in deeds than in words." What stands out in full light in the *Exercises* is "the thought of a distinguished and enthusiastic service, the thought of the will of God to be fulfilled on a grand and magnificent scale." [5]

As a religious institution, the Society of Jesus incorporates this service-theme of Ignatius. In fact, its foundation may be considered a vivid expression and embodiment of his high ambition to render perfect service to God. Significantly the *Formula Instituti* (1540) begins with the words: "Whoever wishes *to serve* under the standard of the cross in our Society, which we wish to bear the honored name of Jesus, and *to serve* our sole Lord and the Roman pontiff his vicar on earth. . . ." God is served by fulfilling his will which is best discovered *in* and *through* the Church. In founding the Society, therefore, Ignatius animated it with a pure ecclesial spirit.[6] By adhering to the Church, his Society would adhere to Christ; and by doing the will of Christ in this world it would do the will of the Father in heaven. The service, which his Society would render, would be neither of words nor of dreams; but rather concrete, real, specific work on behalf of Christ and his Church. Thus Pope Paul III in his bull of recognition, *Regimini militantis ecclesiae* (Sept. 27, 1540), remarks of Ignatius and his companions that they have banded together "to dedicate their lives to the perpetual *service* of our Lord Jesus Christ, to our *service*, and that of our successors."

The Service-Theme in the *Constitutions*

In view of these considerations it is not surprising that the service-theme is dominant in the *Constitutions* which St. Ignatius composed

---

[5] J. de Guibert, S.J., *The Jesuits. Their Spiritual Doctrine and Practice* (Chicago 1964), p. 127.

[6] Cf. R. E. McNally, S.J., "The Council of Trent, the Spiritual Exercises and the Catholic Reform," *Church History* (1965).

between 1540 and 1556. Here the total work of the Society is represented as a supreme act of service of the divine majesty. The words *"Ad maiorem Dei gloriam"* are indeed prominent in the text of the *Constitutions*; but even more prominent is the phrase *"Ad maius servitium Dei."* [7] The personal service of the members is the fruit of their religious obedience, purity of intention and Christian charity. Because Ignatian service is directed purely to God through the Church, it leaves no room for the selfish, the egocentric and the individualistic. The vast, universal apostolate of the whole Society represents the *maius servitium Dei* which is basic to the *Spiritual Exercises* and the very soul of Ignatian spirituality.

If the foundation of the Society of Jesus be looked at from this point of view, its character as a religious organization becomes more intelligible. Since Ignatius conceived the Society as an instrument of service, the *Constitutions* were drawn up to make it an institute whose inner ethos would correspond to this important role. Above all he gave it a flexible, mobile and adaptable structure so that at any and every moment of its existence it could render that service which the crisis of the times demanded. Obviously the elements of stability, complacency and sufficiency were eliminated from this realistic arrangement of things. Thus the *Constitutions,* as they came from the hands of Ignatius, prescribed neither the recitation of the canonical hours in choir, the adoption of religious names at profession, the imposition of regular and obligatory corporal austerities, the acceptance of ecclesiastical dignities, religious exercises in common, nor government by monastic chapter. The members of the Society were to conform the external manner of their life to the customs of the local diocesan clergy. No distinctive religious habit was assumed, nor was stability of residence prescribed. Fundamentally the break with the past was sharp and decisive. It was intended to free the Society from the medieval conception of religious life and to adapt it to the needs of the emerging modern world.

What Ignatius had devised in founding the Society was recognized by his contemporaries as a startling innovation, so novel in fact that certain pompous clerics of that day refused to acknowledge it as an authentic religious order. The negation of the old traditions which

---

[7] Cf. F. X. Lawlor, S.J., "The Doctrine of Grace in the Spiritual Exercises," *Theological Studies* 3 (1942) 524: "In St. Ignatius' mind God is *Dominus,* man is *servus.*"

they found in the *Constitutions* was insufferable.[8] But the revolutionary spirit which moved Ignatius was not in opposition to the past simply for the sake of flying in the face of history; it was rather built on the inspiration that the service of God and his Church was of such primary importance that every obstacle to it should be removed. The whole function of his Society was "to get things done," to accomplish things in the real order. Whatever impeded meaningful work was rejected; what aided service was incorporated. It was a ruthless usage of his own principle, *Tantum-Quantum*.

In breaking with the old traditions of religious life St. Ignatius also broke with its prayer-forms. It is especially in this area of the Saint's activity that his peculiar genius and originality are to be sought; and it is perhaps here more than in any other part of his work that his brilliant creativity comes to the fore. And yet it is this very aspect of the founder's life that is least known and appreciated, doubtless because of an unhistorical approach to the development of spirituality and because of the deep offense that history can give to preconceived ideas. As a master of the spiritual life Ignatius stands not on the side of rigid system, regulation and law, but rather on the side of the human person and his individual liberty, the peculiar needs of his heart, mind and body. This aspect of the Saint's spiritual doctrine is currently out of focus.

Generally candidates to the Society in the time of Ignatius made the *Spiritual Exercises* for a period of thirty days (more or less). The *Exercises* terminated in a reformation, a conversion and a commitment. The exercitant, who entered them with goodwill, was educated in a school of prayer and became "a mortified man." Here he was carefully instructed in a systematic approach to the spiritual life which included meditation and contemplation as forms of mental prayer; but he also came to know other methods of prayer which had their own peculiar function in the spiritual life.[9] But the mental prayer which the *Exercises* inculcated was never intended by their author to be a permanent, universal pattern for all his followers. As the instrument of initial conversion, it formed a *point de départ* for life in the

---

[8] Cf. A. Astrain, S.J., *Historia de la Compañía de Jesús en la Asistencia de España* 2 (Madrid 1905) 73 ff.

[9] Cf. for example Ignatius' letter to Teresa Rejadella (Sept. 11, 1536) in *Monumenta Ignatiana* 1, 1 (Madrid 1903) 107–109, where the Saint describes a method of meditation that does not import physical or mental fatigue.

Society rather than a fixed regime of prayer. In the mind of Ignatius there was no general obligation to meditate daily according to the method of the *Exercises* (or according to any other method).[10] In fact, until 1565, in the generalate of St. Francis Borgia, there was apart from the two examens no definite program of prayer obligatory on the Society as a whole; and before 1608, in the generalate of Fr. Claudius Aquaviva, the mandatory annual retreat, based on the *Spiritual Exercises,* was unknown.

Ignatius looked on prayer as a species of life, something organic that must be nurtured carefully and grow under the inspiration of grace according to its own inner laws. It was not simply a mental exercise that should be shaped and controlled by rigid categories and mechanical patterns. The prayer-experience was unique for each one; and the history of each one's spiritual development was different from all others. Thus Nadal wrote of Ignatius:

In contemplation he finds God as often as he devoted himself to prayer; nor did he think that a definite rule or order was to be followed, but prayer was to be made in various ways; and in meditation God was to be sought now one way, now another.[11]

And again he writes:

Let superiors and spiritual fathers use this moderation with which, we know, Father Ignatius was quite familiar, and which, we believe, is proper to the Society, that if they know that one is making progress in prayer with good spirit in the Lord, they do not prescribe anything for him, nor interfere with him, but rather strengthen and animate him that he might advance in the Lord gently but securely.[12]

Because in this matter one individual could not be the norm for another, superiors and spiritual fathers were to be most discerning in the direction of the prayer-life of those entrusted to them.

[10] O. Karrer, *Der heilige Franz von Borja* (Freiburg 1921), p. 249: "While it is true that St. Ignatius in his Spiritual Exercises employed among other methods meditation, and was the first to work it out systematically, still he never intended elevating it to a permanent way of praying, to a kind of official method of prayer for the entire Order. That would have meant throwing up barriers to the natural dispositions of the individual and to the guidance of divine grace."

[11] *Patrum dicta aliquot,* Nadal, *Epist.* 4 (Madrid 1905) 645.

[12] *In Examen Annotationes,* Nadal, *Epist.* 4 (Madrid 1905) 652.

In writing of prayer Ignatius takes into account a number of personal factors, for example the talents, the age, the depth of experience, the physical and mental vigor, the spiritual progress of each one, especially "the degree of grace imparted to him by God." After all, in his concept of the spiritual life prayer was not an end but a means to developing the perfect servant of God.[13]

St. Ignatius' Spiritual Program

From the point of view of the *Constitutions* of the Society as approved by the First General Congregation in 1558, what program of spiritual exercises did St. Ignatius specify for the interior development of its members? This important question can be posed only on the basis of certain clarifications and distinctions which touch on the different grades—the formed and the scholastics—which make up the whole body of the Society. It can be best answered by appealing to the *Constitutions* themselves. According to the approved text no one spiritual program is obligatory on all.[14] In the matter of prayer, scholastics are to be handled differently than the formed members; and within the grade of the formed no universal norm is of obligation. The ultimate answer, therefore, to the question of how Ignatius thought and spoke about the quantity and quality of prayer which would be basic to the interior formation and development of the members of the Society depends on a number of complex, delicate factors.

Ignatius did not establish a general rule with respect to the prayer life of the professed, and the formed coadjutors. In the Sixth Part of the *Constitutions* (VI, 3, 1) where there is question "of those things in which members of the Society are to be occupied and of those things from which they are to abstain," Ignatius lays down his spiritual program for this category of Jesuits in words which are worth citing here:

Since, in view of the time and approbation of life which is required for admission as professed or as formed coadjutors of the Society, it is to be certainly expected that these will so advance in the way of Christ our Lord that they will be able to race along it, to the extent that physical health, and the external works of charity and obedience

---

[13] Cf. J. M. Aicardo, S.J., *Comentario á las Constituciones de la Compañía de Jesús* 2 (Madrid 1920) 388 ff., 389: "Prayer and contemplation, since they are means, should only be employed according to the needs of each one."

[14] *Const.* VI, 3, 1 A; IV, 3.

will permit, it does not seem in those things which pertain to prayer, meditation and study, nor in the bodily exercise of fasting, vigils and other practices, which concern the austere chastisement of the body, that any rule is to be set down save that which discreet charity will compose for each, provided that the confessor shall be consulted and, where there is doubt as to what is best, the matter be referred to the superior.

Ignatius constructed the thought contained in this chapter on the presupposition that the formed Jesuit is a spiritual man engaged in an active apostolic life. But because the debilitation of bodily strength and the diminution of the works of charity and obedience, which result from involvement in arduous ascetical practices, distract from that service to which the Society by its Institute is committed, the prayer life of the formed Jesuit must be realistically conceived in terms of this apostolate.

For the religious development of the scholastics and their preservation in the Society after they have been admitted to it, Ignatius established certain broad norms in the Fourth Part of the *Constitutions* (IV, 4, 3):

In addition to the sacraments of confession and communion, which they are to receive every eighth day, and Mass, which they will attend daily, let them spend one hour in the recitation of the Office of the Blessed Virgin, and in the examination of conscience twice a day, with other prayers according to the devotion of each one, until one hour of prayer is made up, if it has not already been made up.

The program is almost evangelical in the simplicity of its prescriptions —liturgical prayer, and private prayer which might be either oral or mental. All is to be done "according to the arrangement and judgment of the superiors to whom obedience is due as to those standing in the place of Christ." On the advice of the spiritual father or the superior the order of prayer can be implemented, adjusted, revised in different ways to provide for the personal needs of the individual. The general prescription of the *Constitutions,* therefore, is not to be applied rigidly and uniformly to all alike.[15]

---

[15] Ignatius, *Mon. Ignatiana* 12 (Madrid 1911) 126, and Nadal, *Epist.* 4 (Madrid 1905) 323, 571, 573, indicate the role of both superior and spiritual father in dispensing from mental prayer or in commuting its quantity and quality, but always in terms of individual needs.

In the structure of the Society's ascetical doctrine, prayer is a means, "the most excellent of all means," to a better service of God. It is, therefore, subordinate to the work by which the Society concretely serves the divine majesty and its interests. According to Ignatius it is charity—*discreta caritas*—which preserves this due proportion of means and end. For a prudent, discerning, moderating love of God should control and direct the prayer life of the Society lest the service of God be diminished. Neither body nor soul should be so overcome by that physical and spiritual exhaustion which prayer involves that apostolic work is rendered impossible or difficult. Since each person responds differently to the demands of spiritual exercises, each one must try to discern in the light of his love of God what is truly his level of achievement. There is true charity, where the love of God is expressed more in deeds than in words.

But *discreta caritas* is the principle neither of a purely subjective inclination to, nor an arbitrary aversion from, prayer. It is realistic love; it has, therefore, one foot in the spiritual life of prayer, the other in the apostolic life of service. It looks both ways at once without overlooking either aspect of the religious life. *Discreta caritas* becomes effective in a cooperative way, through the medium of confessor and superior whose counsels should be of paramount importance in helping the religious adopt a manner of prayer suited to his individual needs. The interior disposition of each one should be known to the superior through manifestation of conscience; in consequence, he is in a qualified position to specify a program of prayer and penance that will neither retard nor diminish the expression of the apostolic commitment.

Spiritual counsel should be built on a personal knowledge of the individual, but also on an accurate knowledge of the discernment of spirits which provides a method for discovering and diagnosing the inner motions of God and his grace in the soul of each one. Obviously, both the confessor and the superior must be highly competent men, qualified in human psychology and spiritual doctrine, and capable of determining in each individual case the dictates of charity. For *discreta caritas* is the only rule (*nec . . . ulla regula eis prescribenda nisi quam discreta caritas unicuique dictaverit. Const. 6, 3*) which Ignatius prescribes as normative in fixing the quality and the quantity of the daily prayer of the formed members of the Society. In his mind true apostolic work is inspired by charity, performed with purity of intention and completed under the guidance of obedience. In terms of this concept of service the only *effusio ad exteriora* for Ignatius is egocentric work subtracted from the charity and the obedience of the Society.

Prayer-Work Opposition

To oppose prayer and work as two distinct categories of religious activity, the one to be fostered, the other to be moderated, is to misread the Ignatian concept of both. In his *Memoriale* (Oct. 4, 1542) Blessed Peter Favre provides important insights into this facet of the spiritual life of the Society. He writes:

I was reflecting about the manner of praying well and about different manners of performing good works; also how good desires in prayer prepare the way to good works and the good works in turn prepare the way to good desires. I became aware of this and understood it clearly; he who in spirit is seeking God through his good works will find him later in prayer better than if he had not engaged in these good works. . . . If we seek God above all in prayer, we find him later in good works. Therefore, he who seeks and finds the spirit of Christ in good works progresses in a manner much more solid than he who occupies himself only with prayer. I might even say that one who possesses Christ through the practice of good works and one who possesses him in prayer are like one who possesses him in fact and one who possesses him in affection. . . . You will do better by orientating all your prayers towards the treasures acquired from good works, rather than by aiming during the works at the treasures which are acquired from prayers. . . .[16]

These words were written during the lifetime of Ignatius, whose mind Peter Favre, one of the original members of the Company of Jesus, was well qualified to represent.

Ignatius did not believe that members of the Society should pray for long periods of time. His celebrated dictum is well known: "A man of true self-conquest needs no more than a quarter of an hour of prayer to be united with God." It offers valuable insight into his concept of prayer; and the words, which he addressed (Dec. 24, 1553) to Fr. Caspar Berze in the distant Indies reaffirm his thought on this important matter:

---

[16] *Memoriale*, nos. 126–29, tr., J. de Guibert, S.J., *op. cit.*, pp. 584–85.

And if that land is less conducive to meditation than this, there is less reason for augmenting it there than here. Between work and study the mind can raise itself to God; and, for one who directs all things to the service of God, everything is a prayer. With this idea all in the Society must be thoroughly impregnated. Works of charity leave very little time for long prayers; indeed, it would be false to believe that by work they please God less than in prayer.[17]

This way of thinking perfectly accords with Ignatius' concept of service and its important role in the spiritual and apostolic life of the Society.

For Ignatius work is not merely an exterior task. It presupposes charity, obedience and selflessness on the part of the worker; but, in addition to these personal qualities, work is also sacramental in character; it is a point of encounter with God and has a mysticism of its own. For God who is to be found in all things, is also to be found in work. The phrase, *hallar Dios en todas las cosas*—"to find God in all things"—is characteristically Ignatian, and is an epitome of his understanding of the Christian concept of work. Thus Fr. Polanco wrote to Fr. Urbanus Fernandes, the rector of the College of Coimbra, in the name of Ignatius (June 1, 1551):

Our Father regards it as better that we try to find God in all things instead of devoting too much continuous time to prayer. It is his desire to see all members of the Society filled with such a spirit that they find no less devotion in works of charity and obedience than in prayer and meditation, since they all should be done out of love for the service of God, our Lord.[18]

In the same vein Ignatius wrote (June 1, 1551) to Fr. Antonius Brandanus on the scholastics and the spiritual duties:

In view of their goal of study, the scholastics cannot have prolonged meditations. But over and above [the prescribed spiritual exercises] . . . they can exercise themselves in seeking the presence of our Lord in all things, such as their conversations, their walks, in all that they see, taste, hear, and understand, and in all their actions, since it is true that his divine majesty is in all things. . . . This manner of meditating which finds God our Lord in all things is easier than raising ourselves to the consideration of divine things, which are more

---

[17] *Mon. Ignatiana* 1, 6 (Madrid 1907) 91.
[18] *Ibid.*, 1, 3 (Madrid 1905) 502.

abstract, and to which we can make ourselves present only with effort. This good exercise, by exciting good dispositions in us, will bring great visitations from the Lord, even though they occur in a short prayer. In addition to this, one can frequently offer to God our Lord his studies and the effort they demand, seeing that we undertake them for his love while sacrificing our personal tastes, in order that in something we may be of service to his divine majesty by helping those for whom he died.[19]

The encounter with God in prayer stretches beyond the limits of formal meditation out into the concrete realities of every day life. The totality of human activity becomes a discovery—rooted in charity and obedience—of God in all things.

The *Constitutions* prescribe no formal prayer beyond the two examinations of conscience for the formed members of the Society. This was an important aspect of St. Ignatius' concept of religious life which he strongly maintained until the end of his career, refusing to alter the text of the *Constitutions* by prescribing obligatory prayer for all. There was no Jesuit who could change his mind on this point; and none of the original members of the Company of Jesus dared to try it. In fact, he explicitly stated that it was "his opinion from which no one would ever move him, that for those who are studying one hour of prayer was sufficient, it being supposed that they are practicing mortification and self denial." [20] And this is surprising in view of the fact that of the one hour allotted to prayer for the scholastics not much more than a quarter of it could be devoted to private prayer either mental or vocal, after the two examinations of conscience had been made and the Office of the Blessed Virgin recited. But the point to be noted here is that in the formulation of this prescription Ignatius was realistic in terms of his aims and objectives. From bitter personal experience he knew how thoroughly the mental activity of prayer and study consume human energy. He knew also that the scholastics of the Society were dedicated by their vocation to study, and that their intellectual formation basic to their future apostolic life and consequently to the service of the Church should have primacy over all other considerations.

[19] Cf. J. de Guibert, S.J., *op. cit.*, p. 88.
[20] Gonçalves da Câmara, *Memoriale* 256, *Fontes narrativi de S. Ignatio de Loyola* 1, *Mon. Ignatiana* 1, ser. 4 (2 ed., Rome 1943) 676. Cf. J. de Guibert, S.J., *op. cit.*, p. 89.

Length and Method of Prayer

Whether the formed Jesuit should pray by rule each day for a determined space of time and according to a specific method was not a matter of indifference to Ignatius. An historic exchange between the Saint and Father Nadal after the latter's visitation of the Spanish provinces in 1553–54 is filled with insight into the Saint's mind on this important point. When Father Nadal explained that he had yielded to the Spanish fathers' request for an hour and a half of prayer daily, Ignatius was visibly moved with anger and displeasure. Nadal has described the interview in these words:

By my irreverence and impetuousness in contending that the time of prayer must be increased, I offended Father Ignatius. But at the moment he said nothing. On the next day he sharply denounced me in the presence of others; and, thereafter, he did not make great use of my services.[21]

Father Gonçalves da Câmara, the minister of the house, who was present on this occasion, reports in his *Memoriale* the extraordinary vehemence which Father Nadal's recommendation excited in the Saint. It was in this context that Ignatius uttered his famous dictum on prayer: "A truly mortified man needs only a quarter of an hour to be united with God in prayer."

Father Gonçalves interpreted the exchange between Ignatius and Nadal in this way:

When Ignatius told Nadal that an hour of prayer was enough for those in the colleges, he was placing the chief stress upon mortification and abnegation. Thus it is clear that the Father constructs the great foundation of the Society from all the relevant matters, such as indifference which is presupposed, and the examination after a candidate has passed through his probations and obtained favorable testimony about them, and not from prayer, unless it is the prayer to which all these matters give birth. Thereupon the Father praised highly especially that prayer which is made by keeping God always before one's eyes.[22]

Within the very lifetime of Ignatius there was a tendency among certain members of the Society to increase the quantity of prayer, to

[21] Nadal, *Ephemerides* 2, 42, *Epist.* 2 (Madrid 1899) 32.
[22] G. da Câmara, *op. cit.*, 256, p. 677; J. de Guibert, S.J., *op. cit.*, p. 89.

specify its quality and to make it obligatory on all members of the order. Father Nadal, as we have seen, thought in this direction; but the influence of the great Spanish nobleman, Francis Borgia (d. 1572), proved significant and ultimately decisive in determining the future prayer life of the Society. Though a Jesuit in the generalate of Ignatius, he had not been formed in the religious life of the Society in the same sense that Francis Xavier, Peter Favre and the other early companions had been formed. He had never enjoyed, for example, that intimate personal direction which Francis Xavier had received from Ignatius; nor was he acquainted with the spirit of the Society as it had been from its first beginnings in the Parisian days. The lofty circumstances of his life, the noble traditions of his family, the dramatic character of his conversion were unique, and set him aside in a sense from all the others. His relations to Ignatius and to the Society were not typical of this first generation of Jesuits; and his thinking, his own peculiar religious psychology, foreshadow the second generation whose spiritual life moved more and more in the direction of system, regulation and uniformity.

In the very earliest stages of his conversion he stood under the spiritual influence of Father Andreas Oviedo under whom the members of the Gandia community of the Society were obliged to three hours of mental prayer daily. Francis was austere and penitential, devoted to prayer, mortification and abnegation; so otherworldly and eschatological was his inner conversion that it brought him to a decisive break with the world and all that it represented. It also induced in him a rigid cast of mind marked with monastic inclinations.[23]

In Spain, where religious life in the century of the Protestant Reformation and the Catholic Reform was coming to full flowering with an almost unmatched brilliance, the propensity for long prayer was especially pronounced. Most of the older religious orders had devised elaborate ascetical (prayer and penance) programs which concretely expressed their inner spirit, their fervor and devotion. This *modus vivendi* was a matter of corporate pride. Neither Borgia nor his Spanish confreres could escape these influences. They were too close to

[23] Nadal had his problems with Borgia and his monastic tendencies. For example, he tells us: "When I told him that it was the will of Father [Ignatius] that he should not inflict the discipline and penances on himself, he replied: 'You are going to make me retire into a Carthusian monastery.'" Cf. Nadal, *Epist.* 2, 43.

contemporary religious life to be untouched by it. As members of a new order whose rule refrained from prescribing either a fixed quantity and quality of prayer, obligatory penances or communal religious duties, they felt in a position of inferiority face to face with the asceticism of the day. But more than once, even in the generalate of Ignatius himself, the Spanish provinces moved in the direction of obligatory penance and prayer for their members. Thus in 1554 Nadal describes this situation which he found in the Jesuit College at Alcalá:

The Fathers had six hours of sleep in winter, from ten-thirty to four-thirty, and in summer from nine-thirty to three-thirty; two hours of prayer, one in the morning from five to six, or from four to five, and another before supper from seven to eight in the evening, or from five to six in summer. After dinner and supper they went to the Church to pray and there they passed each time a quarter of an hour . . . Fridays and Saturdays they fasted. They prayed together in the chapel . . . Many times they gathered in the same chapel to take the discipline for any need that may have arisen . . .[24]

Much of this Father Nadal felt obliged to correct in terms of the *Constitutions* which he was introducing into this assistancy.

More than once Ignatius himself had to intervene in the affairs of the Spanish provinces. The rigorist tendencies in the matter of prayer and penance which Fathers such as Andreas Oviedo, Francisco Onfroy and others manifested, had to be corrected firmly and prudently;[25] and a letter which he wrote to Father Francis Borgia as early as September 20, 1548, shows the character of his moderating influence in the whole question of excessive penance and prolonged prayer.[26]

Tendency toward Tepidity

At the same time another tendency is in evidence in the rank and file of the Society, such as it was in the third quarter of the sixteenth century. Already the fervor of the first days of the foundation had cooled, yielding to religious tepidity. The primitive spirit of the Society—its charity and prayer—was disappearing. The decadence that

---

[24] Cf. P. Leturia, S.J., "De Oratione Matutina in Societate Iesu Documenta Selecta," *Archivum Historicum Societatis Iesu* 3 (1934) 92–3; Doc. IV.

[25] *Iudicium de quibusdam opinionibus* 26–7, *Mon. Ignatiana* 1, 12 (Madrid 1911) 650–52.

[26] *Mon. Ignatiana* 1, 2 (Madrid 1904) 233–37.

was setting in and infecting certain areas of Jesuit life is exemplified
by Fathers such as Simon Rodrigues and Francisco de Estrada.[27]
With the passage of time the need of renewal and renovation became
ever stronger and stronger. From the generalate of Francis Borgia
(1565–72) until the death of Claudius Aquaviva (1615), the administration of the Society was seriously occupied with discovering ways
and means of restoring on all levels the primitive spirit of the first
days. Obviously the question of the prayer life of the order—its quality and quantity—were carefully scrutinized and evaluated. Ultimately
the restoration in what concerns prayer in the Society found its method
not so much in implementing the *Constitutions* of Ignatius as in supplementing and revising them.[28]

St. Ignatius died on July 31, 1556. The First General Congregation, which assembled almost two years later (June 21 to Sept. 10,
1558) and elected Father Diego Laynez as his successor, approved
the *Constitutions* as they had been left to the Society by St. Ignatius.
To those delegates who proposed changing the founder's formulation
of the spiritual program for Jesuits in favor of some kind of extended
obligatory prayer[29] the Congregation's answer was decisive: "The
Constitutions are to be preserved and no determination is to be added
which is not already found in them." In the same decree, however,
the Congregation opened a crack in the wall by making room for the
use of epikeia for increasing, diminishing or commuting the prayer of
the different grades of the Society.

But throughout the generalate of Father Laynez (1558–65) the
old custom of the Society was officially maintained. In a letter (Dec.
31, 1560) to Father Antonio de Cuadros in India, who had petitioned
the general for an increase in the time devoted to daily prayer, the

[27] A. Astrain, *Historia de la Compañía de Jesús en la Asistencia de España*
2 (Madrid 1905) 482–500.
[28] Of high significance in this regard is a *postulatum* presented in 1572 by
the Fathers of the Provincial Congregation of Lusitania. With respect to prayer
they observe: here "the Society seems to have suffered no little hurt, not in
that less time is spent on it than the *Constitutions* allow, but that far less fruit
is harvested from it than formerly; and the clear proof of this situation is the
slender fervor of spirit which is evinced in hearing confessions, in preaching
to the people and in the other ministries of the Society. Many things, which
are said by the Fathers, in no small way lead to the conclusion that prayer
should be restored to its pristine state." Cf. P. Leturia, S.J., *op. cit.*, p. 94: Doc.
VII.
[29] Not only was Borgia not present but his *postulatum* on increasing the
time of prayer arrived in Rome only after the Congregation had dispersed.

direct answer was given: "It does not seem to our Father that generally the time of prayer should be altered by devoting an hour and a half to it." [30] At this time (1558–65) the Spanish provinces seem to have unofficially practiced a continuous hour of daily prayer. Thus there grew up in the most powerful provinces of the Society what amounted to a custom contrary to the *Constitutions*.[31]

On July 2, 1565, Francis Borgia was elected third General of the Society by the Second General Congregation, which he had convoked as vicar. In its twenty-ninth decree it resolved to leave the decision on increasing (but without specifying) the amount of time assigned to prayer to the newly elected General. This was the fruit of prolonged discussion (*per aliquot dies disputatum*) with spokesmen on both sides of the delicate and important question. The Germans and the French "and with them probably the future General Everard Mercurian and perhaps St. Peter Canisius" opposed any increase in the time devoted to prayer by rule, while "the provinces not only of Portugal and Spain but also (and this was decisive) of Italy," with Father Salmeron, Fr. Nadal and probably Fr. Polanco, supported the new approach which Francis Borgia advocated.[32] In formulating their decree the Fathers of the Congregation intended that the General, prudently using the power which they had entrusted to him, might increase the time of prayer, "after taking into account persons, nations and so forth." But this care for the minority—specifically the north European provinces—and its individual needs seems never to have been taken seriously.

On October 5, 1565, approximately one month after the closure of the Congregation, Father General Borgia sent his directive to the whole Society on the prayer-life of all its members, both scholastics and formed.[33] In addition to Mass and the two examinations of conscience he required all to make one hour of prayer each day. At first this hour was not conceived as a unit. For example, fifteen minutes of it could be joined to the night examen. But finally this quarter hour of night prayer was transferred to the morning where it constituted one continuous hour of prayer either mental or vocal (for example, office, rosary or the like), but with growing accent on the former. "Thus

---

[30] *Lainii Monumenta* 5 (Madrid 1915) 357.
[31] Cf. O. Karrer, *op. cit.*, p. 261.
[32] Cf. P. Leturia, S.J., *op. cit.*, p. 71.
[33] Nadal, Epist. 4 (Madrid 1905) 250, n. 1.

the hours of prayer were regulated forever and for all in the Society of Jesus." [34]

In 1566 litanies as a community prayer were introduced into the *de more* life of the Society, as Borgia's response to the request of Pope St. Pius V that prayers be offered by all in the Church for a successful issue to the Turkish problem in Eastern Europe. But even after this crisis had passed, the litanies remained.[35] Gradually communal visits to the Blessed Sacrament after meals—a practice unknown in the time of Ignatius—became normal. At the same time the *exercitia corporis*, a series of menial, manual tasks in the kitchen, the refectory and elsewhere became part of the order of the day. Rosaries were worn as an appendage to the clerical dress which tended to become stylized as a religious habit. As more and more of the morning prayer was devoted to mental prayer, the recitation of the rosary and the Office of the Blessed Virgin was transferred to another part of the day. In 1571 Borgia made the celebration of daily Mass obligatory, and in the following year spiritual reading as a prescribed religious duty entered into the daily order. About the same time the giving of points in common for the morning prayer and the use of special point-books came into greater vogue.

Efforts to Return to the *Constitutions*

In the Third Congregation (April 12 to June 16, 1573), which elected the Belgian Everard Mercurian fourth Father General of the Society, delegates from the northern provinces presented *postulata* that the prayer-pattern of the original *Constitutions* be restored.[36] The appeal was denied. In fact, to the *propositum* of the Provincial Congregation of the Province of Aquitania: "That the program of prayer set forth in the *Constitutions* (IV, 4, 3) as to the manner and time henceforth be observed everywhere in the Society"—and, hence, that the regulation of Francis Borgia be set aside—Father Mercurian gave the curious response: "*Nihil est innovandum.*" Notwithstanding the

[34] Cf. H. Fouqueray, S.J., *Histoire de la Compagnie de Jésus en France* 1 (Paris 1910) 480.

[35] By 1608 the litanies had jelled into a *pia consuetudo*, a private devotion obligatory on all as a communal exercise.

[36] At the same time (1572) the Provincial Congregation of the province of Naples, which Alphonsus Salmeron and Bernardino Realino attended, was asking that the integral hour of mental prayer be decreed as a necessity. Cf. P. Leturia, S.J., *op. cit.*, pp. 97–8: Doc. VIII.

formulation of the so called *Canones trium Congregationum,* the practice, which Borgia had inaugurated, remained normative for the Society, while a restitution of the prescriptions of the *Constitutions* of
Ignatius seemed an innovation.

But even in the course of the decade after the Society's adoption of
the Borgian usage there still existed a pronounced confusion, dissatis-
faction and resentment. The desired renewal had not been secured.
Apropos of certain doubts about the question of the Society's prayer
the Belgian Provincial, Badouin de Lange, wrote on April 22, 1574,
to Father General Mercurian for clarification. The official documents
seemed to create an obscurity which required explanation. According
to the thirty-sixth canon of the *Canones trium Congregationum,* he
writes:

the *Constitutions* are to be preserved and nothing else is to be pre-
scribed about the time of prayer. But from an ordinance of the late
Father Borgia of happy memory we have, in addition to Mass, two
hours of prayer daily. At the same time the fourth chapter of the
Fourth Part of the *Constitutions* prescribes only one hour of prayer.
Will Your Paternity, therefore, please tell us what we should do.
Should we follow the canons and the *Constitutions,* or the ordinance
of the Reverend Father of happy memory . . . ? [37]

In solving the doubt the Father General simply refused to yield on
the practice of Borgia, which had become customary in the Society.

In 1576, the Provincial Congregation of the Province of Aquitania
once again petitioned Father Mercurian to rescind the obligatory hour
of prayer which had been introduced eleven years before by Father
Borgia. The ten *rationes adversae* which accompanied the *postulatum*
are striking in their frankness and are worth citing, at least partially:

First. According to the original Institute (IV, 4 and VI, 3) there is
expressly granted to Jesuits one hour of prayer each day; for this reason—that the ministries of the Society consume the whole man and,
therefore, its members should not be burdened with long prayer and
meditation.
Second. When in the First Congregation there was question of increasing the prayer, the response was given that the *Constitutions*
should be preserved and no determinations added to them.
Third. When in the Third Congregation there was question of remov-

[37] *Ibid.,* p. 99: Doc. XI.

ing the increase in the time of prayer, the matter was referred to
the General that in virtue of his charity and prudence he might act
in accord with the power granted to him by the Second Congregation.
Wherefore it was the hope of some that the increase in prayer might
be removed.

Fourth. We should consider what fruit this increase has yielded.
Generally speaking we seem to have been better, or at least less bad,
before its introduction than after.

Fifth. Our teachers complain that they do not have enough time for
preparing their lectures when they are forced to pray for a whole
hour in the morning. This verges on working a detriment to the youth
whose education we have undertaken.

Sixth. Priests and many administrators complain that they are severely
burdened with the Breviary, which is now much longer than before,
moreover with daily litanies and with [meditating on] the rules of
office, when an hour of morning prayer is added to all this.

Seventh. Many complain, those especially who have not acquired
the habit of meditating, that because of the long period of prayer
they are discouraged from it or at least fatigued. This would not
happen, if prayer were for the space of a half hour.

Eighth. Others complain that after a half hour they are swamped
with phantasms and thoughts which not only take away from them
the relish of prayer but also a great part of prayer itself.

Ninth. It seems that the incrementum should be removed that all
might more easily bear the other burdens of the Society and perform
their work more expeditiously.

Tenth. It seems that the increase in the time of prayer should be removed that that former relish for it might return and be conserved.[38]

To this *postulatum* Father Mercurian answered: "It seems now that
nothing should be changed, but the superior can dispense those who
are very weak (*imbecillioribus*) and those who are very busy."

A realistic insight into the situation, which the introduction of the
hour of morning prayer had created, is afforded by a letter which the
astute French Provincial Claude Mathieu directed (Feb. 26, 1576) to
Father General Mercurian. It foreshadows in a certain sense the modern problem of religious tepidity.

Will Your Paternity please consider whether in the Society it is fitting
that that period of time for prayer be observed which is prescribed
in the *Constitutions,* and that the incrementum of prayer be removed
which was introduced some years ago. For I notice that Jesuits are
less fervent in prayer now than previously. Indeed in the past they

[38] *Ibid.,* pp. 100–101: Doc. VIII.

used frequently to ask permission to give more time to prayer, and perhaps they spent more time then on prayer than they do now . . . But nowadays many ask to be dispensed from the increase in prayer. Thus in a very short time there will be more who are dispensed—or what is worse, more who will dispense themselves—than those who (as is now the case) observe the rule. It has always seemed to me that we will accomplish not a little, if we simply and perfectly observe those things which are in our *Constitutions,* because if we wish to adopt other things, there is fear that little by little the practice of what is prescribed in our *Constitutions* will cease; and finally we will learn to our discomfort that it would have been better if we had remained in the simplicity of our fathers.[39]

Aquaviva's Generalate

On February 19, 1581 the Fourth General Congregation elected the young (thirty-eight-year-old) Neapolitan Fr. Claudius Aquaviva fifth General of the Society. His tenure of office, the longest in the history of the Society, lasted thirty-four years, and was marked by a concentrated effort to renovate and restore its depleted spirit. Following the lead of Francis Borgia, this Congregation in its fifth decree made it a matter of law that every member of the Society, both scholastic and formed Jesuit, make one integral hour of prayer every day in addition to the two examens of conscience and attendance at Mass. It decreed that "the pious and salutary custom . . . as it was introduced by Reverend Father Borgia, should be retained." But the decree did not say that the hour must be in the morning nor that it must be continuous; nor does it specify the quality of this prayer, whether it should be mental or vocal.

Francis Suarez in his monumental *Tractatus de religione Societatis Iesu* (1608–09) remarks that the hour of mental prayer in the Society is a matter of custom rather than of positive law:

The time of that hour in virtue of the *Constitutions* is not so ordered to mental prayer that the Rosary or the Office of the Blessed Virgin cannot be recited during it, in view of the devotion or the greater fruit of those praying . . . Even though the fifth canon of the Fourth General Congregation says that "the custom of praying for an integral hour be retained," it does not declare that the whole prayer is to be mental.[40]

[39] *Ibid.,* p. 102: Doc. XIV.
[40] F. Suarez, *Tractatus de religione Societatis Iesu* VIII, 2, 2 (Paris 1857) 402.

He concludes that by the *custom* and *practice* of the Society the whole hour of morning prayer is mental (meditation and contemplation) and thus it should be considered a *ius ordinarium Societatis.*

In the generalate of Aquaviva the hour of daily prayer as an hour of *mental* prayer became more and more a general rule for the whole Society. In writing, for example, to the Polish Province in 1581 the General says: "Let superiors take care that an hour in the morning be devoted to mental prayer"; and later, in 1582, he writes to Fr. Henry Herveus of the Lower German Province: "Even though we do not totally prohibit vocal prayers, since in the judgment of a superior or a spiritual father it may be that one might be assisted by them spiritually, nevertheless we desire that among Jesuits mental prayer thrive as much as possible." The movement of ideas was clearly in the direction of meditation and contemplation.

Nor did the General consider that the Fourth Congregation in making an hour of daily prayer obligatory on all had in any way revoked the principle of *discreta caritas* which Ignatius had explicitly laid down in the *Constitutions* as the norm to be followed in establishing the prayer-life of the members of the Society. It has been seen above how adamant Ignatius was in rejecting any and every attempt to infringe this key principle of liberty and diversity in the spiritual life. And it is an anomaly in the history of spirituality that to this day the hour of morning meditation is represented as an authentic tradition of Ignatius, almost as a measuring rod of Jesuit asceticism.

In setting down his principles on the prayer-life of the formed Jesuits, Ignatius shows a remarkable broadness of judgment and liberality. He always provides for the exception and the exceptional. Thus he remarks in the *Constitutions* (VI, 3, 1): "When doubt arises about what is fitting, the matter should be referred to the superior"; and later (VI, 3, 1A): "If it be judged wise that a definite time be prescribed for certain ones to prevent their being either excessive or deficient in spiritual exercises, the superior will have the power to do this." Qualifications such as these are often used by Ignatius in his directives and laws. They are prudent provisions allowing superiors to make exceptions for individuals or even for groups, "for certain ones," as he says, who for one reason or another are incapable of fulfilling the law or fulfilling it only with difficulty. But with respect to the quality and quantity of prayer prescribed for the whole Society, Ignatius had already explicitly precluded any change of the text of the *Constitutions.*

On the other hand, he respected the individual religious and his needs to the extent that he did not wish to exclude the possibility of changing general norms in favor of particular needs, even to the extent of allowing this or that one more time, if it should be needed. But the sources do not show that Ignatius intended or would have approved a basic displacement of the spiritual program which he outlined in this part of the *Constitutions*.

What is most novel in the trends that have been described here is not that Jesuits meditate for one hour in the morning (Ignatius was not really opposed to that), but that the administration of the Society should determine by law universal norms for the spiritual life of all its members, regardless of their individual differences. It is here that one notes a drift from that freedom of spirit on which Ignatius' spiritual doctrine rests and which gives it its peculiar excellence. It is here, in legislation which prescribes the same spiritual regime for all the religious of the Society, however diverse in age, talent, experience, work and energy, that a sharp displacement of the Ignatian insight is discernible.

It can be freely granted that both Francis Borgia and Claudius Aquaviva, as well as the Second and Fourth (1581) Congregations, had serious religious problems to face which could only be solved, or at least mitigated, by the ascetical prescriptions which they provided. The facts of history seem to incline to this conclusion. These Generals had full authority to act; and their decrees in the matter of prayer are part of the law of the Society to be observed by all its members. But a further question can be posed apropos of the *Constitutions* of Ignatius and their historical development. In view of the modern problems which confront the Society, does its prayer-life require new thinking, evaluating and adjusting? The question becomes especially relevant when one considers that historical scholarship over the past half century has thrown so much light on the character of the spiritual doctrine of Ignatius and his personal insights in the formation of religious.

Picture of St. Ignatius

The picture which emerges from contemporary research shows that St. Ignatius was truly adept in psychology and a master of prayer, perhaps more skilled in this precious art than has yet been fully appreciated. His own interior development was a marvel to those few who knew him sufficiently to comprehend the wondrous depth of his prayer-life. But apart from his personal sanctity, Ignatius had a very fine appreciation of the richness of human nature and of the diversity of its approach to God in prayer. For him man was complex, not in the way that the structure of a machine is intricate, but rather with the dynamic multiplicity of a living (spiritual, intellectual and sensitive) organism, which must be cared for in terms of its own individual stage of development and achievement. In this area of human activity fast norms cannot be drawn to provide for all aspects of growth and evolution, for the life of the spirit knows no universal categories.

Ignatius also had a meaningful perception of the nature of work, of the concrete act of service, of the manifold tasks that integrate a day of apostolic life. This aspect of the human existence Ignatius conceived as the point of encounter with God who is to be found in all things, in work therefore, as well as in prayer. Ignatian spirituality does not rest on the dichotomy—work and prayer; rather it envisions the entire activity of the formed Jesuit as a continuous band of service proceeding from charity, obedience and selflessness. Here, in all the work which the apostolic life involves, the Jesuit meets God. In the service of the divine majesty the heart and core of Ignatian spirituality finds its fulfillment. It does not seek to burden the human spirit.

In this study I have not tried to say everything that could be said. In the course of so few pages no one can settle definitively the complex issues—from the point of view of spiritual doctrine and religious history—which this study raises. The theme which is under consideration here is delicate not only because it infringes venerable traditions but also because it touches the commitment of so many individuals who have a precise understanding of their historical past. If this discussion has raised important questions, agitated them in the minds of the readers, opened up new vistas or even cast doubts on the validity of old ones, it has succeeded. No one is really worthy of a great heritage unless he understands its origins, character and value; and no heritage is really great unless it can endure the wear and tear of time. The heritage which the contemporary Society of Jesus has received from its holy Founder is far in excess of the value at which it is commonly assessed. It is our present obligation to seek out this treasure, study, know and restore it.

APPENDIX

This study is not presented as a totally original contribution to historical research. It rests on the excellent scholarship which has been made possible over the past fifty years by the publication of the various parts of the *Monumenta Historica Societatis Iesu*. On the basis of this vast source collection historians of the Society are now better acquainted with the genetic development both of its history and its spirituality. We are approaching the time when it will be possible on the basis of historical evidence to make valid value-judgments on certain aspects of our past which have been obscure. The scholarly work that has already been accomplished in this area of concentration—the spirituality of St. Ignatius—has enriched the Society with a deeper understanding of its origins, character and possibilities of future development.

I add here a list of some of the more important titles that handle various aspects of Ignatian spirituality, which is the central theme of this paper:

J. Aicardo, S.J., *Comentaria á las Constituciones de la Compañía de Jesús* 2 (Madrid 1920) 386–409.

A. Astrain, S.J., *Historia de la Compañía de Jesús en la Asistencia de España* 2 (Madrid 1905).

A. Astrain, S.J., *De oratione matutina in Societate Iesu* (Bilbao 1923).

P. Bouvier, S.J., *Les origines de l'oraison mentale en usage dans la Compagnie* (Wetteren 1923).

J. de Guibert, S.J., *The Jesuits: Their Spiritual Doctrine and Practice* (Chicago 1964).

B. Duhr, S.J., *Geschichte der Jesuiten in den Ländern deutscher Zunge* 1 (Freiburg 1907) 570–73.

H. Fouqueray, S.J., *Histoire de la Compagnie de Jésus en France* 1 (Paris 1910) 435–36.

O. Karrer, *Der heilige Franz von Borja* (Freiburg 1921) 249–67.

P. Leturia, S.J., "La hora matutina de meditación en la Compañía naciente," *Archivum Historicum Societatis Iesu* 3 (1934) 47–86.

P. Leturia, S.J., "De oratione matutina in Societate Iesu documenta selecta," *Archivum Historicum Societatis Iesu* 3 (1934) 87–108.

The Origins of
the Jesuit Tertianship

Anthony Ruhan, S.J.

When Favre, Laynez, Broet, and the other companions of Ignatius decided to remain in Venice in 1537 and not seek God's greater glory as galahads in the Holy Land, they spent tedious days and nights caring for the sick, hearing confessions, and preaching to the poor. Years later, Ignatius wanted the young men studying to be Jesuits to share in the experiences of first companions at Venice. Ignatius knew that many years of study did not constitute a complete preparation for the apostolate: maturity and compassion come when dealing with people. Thus tertianship was started not as an experiment for leading a contemplative life regulated by definite patterns and practices, but a time when young Jesuits could experience and perceive the needs of their fellow men.

In this article an explanation is sought of the statements found in the *Constitutions* of the Society of Jesus concerning the last year of probation, or tertianship, as it is often called. The aim, then, is exegetic. The question of meaning, however, leads to the problem of interpretation, and this, in its turn, poses almost inevitably the problem of development. As is the case with every body of legislation, the statements embodied in the *Constitution* of the Society can be traced to various strata, each of which had its origin in different historical situations, but which were all united by the legislator into a series of terse legal phrases.

As it is only by discovering the historical situations which gave rise to the different questions and their corresponding answers that we can understand the answers themselves, so it is only by viewing the way in which these questions and answers follow one another in time and are related to one another that we can understand fully the meaning of the *Constitutions*. In other fields the importance of the idea of development has been shown, and, if it has been regarded as essential to an understanding of Christian doctrine, whether in the matter of the Trinity or in that of the sacraments, it should prove to be no less useful when applied to the interpretation of the *Constitutions* of the Society.

The *Constitutions* and the *Examen Generale* call the tertianship a year of probation: they mention it as a time in which the candidate for final vows is tested and examined with a view to determining once for all his suitability for Jesuit life.[1] Besides the testing of the candidate for religious profession, however, there is mentioned, almost in parenthesis, another reason which it is possible to pass over without further reflection as being merely an amplification of the idea of probation, but which, on second thoughts, is not so easily reduced to it. This is the statement that, after completing his studies (which were concerned with the cultivation of the intellect), the scholastic should apply himself to the *schola affectus* (which deals with matters of the heart), by turning now to "spiritual and corporal" works, which will help him to make progress in humility and in the denial of selfishness and self-will or self-opinionatedness.[2] These qualities will fit a man better to work in the apostolate.

Here we see two themes laid down quite clearly by the *Constitutions,* and it seems that they are obviously closely united. Within the legal context of determining a candidate's suitability for admission to final religious profession, the idea of probation appears primary. However, in the background there lies the pedagogic purpose of the tertianship: if the qualities desired are lacking in the candidate, the probation has as its purpose to produce them in him, and it may even be prolonged for this reason. But both of the purposes derive their meaning from the necessity of having religious with the type of character mentioned. These characteristics are obviously valuable in themselves, and they can only be understood in this context when we grasp why the men who wrote the *Constitutions* thought they were necessary—for the *Constitutions,* although put finally into words by one man, were certainly the work of a community.[3]

[1] *Constitutiones,* Pars V, C. 2, n. 1. *Examen Generale,* C. 1, n. 12; C. 4, n. 16.
[2] *Const.,* P. V, C. 2, n. 1.
[3] *Monumenta Ignatiana Constitutiones* I: Monumenta Praevia.

I: THE MEANING OF THE *CONSTITUTIONS*

St. Ignatius and His Early Companions

The early companions of St. Ignatius who mention the last probation place its origin in the religious experience which they all had
together during the time which elapsed between their departure from
Paris on December 15, 1536, and their final arrival in Rome in
1538. As Aicardo suggests, that this is true is first of all rendered
probable by the saint's habitual way of acting.[4] For he ordered the
book of the *Exercises* according to his own experiences and that of
the others who made them; the steps in the spiritual life described
in the *Examen* are those which he himself had passed through and
which he made his followers go through and practise; the successes
and failures of his student days in Alcalá and Paris provided the guide
for the method of study and life in the colleges of the Society; the
procedure for the congregations he took from that of the first reunions
which the early fathers had had among themselves; and, finally, the
traits and method of government of the general he based on his own
traits and manner of ruling. Hence, it was natural that here, too, in
the matter of the last probation of the Society, he should have had
recourse to the same experiences which had guided him in other considerations. As we shall see, all of the first generation of Jesuits regarded the experiences, or experiments, as they came to be called,
as of primary importance. This was especially true for those of the
last probation. In order to understand their attitude, we must try to
reconstruct for ourselves briefly the life of St. Ignatius and his companions from the time of their departure from Paris to their arrival in
Rome in 1538.

After the completion of his studies in Paris, St. Ignatius rode to
Azpeitia, where he lived in a hospice for the poor and supported
himself by begging. There he carried on three months of apostolic
activity in the seignorial domain of his brother, Don Martin. He
held classes in catechism for the children each day; he preached
and worked in every way to convert those whose lives needed
emendation. He also organized relief for the poor. In July, 1535,
he began a journey on behalf of his companions, whom he had left

---

[4] J. M. Aicardo, *Commentario a las Constituciones de la Compañía de Jesús*
(Madrid: Blass, 1930), V, pp. 667 ff. *Fontes Narrativi de Sancto Ignatio Mon.
Ign.* II, p. 9, n. 22. Exhortation of Nadal.

in Paris. On foot he crossed a great part of Spain, from Pamplona through Toledo to Valencia, visiting the families of Francis Xavier, of Laynez and Salmerón and some of his former friends. From Valencia he took ship for Genoa, despite warnings as to the dangers of pirates, and passed through storms before reaching that city. On foot from Genoa to Bologna he endured great trials and dangers by road and not a little inconvenience in begging for food and lodging. Sickness, which had hindered his studies in theology at Paris, recurred and prevented him from doing them there at the university. Hence he set out for Venice, where he arrived in the last days of 1535, and began giving the *Exercises* and helping others by his conversation. Here he was able to continue his studies, in addition to performing his apostolic work. Here also he endured misunderstanding and persecution.

His nine companions, after obtaining their master's degrees in Paris, left that city despite the threat of war between France and Spain, and came by foot, in the middle of winter, through Lorraine, part of Germany and Switzerland, begging their way and carrying only a few books and their breviaries in satchels on their backs. On the way they engaged in occasional debates with the Lutherans, insisted that the priests among them say Mass every day, and arrived to meet Ignatius in Venice in early January, 1536. Since no ships were leaving for Palestine, they decided to occupy themselves in the interim by working in the hospitals of the city. The type of work was back-breaking and unremitting service of the most heroic kind.[5] Granted the conditions in the hospitals of the day, what the early Jesuits were doing was rendering service of the most elementary kind to those who were often almost abandoned. Of these activities Pedro de Ribadeneyra says that "our fathers there laid the foundations of the probation which the Society would afterwards have to undergo." [6] After a further journey to Rome, during which they once more walked their twenty to thirty miles a day, begging their way, the nine companions returned to Venice and Ignatius with the blessing of the pope on their pilgrimage to Jerusalem. Back in Venice they

[5] *Mon. Broet,* p. 475. *Mon. Ign. Font. Narr.* I, p. 110: letter of Laynez concerning St. Ignatius. Tacchi Venturi, La Prova dell' Indifferenza e del Servizio negli Ospedali nel Tirocinio Ignaziano, *Archivum Historicum Societatis Jesu* 1932, I, pp. 14–23.

[6] P. Ribadeneyra, *Vita di San Ignazio di Loiola* (Roma: Coi Tipi della Civiltà Cattolica, 1863), pp. 112–13.

renewed their work in the hospitals, and those of them who were not priests received orders. Then followed a diaspora, the company breaking up into groups of three or four and going to Vicenza, Padua or Monselice, Bassano, Verona and Treviso. In these cities they sought out solitude and made the *Exercises* for forty days, in the meanwhile living in great poverty. Then began their effective, if unusual, evangelizing of the cities, shouting to attract attention in the market places, preaching and hearing confessions in a language which they had imperfectly learned. In the autumn they reassembled in Vicenza and continued their activity. The abandonment of their hopes of going to the Holy Land led them to resolve to offer their services to the pope, and from this point onwards the foundation of the Society proceeded apace.

This, it would seem, was the seminal period for the final probation of the Society. Hence, it will be necessary to make an evaluation of it in terms of the men who lived and experienced it. Certainly, here there was no talk of probation. As yet there was no explicit talk of any corporate endeavor, and hence no question of associating others with themselves. If there is a key to the understanding of this period in the life of the Society, it lies not in the word "probation," in any proper sense of the word, but rather that it was a school to develop and foster the affective life of those concerned. Let us try briefly to delineate the features of this phase in the development of the ten companions.

Their association had begun in Paris under the influence and guiding hand of St. Ignatius. At first, the common feature of the members of the group was that each had undergone a religious conversion. In turning to God they drew nearer to one another, and the logic of the Gospel led them soon to the idea of service—at the beginning, of a whole-hearted, if somewhat vague, service. It was a time when the Turks were menacing Christendom, and the spirit of the crusades was in the air. That spirit had already led Ignatius once to the Holy Land, and it was to spread its infection through his followers. Acting under this impulse they set out in their groups, as already described, for Rome, but met with obstacles.

At the same time they were academics, or at least educated men, with their minds set to some extent upon an ecclesiastical career. Ignatius himself had perceived dimly that, in order to be of service to God, he would have to become an educated man, and it was this perception which had directed him to Paris. Yet the connection between learning and the spreading of the kingdom of God was in many ways a formal one. The ecclesiastical studies of the late fifteenth century were languishing in the long decline which began at the end of the golden age of Scholasticism. Theology was infected with nominalism, and positive studies were neglected. The revival of theology, which had just begun, was a long time in making its influence felt, and the cultivated classes were at pains to keep clear of Scholasticism.

The studies, then, that had just been occupying the first companions of Ignatius might well have been called desiccating. The famed "order and method of Paris," so beloved by the Saint, with its endless cycle of preparation for the lecture, attendance at the class and repetition of the matter heard, when not supplemented by more widening reading, would have suppressed the emotional life of the students. Of course, the students in general had their own means of entertainment, but earnest young men, trying at the same time to lead a devout life, would have found life by and large a grind. And it was from this life that they turned to the journey to Venice and the work in the hospitals and to the evangelizing of the surrounding countryside. Within two months they had begun to care for the poor and abandoned, washing and feeding the sick, digging the graves and burying the dead, and this experience could only have been profoundly moving. In the *Memoriale* of Gonçalves da Câmara we read St. Ignatius' own account: "I had many spiritual visions and more consolations than ordinary, contrary to the period in Paris. Especially when I commenced to prepare for the priesthood in Venice and to say Mass I had more consolations than at Manresa." [7] Of the period of study in Paris, Laynez writes that Ignatius had then many difficulties in prayer.[8] Then, their apostolic activity of preaching, hearing confessions and teaching children the catechism would have provided one more affective release to the erstwhile students. Here was the first use of the tools of learning which they had so laboriously acquired in Paris. And both the spiritual and corporal works had the effect of focusing in their minds the initial, admittedly vague desire of winning back the Holy Land in order to save the honor of the King who had once ruled there. Yet, in another sense

[7] *Font. Narr.* I, pp. 494–95.
[8] *Ibid.*, pp. 99–100.

that they had not at first perceived, the kingdom of God was lying in ravages all around them in Italy, and in the Germany and Switzerland through which they had passed. These perceptions at first lay fallow in the fertile soil of their hearts, but it did not need more than the shrewd remark of Paul III to bring them to fruition: "Italy is a good and true Jerusalem, if you wish to produce fruit in the Church of God!" [9] The main lines of the Society's structure were laid down during this year or more of labor after the companions' studies. The relation between the religious idea (grasped by Ignatius in his experiences in Manresa and communicated to his companions through the *Exercises*) and studies in the service of the Church was also established here, and received practical application within the next few months when first Favre and Laynez, and then Broet, received special missions from the pope.

To summarize, then, the results of our analysis of this period, we can say that the first community of Jesuits-to-be was dominated by the idea of service in the Church, i.e., to rescue the kingdom of God from its enemy, where it had fallen under his control, or spread that kingdom and increase the honor of the king. Their spirit may fairly be described as a crusading one. What had remained during their course of studies an abstract idea now became, under the pressure of circumstances and through contact with reality, a living one, although not yet so clear as to admit of its being exactly and fully formulated in writing.

Probation for the New Entrants into the Society

Scarcely had the companions arrived in Rome to seek the blessing of the supreme pontiff than the latter had commissioned Favre, Laynez and Broet for special work on his behalf; and the demands for their services multiplied immediately and beyond the possibility of their answering them. Since it was evident that the first intention of St. Ignatius—to receive only priests—would restrict the scope of the nascent Society's effectiveness too much, he early decided to accept young students, with a view not only to educating them, but also to giving them a religious training which would make them in time fellow workers with the first companions. This determination was expressed already in 1539, in the summary of the Society's In-

[9] *Mon. Bobad., Autobiographia,* p. 616.

stitute and later appears as the theme of the deliberations *De Fundandis Collegiis* of 1541 and 1544.[10]

From the beginning the existence of a class of students in or connected with the Society posed many problems. Their exact status was also problematical. After an initial period of trial, they first took a vow or promise to enter the Society after the completion of their studies, with the condition that the vow or promise should become effective only after the first year of their studies. If they were not then satisfied, they could sever their connection with the Society.[11] Later, vows of poverty and chastity, and, in some circumstances, of obedience, were pronounced. The vows were merely vows of devotion, and there was great variety in the formula for pronouncing them.[12] However, the details of the history of the canonical status of the scholastics need not detain us here. It is enough to know that the idea of a scholastic was at this period of history somewhat anomalous, and that their connection with the Society was initially a loose one. Later, with the increase in number of the colleges run by the Society, the life of these students normalized itself, and was, to some extent and on some occasions, lived with the Society itself.[13]

What was characteristic of the training of the scholastics was that they were required to undergo certain experiences or "experiments," as they were called. These experiences were precisely of the kind which the first companions had themselves undergone in the period after their studies in Paris. Thus, in the first deliberations concerning the Institute in 1541, we read that, "first of all, he who is to study in such a college must pass through three experiences: the first being that the Society or someone ordered to do so on its behalf must talk with the prospective student during the period of one month, more or less, while he makes the *Spiritual Exercises* or something equivalent, in order that some judgment may be made as to his nature and constancy, his ability, inclinations and vocation. For another month he must serve the poor in a hospital doing every kind of menial work which shall be required, so that, by overcoming

[10] *Mon. Ign. Const.*, pp. 19, 48 ff. See *ibid.*, Prima Soc. Iesu Instituti Summa, p. 19.
[11] *Mon. Ign. Const.* I, pp. 53–55, n. 6–9 of 1541; and p. 56, n. 5 of 1544.
[12] Vow formula for 1549, *Mon. Ign.* II, p. 202. Cf. formula of Ribadeneyra, *Rib. Epist.* II, p. 297. See also unpublished manuscript of Rev. I. Miller of Innsbruck, *Das Eintrittsgelübde.*
[13] See letter of St. Ignatius to Araoz, *Mon. Ign. Epist. et Instruct.* V, pp. 5–9.

himself, any sense of shame may depart or be lost in this victory. For the space of another month he should go on a pilgrimage on foot and without money, so that he may place his every expectation in his creator and Lord, and grow accustomed to sleeping and eating poorly, since anyone who does not know how to live or go one day eating and sleeping poorly would not appear likely to persevere in our Society . . ." [14] In the application of these methods of training to the individual, however, great flexibility was recommended. After, or even during the period of studies, according to the demands of circumstances, another three months of similar experiences were required; and at the completion of the whole period a complete year in making the *Exercises* and in similar activities, although with the addition of apostolic ministries, was laid down as necessary.

The purpose which St. Ignatius and the first companions always give for making the students undergo these experiences was as follows. Other religious orders live in a cloister and have a protected life, whereas men of the Society must renounce this solitude in order to live in the world. Consequently, they will have in the normal course of events many more temptations to sin. A man with sinful habits who enters a monastery will have the opportunity of amending his life without exterior stress, whereas the Jesuit must mix with men and women, with the virtuous and with those of evil life, and hence must be tried to begin with. The only way to become seasoned is to plunge into life and experience its pushes and pulls. There was no mollycoddling in the early Society. The hospital experiment, as we have seen, was no formality. Tacchi Venturi has given a graphic description of this experience as it was practiced in the time of St. Ignatius, and he notes that some did not come through it successfully: there were those who died or became ill through catching infections or from overwork; there were those who simply fled the Society because they could not endure its rigors; and there were those who fell into sin and sinful habits and were lost to the Society in this way.

However, the aim was not merely the negative one of finding out weaknesses. The theory behind the subjection of the young Jesuits-to-be to these experiences was a sound one, well known to modern psychology: it was simply that human beings come to maturity by living contact with other human beings in rather intensely emotional

[14] P. Tacchi Venturi, *AHSJ* 1932, I, pp. 14–23. See also Ribadeneyra, *Vita*, p. 112, and *Mon. Broet.*, pp. 474–78; Polanco, *Chronicon* I, p. 57.

circumstances—the psychologists call it "involvement"! The particular nuance which the early Jesuits thought so valuable for the purposes of the Society was to have these circumstances dominated by the idea of service. Performing the most elementary services for the helpless wrings one inside out, just as preaching the Gospel or explaining the truth to the ignorant can also be a moving experience.

The reason why the early Jesuits saw this time of raw contact with life to be necessary may also be sought partly in the nature of the studies. The case of Frusius and Polanco will serve to illustrate both this wearing and wearying effect of the studies and also the way in which the first students of the Society were put to study. Polanco and Frusius were sent to study in Padua, presumably after some time spent in experiencing life in the hospitals and in similar activities, Polanco to repeat the course and Frusius to begin it. They lived together in a room near the university, attending lectures and working at home. Polanco remarks that the lectures were rather mixed in quality, and that it was sometimes more profitable for them both to stay at home and work together. He says that he himself repeated some courses quickly; omitted others which did not seem useful; worked at Scholastic theology, both old and modern; studied Scripture; but, then, "a number of other authors, who appear to help the practical ministry of preaching to our neighbors, hearing confessions and interviewing." [15] It is good to see that exasperation with the lack of utility of parts of the course of theology was no modern malady! Indeed, as we have seen, the students of those days had probably more grounds to complain than those of today. But the change to three months of experience of the type mentioned above would have been both necessary and welcome: it would have been in every sense a *schola affectus,* orientating the personality of the student once more towards the ideal of apostolic service in a very concrete and salutary way.

But there was obviously in the minds of the early companions of St. Ignatius another facet of the problem of studies with which we have not yet explicitly dealt. For many in those days studies were the necessary first step on the path towards ecclesiastical preferment. The case of Erasmus was the classical one, but it was by no means rare. It is a commonplace of the history of the Reformation

---

[15] *Polanci Compl.* I, pp. 50–51. See also pp. 3–4.

that service in the Church was used by many in order to achieve positions of comfort, honor and wealth. This was merely one feature in the general decline of religious life at this time. Once a young man had been launched into ecclesiastical studies, even though his original intention had been one of apostolic service, there was always the temptation to think more of himself than of the needs of the kingdom of God, and so to lose the ideal of the Society.[16] For this reason the early Jesuits insisted upon just that kind of wholehearted service for three months after the completion of the studies, and then, in addition, of another year, more or less as a complete repetition of the year which the ten first companions had spent in the territory of Venice in 1537–1538. The case of Polanco was in every way typical. Ferronius, writing from Rome in March, 1547, to Turrianus says: "Since Master Juan de Polanco has been six years in association with the Society and he has finished his studies in Padua, he has begun to do the customary year of probation. . . . He has produced great fruit for souls by his four months of preaching in Bologna and Pistoia, as well as by hearing confessions and giving lectures, sermons and interviewing people, moving on to the city of Florence about six months after leaving Padua in order to perform the same ministries there." [17] The subsequent history of Polanco's doings in Florence need not detain us here. It is sufficient to know that the course of the year's probation followed that of the first ten companions more or less exactly: the religious experience of making the *Exercises* and serving the poor and the ignorant with the utmost generosity. If the erstwhile student was not content to do this, he should leave the Society.[18] It is interesting that Polanco himself states, in the period from 1547 to 1549, that the time of this last probation can even be extended so as to achieve its aim, thus taking up the words of the *Examen Generale* (C. 1, n. 12).

By way of conclusion to this section we may note that the experience of working in the kitchen and doing other menial work around the house had not the overtone of artificiality in the early Society. One of the practical effects of the shortage of numbers in

---

[16] Nadal in 1554 speaks of the danger of a *spiritus debilitas* and *spiritus distractiones*, *Mon. Nad.* V, pp. 64, 306.

[17] *Mon. Ign. Epist. et Instruct.* I, p. 467.

[18] Polanco, letter of Oct. 31, 1547, to Araoz, *Mon. Ign. Epist. et Instruct.* I, p. 615.

the Society was that its members had to do housework themselves, simply because there was no one else to do it. We have the charming story of the visit paid by Araoz to Ignatius in Rome. He found Francis Xavier in the porter's lodge. Francis called out: "Ignatius, here is Araoz to talk with you! [19] Yet we need not imagine that it was more than necessity which compelled Francis or any of the early Jesuits to do this. As Paul III so courteously expressed it, their intentions were just the opposite,[20] and in this they were merely following the example of the apostles (Acts 6:1–6). But the tradition of healthy, practical realism remained, and no one could regard himself as too good to do the ordinary housework if it proved necessary.

From 1548 onwards it was agreed that St. Ignatius should begin the drafting of the *Constitutions* of the new order. Into this book were incorporated the religious experiences and the acquired wisdom of the first companions. As Karl Rahner has suggested in his essay on the inspiration of Scripture, the New Testament was the book of the primitive Church, and hence the model for the Church of all time. In it was expressed the unique experience which the men of the apostolic age had had in their fellowship with the Lord Jesus Christ; it was the literary crystallization of the experience of the first Christian community. In an analogous way the *Constitutions* were the literary expression of the authentic religious experience of the first and founding Jesuit community, which had grouped itself around Ignatius Loyola under the inspiration of the Spirit of Christ. Their unique desire for a completely free and utterly dedicated service of Christ the King by reconquering the Holy Land was gradually transformed in their minds by the logic of the experiences which they had had following the years after leaving Paris. The trials and errors which resulted from their novel conception of the religious life had gradually come, after the protracted discussions over the nature of the Institute of the new order, to final expression in the document which their leader presented for their final consideration and further experimentation in 1551.

In the light of this apostolic aim to serve where the need was greatest in the Church we can now understand the meaning of the words of the *Constitutions* that the last year of probation, or the third, as it now was in law, was the final proof to the Society and to

[19] *Font. Narr.* I, p. 613.
[20] See Litterae Apostolicae Pauli III, *Mon. Ign. Const.* I, pp. 170–73.

the man himself that the candidate for final admission to the order did indeed possess the spirit of the Society. His studies had been made not with a view to his own advancement in the Church or merely as an academic exercise, but were merely tools for the service of the poor, and, in order that this noble profession might not remain merely a verbal one, he now turned to just this service in its most radical form, to the corporal and spiritual help of the most abandoned. In this way he would be able to make the final discernment of spirits which is necessary for every man who will give his life a direction under the guidance of God. In this sense the tertianship was the school for men after Ignatius' heart.

II: THE INTERPRETATION OF THE *CONSTITUTIONS*

The Tertianship during Generalates of Laynez and Borgia

As Aicardo remarks, there is not a great deal in the sources of the early Society's literature about the tertianship apart from what we have already examined.[21] The *Constitutions* were experimentally promulgated in 1552, and Nadal travelled about Europe explaining their meaning. They became the Society's law in 1558. There is no reason to doubt that the last probation was practiced as it had been during the previous period. Until the time of St. Francis Borgia's government of the Society we have no explicit reference to it, but it was at this time that there began in all probability a tendency to interpret the *Constitutions,* which we have mentioned as the correlative problem to that of grasping their original meaning. For the purpose of appreciating this particular interpretation, which perhaps did not make itself felt until the reign of Claudius Aquaviva, it will be necessary to sketch the character of St. Francis, or at least its distinctive traits insofar as it determined his manner of governing the Society, as well as the influences he underwent. Even during the time of St. Ignatius, as is well known, there existed in the Society two ascetical tendencies. There were those who favored a contemplative manner of living, much devoted to bodily penance and long prayers. Of these the Jesuits Oviedo and Onfroi, together with his former

---

[21] Aicardo, *op. cit.,* p. 674. Aicardo states that Nadal has nothing in his instructions upon the subject of the tertianship. We do, however, possess some of his remarks made in letters and exhortations. See, e.g., *Font. Narr.* II, p. 9, n. 22, and *Mon. Nad.* V, pp. 64, 806.

court chaplain, the Franciscan Tejeda, exerted a marked influence upon St. Francis.[22] Others maintained that the Ignatian spirit demanded a more moderate practice of prayer and penance. During the period when St. Francis was General-Commissar for the Society in Spain, i.e., from 1544 onwards, he was friendly with and trusted Fr. Bartholomew Bustamante. Bustamante's character and his deeds can be discovered by a perusal of the volumes of the *Monumenta* of Borgia and Nadal. Here it is enough to cite a brief estimate of his character, which does not depart from that of other historians. "Bustamante, an able and ascetic man who fancied himself as an architect, was provincial of his brethren in Andalusia and had nearly driven them to revolt by his high-handed methods of government. Believing strongly in the good old medieval ways of doing things, he had introduced into the houses under his obedience prisons, stocks and even stripes for offenders against rule. He imposed a new style of recreation also, requiring the brethren to sit around in silence until each in turn was called upon to analyze some virtue or vice propounded by the superior." [23]

Doubtless due to the influence of St. Francis, Bustamante was appointed master of novices in 1554–1555 in Simancas. Here he was able to give free reign to the tendencies which he later tried to impose upon the Province of Andalusia. His attraction for the monastic life showed itself then by his introduction of such practices as monastic forms of greeting, extreme outward regularity in observing the discipline of the house, calling the private rooms cells, saying *Deo Gratias* and using other monastic expressions, and many other such practices. In addition he was severe and unapproachable in his manner and in his dealing with others. His letter to St. Ignatius describing the life of the novices is instructive: "Here young men seem old. . . . Anyone who converses with them would believe that he was in the midst of the Scythian or Egyptian monks. I can say without exaggeration: whoever looks on this house during the hours of recreation, might imagine that he was seeing one of the Collations of

---

[22] J. de Guibert, *La Spiritualité de la Compagnie de Jésus* (Roma: PU Gregoriana, 1953), pp. 179–80. H. Rahner, *Ignatius von Loyola: Geistliche Briefe* (Einsiedeln: Benziger, 1956), pp. 160–61, 177–78.

[23] J. Brodrick, *The Progress of the Jesuits* (London: Longmans, 1946), pp. 127–28. See the fuller and severer judgment of A. Astrain, *Historia de la Compañía de Jesús en la Asistencia de España* II (Madrid: 1905), pp. 267 ff.

Cassian." [24] His ideal seemed to be the training of young monks, and his departures from the Jesuit Institute brought more than one check from authority.

It is interesting to see, then, that the same Bustamante was appointed by St. Francis Borgia, on his accession to the post of General of the Society, as Provincial of Andalusia (from which post he was removed by Nadal in his function of visitor), then as director of a college in Seville, and then to a college in Trigueros. Never a man who brooked opposition to his own authority, he did not submit so easily to that of others, and he had difficult relations with his superiors. It is all the more surprising to find Bustamante appointed about the middle of 1566 and in 1567 as visitor to the Provinces of Andalusia and Toledo. (His exercise of these offices was likewise in the end discontinued.) It is here that we find traces of his influence in the formation of the tertianship. A letter of Borgia of March 11, 1567, reprimands him for excessive rigor and for innovations, of which he notes the main ones: "In the course of your visitation, you hold the confessors incarcerated in the *Spiritual Exercises,* as has happened twice before in Placentia, from which one gathers that they remain shut up, not living outside the house or hearing confessions in the church. In the same manner, you make the students work on the building . . . in the heat of the summer sun. You sent them on a pilgrimage in summer to Guadalupe, to the poor village of Loarte, so that they returned sick and exhausted. Similarly, after the studies you shut the fathers up in seclusion in such a way that you allow them neither to preach nor to hear confessions, and make the probation as strict as the first (i.e., the novitiate), and, finally, there is lack of sweetness and show of charity which one ought to find in superiors." [25]

If St. Francis Borgia was moved to such strictures, the regime in the tertianship must have been strict indeed! In the novitiates begun under the saint, which agree as far as their running is concerned in almost every legal detail with the Society's present ones, the practice of meditation, spiritual exercises and separated periods of work did harm to the health of the novices. The Neopolitan Provincial complained of this in 1571 and added that "almost everyone, to the last man, who is in this novitiate or comes here from Rome, suffers

---

[24] *Mon. Ign. Epist. Mixt.* V, pp. 118–20. See also p. 48 ff.
[25] *Mon. Borg.* IV, p. 428.

from headaches or chest pains or in some other way." [26] From Belgium, the Provincial, Fr. Coster, had already in 1568 obtained a modification.[27] This was in marked contrast to the novitiates of St. Ignatius' time, as is shown by a perusal of Polanco's letter of October, 1547, to Rodriguez, which advises the setting up of separate houses for training novices,[28] and by the gloss of Gonçalves da Câmara on the margin of his diary for March 2, 1555, where he notes that "in this (Roman professed) house the novices are trained. Each one shows his own particular traits. . . ." In 1573 a similar remark follows: "At that time the novices were allowed to exhibit their temperament. We were able to know them, and therefore distinguish among them, for they lived in greater freedom—that is, without so many regulations and external ceremonies, with which today one can veil his personality." [29]

One can conjecture what must have been the order which Bustamante had imposed upon his unfortunate tertians in Andalusia! The reactions of the General were healthy, but one cannot help wondering what he himself would have regarded as desirable. Further, one wonders whether it is possible to discern here the beginnings of a tendency to stress something else in the probations, and particularly in the one immediately before final vows, which was quite different from the accent and orientation in those of the early Society.

The Generalate of Mercurian

There is little of interest as regards the development of the idea of the tertianship during the reign of Mercurian.[30] From Sicily Juan Polanco wrote on March 20, 1576, to the General that, of the six candidates for final profession proposed to him for approval, most are sound in the main, but require a little more self-command in some respects. It is intended that they now do the third year's probation, so that they may be helped to improve in these matters, and so that they can be professed straightway. The reason for delaying their tertianship had been to ensure the legal number of attendants at the

---

[26] Quoted by O. Karrer, *Der Heilige Franz Borgia* (Freiburg: Herder, 1921), p. 231.

[27] *Ibid.*

[28] *Epist. et Instruct.* I, pp. 603–06.

[29] *Font. Narr.* I, p. 678.

[30] See de Guibert, "La Généralat d'Aquaviva de l'Histoire de la Spiritualité," *AHSJ* 1940, 9, p. 65 (text and n. 15).

provincial congregation, and these grounds were no longer valid. Some grounds were advanced for having a house for tertians separate from the noviceship.[31]

Organization of Tertianship during Generalate of Aquaviva

Speaking of the houses of probation in the Society, De Guibert writes: "However, while the institution of novitiates became general under Borgia and while, under Mercurian, there existed already the Rules for the Master of Novices, it is only under Aquaviva that the tertianship took a regular form, that under which it has been so justly admired and so largely imitated, that which it has even today without notable change: grouping of the tertians under the direction of an instructor, spiritual exercises made again throughout an entire month, retired life given to prayer, penance and interior and pastoral formation, to the exclusion of all study properly so called and of every sort of showy or absorbing ministry." [32]

The impression which one gains from reading the third chapter of the *Ordinationum Generalium* concerning the tertianship, which had Aquaviva for its author, is strikingly different from the impressions one has of the last probation in the time of the early Jesuits.[33] If one were to describe briefly this difference, one would say that the picture of the tertianship as it emerges from this document of Aquaviva is that of a very rigorously controlled life, controlled down to the last distribution of the hours of the day, secluded, with a strict monastic silence, dictation of what books the tertians shall read (and these from a narrow range of spiritual writers), and even of the way in which they shall read them (i.e., what they shall look for in their reading). Without doubt, the main preoccupation which pervades this document is precisely with that external religious observance and with the psychological conditions pertaining to it, which we found (to an exaggerated degree, admittedly) in the probation directed by Bustamante. Let us take an example from the treatment which this document of Aquaviva gives to seclusion and silence. In the thirty-odd paragraphs which the chapter contains, nine deal with separation from normal intercourse with one's fellow men. The way in which the experiences or experiments are mentioned

---

[31] *Polanci Compl.* II, pp. 301, 431, 495.
[32] De Guibert, *op. cit.*, p. 65.
[33] *Institut. Soc. Iesu,* Ord. Gen. C. 3, pp. 210–15.

is remarkable in comparison with the attention given to spiritual reading and to the kind of instructions obligatory, and to what dispositions of soul must be fostered. The experiences received four mentions, reading ten, and disposition of soul nineteen. The whole tone of the document is negative and preoccupied with the individual; the experiences are viewed merely as a means of exciting affective states of soul in the individual. Coupled with the absence of any normal community life, for such would be impossible under the conditions laid down restricting spontaneous fraternal communication, the routine envisaged in this instruction is chillingly individualistic and lacking in apostolic spirit. The tertianship is viewed in a legal framework; it is regarded merely as one more step in a system of training. It is not looked at primarily in relation to the apostolic aim of the Society, the contact with one's fellow men and with the harrowing exigencies of life as the early companions in the Society delighted to experience them.[34]

Whatever were the sources which led to this document and to the practices which it was influential in inculcating, it is certainly possible to discern in it the beginning of a process in which the individual person is faced with a code of conduct, i.e., with a body of law, whose meaning he can understand only indirectly. When reading, prayer, silence, seclusion and states of mind appear in a document on the same footing as, and more frequently than, apostolic work and converse with one's fellow men and with God, then the person interpreting the document is in danger of mistaking the wood for the trees! This process is a general and well-known one in the history of religion. When the will of God ceases to speak to us directly in our individual lives through the needs of our fellow men, as it always will to the man of faith who contemplates and wishes to assist in the salvation of the world, then the law which expresses this divine imperative is in danger of being separated from the

---

[34] In his brief exposé of the spiritual doctrine of Aquaviva, De Guibert says that the main care of the General was to procure regular observance and effective execution of what was commanded the subjects. The formal prayer of the individual was held by Aquaviva to be the condition of all the rest, and the recurring theme of his letters and teaching to the Society was the need for a constant spiritual renewal, which occurred in this prayer and in the special periods of reflection set aside from other activity. It was the formation of the young religious in this spirit which seemed to Aquaviva to be the secret for the success of the Society. See De Guibert, *op. cit.*, pp. 67–68.

period and circumstances which gave rise to it and elevated into an absolute magnitude, and its observance will begin to be the cultivation of an interior attitude alone. As Asting writes: "The stage which we call legalism is reached in the first instance, when the need which produced the legal prescription is no longer fully living. Then the prescriptions are no longer an expression for requirements which the liturgical community finds by force of circumstances from life, but they stand opposed to life, strange and self-sufficient; the life which has produced them fills them no longer, and hence they stand in stiff authority, and become commands which are fulfilled precisely because they are commands made by authority. What came into being as a natural growth from the interior life, now becomes something which comes to man from outside, and this fact influences powerfully the liturgical community as something new and leads it into quite different paths." [35] As Von Rad himself remarks: "By this means the revelation of the divine commandments becomes something different from what it was. It is no longer the saving and ordering will of the God who leads his people through history, but it begins to be now a law in the theological sense of the word." [36] While it is merely the existence of a tendency which we wish to suggest here, the truth of this suggestion is reinforced by the admission of De Guibert that the institution of the tertianship has remained unchanged since the days of Aquaviva. A theology which developed from a living contact with life and derived its force from the vivid perception of the urgent needs of men around one has come to be a self-sufficient theology, capable of providing food for thought in its own right, and of absorbing attention which was once held by experiences which lay at its origin.

[35] Quoted in G. von Rad, *Die Theologie des Alten Testaments* (München: Kaiser, 1961), I, pp. 98–99, n. 47. Asting speaks here of cultic laws, but his remarks apply quite generally.

[36] *Ibid.*

PART III

Obedience

Introduction

Few questions in recent years have stirred up as much discussion
and controversy in religious communities as has the question of
what it means to take and live a vow of obedience. The question
grows out of—and in turn gives rise to—a series of closely related
problems: What is the proper function of authority in the Church
and in a religious congregation? How should this authority be
exercised? How should superiors arrive at the decisions they impose upon those they govern? What does it mean to say that the
superior's will is the will of God? What part does the delegation of
authority or the principle of subsidiarity have to play in the life of
religious obedience? Does the vow of obedience leave any room
for a conscientious objector? What is the relation between supernatural faith and religious obedience? How can the obedient religious
grow into a mature person able to make responsible choices? Is
the crisis of obedience not really a crisis of community?

The concept of Ignatian or Jesuit obedience is frequently brought
into the discussion of all these areas. St. Ignatius, who wished his
Society to be truly outstanding in its life of obedience, is rightly
considered to be one of the Church's foremost exponents of religious
obedience. Many religious congregations owe much of their understanding of obedience to Ignatius' famous Letter on Obedience
written to the Jesuit scholastics in Coimbra, Portugal. Recent historical and theological studies, however, have helped to place this important document in its proper context. Viewed in the light of the
sources now available, the Letter on Obedience appears as only
a partial exposition of Jesuit obedience. Jesuits now tend to attach
more importance to the teaching on obedience to be found in St.
Ignatius' *Constitutions of the Society of Jesus*. In showing how
Jesuit obedience began and what functions it was supposed to have
according to Ignatius' original intuition, Fr. Miguel Fiorito indicates
some of the consequences of this present tendency. Theological

121

support for the conclusions of historical research comes from Fr. Karl Rahner's now well-known reflections on obedience, a study that clarifies and enriches our understanding of the life of religious obedience.

James P. Jurich, S.J.

A Basic Ignatian Concept: Some Reflections on Obedience

Karl Rahner, S.J.

In recent years, many authors have expanded upon Fr. Rahner's statement that religious obedience is not a quest for an "Olympian papa," nor a "regulation of traffic" to insure the rational functioning of a human organization. Religious obedience is not that of a child toward a parent, nor is it an imitation of Christ's obedience to the Father, since Christ did not obey a fallible human being. To understand fully and positively what the vow means, it must be examined in the context of the life of the Church; hence, initiative is a sign of vitality and the obedience of the rational man a sign of harmony within that life. The renunciation of one's will, seen so often as the Ignatian ideal of obedience, is nothing other than the unconditional acceptance of God's presence in the Church.

In contributing to a periodical which is commemorating the fourth centenary of the death of St. Ignatius, the founder of the Jesuit Order, what theme should a writer choose? If he prefers not to speak directly of the Saint himself and still wants a fitting topic, he could choose nothing better than the concept of obedience. Jesuit obedience—some like to call it *cadaver* obedience—is a well-known and even notorious tag. It is also something which is poorly understood. Ignatius stressed the importance of this virtue for members of his Society, since it is a matter of great moment for an order engaged in the active care of souls. But in reality Jesuit

Note: The German original of this article: "Eine ignatianische Grundhaltung: Marginalien über den Gehorsam," appeared in *Stimmen der Zeit,* 158 (1955–6), 253–267. The present translation was made collectively under the direction of Joseph P. Vetz, S.J., and the supervision of Gustave Weigel, S.J.

obedience does not differ from the obedience found in the other religious orders of the Catholic Church.

In choosing obedience for his topic this writer does not flatter himself that he is rediscovering a long neglected subject. In the last ten years, in Middle Europe alone, at least fifty books and articles have been devoted to this theme. In attempting to say something on the subject of obedience the writer is troubled by a suspicion that possibly he merely wants to be numbered among those who have had something to say on the point. Besides, in a short article like this, one can scarcely hope to say anything that is at all comprehensive or conclusive. Hence these few lines do not pretend to be more than marginal notes, and the writer is resigned to face the possible accusation that he was incapable of conceiving a livelier topic for discussion.

Various Misconceptions

Considered in its essence, obedience in religious life has nothing to do with the obedience which children owe to their parents and to others who are in authority, supposedly equipped to care for their upbringing. The reason is that this latter type of obedience has as its very aim its own eventual transcendence. By means of this training in obedience, the obedience of childhood later becomes superfluous, since the adult, having achieved liberation from the domination of blind instinctive drives, is able to command himself. On the other hand, in the case of obedience in religious life, we assume that the subject is already an adult. But we do not assume that the person who commands is necessarily more intelligent, more gifted with foresight or morally more mature than the person who obeys. If such an assumption were in order, the relationship of superior to subject would be an educational relationship. The one obeying would be a child or a man of infantile character, who is not yet responsible for his own behavior. Human nature being what it is, there are such persons even in religion. Still their percentage should not be greater than that found in other walks of life. And I suppose that, generally speaking, it is not. After all, childish persons can find too many havens to which to flee from their unfitness for life without having to seek out religion as their only refuge. One conclusion that can be drawn from these rather obvious considerations is this: Superiors should not act as if by nature or by reason of their office they are more intelligent, more clever persons, more morally steadfast, more provident and wise in the ways of the world. This may be true in individual cases, for the world is not so constructed that only the more stupid become superiors. But it should be soberly stated (for subjects, lest they demand too much of superiors, something which would be unjust and show a lack of charity; for superiors, lest they delude themselves): the higher the office, the smaller the possibility, humanly speaking, of fulfilling it as well as in the case of a man faced with a lesser post. For we may reasonably presume that the degrees of variation in mental and moral gifts among men are less than the degrees of difficulty found in the management of various social enterprises. From this it follows that, as a rule, more important duties will unavoidably be more poorly performed than lesser ones. No judgment is passed here on any particular case. As a matter of fact, sometimes people do grow in stature in performing more difficult tasks. But for the most part, the opposite takes place. Along with the assumption of a more important responsibility comes the painful realization, felt both by the superior and those about him, that the man is far from being equipped for his task. The defective fulfillment of higher obligations cruelly lays bare the shortcomings of a man's capacities which previously escaped our attention.

Let us repeat once more: obedience in religious life is not the obedience of children. Therefore, the religious superior should not play the role of an Olympian papa. In the life of the cloister (even in orders of women) there are still to be found age-old rituals governing the etiquette of superiors, involving demands of respect from subjects, secretiveness, manifestations of superiority, appeals of superiors to a higher wisdom, displays of condescension, etc. All this should gradually be permitted to wither away. Superiors should cast a long and quiet glance at the world around them: those who are truly powerful and influential, who receive a great deal of unquestioning obedience, place no value on ceremonial of this sort. They find no need of concealing their weakness, anxiety, and insecurity behind a pompous front. Superiors should quietly admit that in certain circumstances their subjects know more than they do about the matter at hand. Given the specialization of modern life with its need for countless types of ability to cover its many areas, present-day superiors can no longer act as if they can understand any and every matter that falls under their authority. In the good old days a superior could do everything that he commanded his subject to do. He had previously done the very thing himself. He had distinguished himself (otherwise he normally would not have been made superior) and so had given proof that he understood at least as much as his subject. At least this was the rule in the past, though naturally there were exceptions to it even then. Today it is quite inevitable that what formerly was the exception should become the rule. Every religious superior has many subjects who necessarily possess a knowledge of science, of pastoral functioning, of current affairs, which the superior (who can be a specialist himself only in a single limited field) cannot possess. He finds himself, or ought to find himself, in the same position with regard to the knowledge of others as a leader does with respect to the mysteries about which his atomic experts advise him. The superior, therefore, is dependent upon the information of counselors to an extent not required in the past. The advisors, usually provided for superiors by the constitutions of an order, today in many ways possess an utterly new and more urgent function than in former times when they were in practice only a democratic check on an excessively authoritarian and uncontrolled government of one individual. It would be well, therefore, if superiors would always seek the information they need in a spirit of objectivity and concreteness, for they must give commands for objective and concrete situations, no matter what be the value of obedience to an objectively erroneous command. This is not always done. A secret-cabinet policy may often be a well-intentioned means of acquiring such objective counsel, but it is not always effective. In religious life, on final analysis, there can be no real democratization of obedience, as will later be shown. But there can be objective and clearly determined methods of procedure for achieving the counsel and information needed for decision. Unfortunately this is not always the case. Once again I insist, mostly for the benefit of the secular opponent and hostile critic of religious obedience: the people in religious life realize that religious obedience is not the obedience of children. It does not presuppose children, but mature adults. And only in the measure that it can legitimately presuppose this can it be at all true to its own proper nature.

Again, religious obedience is no mere "regulation of traffic." Certainly where men live together in a community there must be order. That there be order, the power to command must be present. Not everyone can do as he pleases, and moreover, not everyone can discover for himself just what is required by the total whole. Command, however, implies obedience. When obedience is conceived merely as a rational or rationally prescribed function of order for the life of a community and for the coordination of its organs and activities toward a common goal, then perhaps the pattern has been discovered which can intelligently explain civic and national obedience. But in this concept the peculiar nature of religious obedience has not been grasped, even though it cannot be denied that in religious life this aspect of obedience is also present, and necessarily so. Religious obedience is no rational and inevitable regulation of traffic, by which every sensible person submits himself to the traffic policeman, and in which a coordinating agency takes care that everything moves without friction toward the common good. At times attempts have been made to explain religious obedience in this merely rational fashion. But this explanation is too easy and cannot reach the real roots and depths of religious obedience. And yet the obedience entailed in the rational regulation of traffic and of the sensible coordination of work in a common effort is part of religious obedience, though it is not the most characteristic nor the most profound element of the evangelical counsel. For the daily functioning of obedience in religious life it ought to be noted that this element of obedience is present; yes, that it is almost identical with the superficial tasks of quotidian obedience. For day-to-day life, therefore, a certain de-mystification of obedience should quietly take place, perhaps to a greater extent than is now permitted in some parts. In the many small details of daily life, obedience is in reality nothing else than a rational method by which rational beings live together. Therefore, the superior should not try to give the impression that he stands under the immediate inspiration of the Holy Spirit, but should be courageous enough to seek approval for his commands by giving reasons for them. It is incomprehensible how such an approach to mature and much-loved brothers or sisters in the Lord should be a threat to the authority of the superior, who, according to the command of Christ, should see in the authority of his office only the greater obligation to serve. This does not mean that there should be long debates and discussions over every small decree of a superior. That was the folly of the Parliaments in the past.

This would be irrational and childish (although unfortunately it does occur). The problem can be met and overcome by an appeal to higher ascetical motives. Without irritating himself or others, the subject should calmly and maturely consider the many unavoidable regulations of daily life in a religious community for what they really are: inevitable burdens of earthly life which weigh upon people in the world just as much as they do on people in religious life. Much irritation among religious persons caused by details of common life flows solely from immaturity which does not comprehend that a person does not prove his independence and personal integrity by rebelling against communal rules and regulations. And yet it still remains true: religious obedience, according to its own proper nature, is more than a merely rational regulation of traffic.

There is a third consideration which will preserve religious obedience from misconception and excess. It is not true, even in religious communities, that all initiative should take its rise from superiors. Nor should we be too quick to consider this statement a mere platitude. To comprehend it really, we must make use of metaphysics, a metaphysics which consists in pondering with wonder on the commonplace and the obvious and then drawing some conclusions. Human authority (even when exercised in God's name) must not be conceived as adequately and exclusively competent to monopolize all initiative, all effort and all personal decision. Nor does it imply that subjects are called to initiative and decision only when authority gives the signal.

One frequently gets the impression, both in religious orders and in the Church in general, that initiative, action, militancy, and the like, are indeed considered necessary and desirable in subjects, but only on condition that the go-signal be given "from above," and only in the direction which has already been unequivocally and authoritatively determined by superiors. Unconsciously and spontaneously a tendency is vigorously at work to make the subject feel that he is so built into his order or the Church that only the total structure through its hierarchy is capable of initiative, that opinion or enterprise finds its legitimacy only in the express, or at least tacit, approval from authority.

Unless we wish to absolutize the community, the principle of subsidiarity has application not only between smaller and larger societies, but also between individuals and their communities as well. Yet there can be no subordination of the individual to a community and to the authority representing it, if it tries to make the individual an exclusively dependent function of the community and its authority. We need only put the question in all simplicity: may one propose a wish to a superior, or, with due modesty, propose an alternative policy? Everyone will answer: "Obviously, yes." Hence it is unnecessary first to ask the superior whether he wants the request to be presented or the alternative proposed. Yet this request, this alternative suggestion is also initiative, in which one must take the responsibility of deciding whether it is to be presented or not. For even when with all obedience and modesty the decision is left to the superior, the suggestion alters the situation of the superior in making his decision. It broadens or narrows the field of choice. Indeed even when the subject shows the greatest discretion, the superior is "influenced," whether he likes it or not, whether or not he would have followed the suggestion on his own. In the whole world there is no autarchic human authority which is pure activity and in no way passivity. To command absolutely is proper only to the creator who is not faced with opposing structures and unavoidable initiatives, because he himself in the strict sense makes everything out of nothing. All other authority, even in the Church and in religious orders, is not the only determining initiative but is one force in an immense network of forces, active and passive, receiving and giving. Authority has and should have the function of directing, coordinating, overseeing, and planning the whole interplay of human initiatives. It is not, to speak strictly, even in the ideal order, so representative of God that it alone is the autarchic planner and designer of all human activity. This would be the hybris of a totalitarian system which cannot exist, and, more significantly, should not exist.

Hence, authority, even in religious orders, in practice needs, calls for, and puts to use the initiative of subjects. Even in the abstract, there can be no *absolute* ruler and director of it. Independently of authority there exist initial sparkings of forces which cannot be controlled by authority. Because this is so and cannot be otherwise, it also *should* be so. That is to say, in no community or society, not even the Church or religious orders, *may* authority act as if all good initiatives originated from it, so that every execution of plan, command, and wish originated in authority alone. Even the most laudable initiatives of the Holy See often are only the reaction to an action which originated elsewhere, and this is important. The same is true in the case of authorities of religious orders. Subjects are not mere receivers of commands, because that is simply impossible. The aim of obedience is not to make merely passive subjects. This is not even an "asymptotic" ideal, but a chimera and the usurpation of the creative power reserved to God alone, which he can delegate to no one. Only God has "all the threads in his hand," and he has empowered no one to act in his fashion.

Consequently the superior cannot be a god in the fulfillment of his office. Not to prevent his subjects from assuming initiative is not enough for a superior. He must positively count on it, invite it; he must not be irked by it. He must, to a certain degree, recognize himself also as only *one* of the wheels in a heavenly mechanism whose ultimate and comprehensive significance is directed by one only, by God and no one else. The superior always remains something moved. In an ultimate sense, he does not know exactly to what end evolution is moving. In spite of all the authority given him, and in spite of all the supervision he is charged with, he acts in trust and ventures into the unknown. He too never knows exactly what he is doing or starting when he commands or refrains from doing so. He must remember that authority is not the only source for heavenly impulse, direction, and stimulation. He must realize that God never took on the obligation first to advise the authorities selected and authorized by himself about God's own activity in the Church for the salvation of souls and the progress of history. The superior has no exclusive vision of the divine will with the mission to pass it on to his subjects. There is no God-given warrant for such a process of communication. Rather the superior must also be an obedient man, a hearer. The formal correctness and juridical validity of his commands does not guarantee that they are likewise ontologically guaranteed. If the subject must obey in order not to be disobedient before God, this fact is no proof that the command given was the command which, according to God's antecedent will, should have been given. It can be the product of a permitted fault in the superior. It can proceed from dead traditionalism, from human limitations, from routine, from a shortsighted system of uniformism, from a lack of imagination, and from many other factors.

There is in the world a plurality of forces which can in no way be hierarchically subject to authority—though such forces cannot contradict authority as far as the latter succeeds in bringing them within the field of direction and command. This latter task, as has been said, can and should be only partially achieved. Hence the subject in religious life has no right simply to take refuge behind obedience, as if he could thus be free from a responsibility which he himself must bear, the responsible direction of his own personal initiative. We often hear apologies of obedience which praise this supposed advantage. It does not exist. At least not in the sense that the religious can thereby escape from the burden of personal responsibility. He himself chooses obedience; otherwise he would not be in religious life. He must then answer for the consequences of his choice.

The received command is a synthesis of elements. One is the superior's personal and original activity, the other is the external condition for that activity. This condition is constituted by the subject himself: his mode of being and action, his capacities and incapacities (perhaps culpable), his approach and attitude to the superior. This conditioning is prior to the command and makes the subject co-responsible for the command itself. Certainly the religious can often say to his own consolation that the superior has to answer for this or that decision and not the subject. But the extent of this consolation is not great. Taken as a whole, the religious cannot escape the responsibility for his own life, down to its last details. He simply hears in the command the echo of his own character and activity. There does not exist in this world a control center of action from whose uninfluenced motion all else in existence originates. A human being cannot relinquish his personality to a representative, not even in religious life. That is in no way the purpose of obedience

True Obedience

To provide a positive definition of religious obedience is by no means a simple matter. We could immediately and without further examination maintain that religious obedience is an abidingly vibrant obedience to God and the fulfillment of the divine will. But if we were to do that, we would have to determine how it is possible to know in what sense it can be said that that which is commanded is the will of God. For the fact remains that there can be commands which the subject must obey, provided that the things commanded be not sinful, but which in the objective order, are wrong, and which, in given circumstances, have been commanded with real culpability on the part of the superior. In cases of this kind it is no simple task to say why and in what sense the fulfillment of such a command could be the will of God. Nor should we oversimplify the matter by praising without qualification the "holocaust" and "renunciation" which obedience entails. For it is obvious that pure subjection to the will of another who is not God has no value as such in the realm of morality. In itself, pure dependence of self on the will of another is amoral, not to say even immoral, unless some further element be added to it.

We might add that if religious obedience is subordination of one's own will and decisions to those of another who holds the place of God and is the interpreter of the divine will, we must at least determine how we are to know how this other person received the divine commission to be the expositor of the will of God. This question is a difficult one; even more so than that of poverty and of the evangelical counsel to renounce the blessings of conjugal love. For these two evangelical counsels are recommended directly in the words of holy Scripture and by our Lord himself. As far as these two counsels are concerned, it is always possible to fall back on this recommendation, even when we do not succeed in achieving a crystal-clear understanding of their inner meaning. In this matter it can be said that the religious is walking in the way of the Gospel. And to him who has set out on this path in unquestioning surrender, the meaning of these counsels will be more and more fully revealed. He can always say that he is imitating Christ. And hence he needs no further argument over and above the fact that the disciple does not wish to be above his master, and that love understands what it recognizes as a fundamental characteristic in the beloved Lord.

Concerning obedience, however, the problem is not as simple as all that. As a matter of fact, we see that in the days of the early Church, in which a continuous procession of ascetics and virgins was already a fact, there was as yet no mention of religious obedience. Nor can any direct affirmation of this concept be found in the pages of the gospels. The early ascetics lived the life of solitaries, and so there was no stimulus to the evocation of a notion of obedience. And even for a long time afterwards, obedience was not praised as a third vow. The religious accepted a celibate or monastic life in any form, and obliged himself to remain in a definite community which lived such a mode of life. It is clear that we will have to proceed carefully if we are to specify the content and arguments for religious obedience.

Before we proceed in the question of the meaning of obedience precisely as it exists in a religious community, we must be clearly warned against another simplification which superficially gives a quick and easy solution to these questions. We cannot simply refer to the example of Christ. Beyond a doubt he was obedient. Obedience to his Father, according to his explanation, was the form, the driving power and the content of his life. We must by all means imitate Christ. But this is precisely the question: how do we know that in subordination of self to human authority we exercise the deepest obedience to God? Christ did not do it. Certainly the apostle knows that there are human authorities which in some fashion take the place of God as far as we are concerned, and whose decrees ought to appear to us as the will of God. But Paul is speaking of the authorities which are not freely chosen nor created by us, but exist prior to us and prior to our will, namely, parents, masters, and the civil governors. Can we extend and complete this divine will imposed on us by subordinating ourselves to new régimes of our own making? If we answer that religious superiors have ecclesiastical authority because they are appointed by the Church, this reply alone does not lead us to any clear-cut doctrine. Subordination to the authority of religious superiors is not imposed on men by the Church without their own free and deliberate consent as implied by the vows. Hence the question remains: why is it meritorious to submit to the authority of another, when it has not been imposed on us by God himself? Should we not safeguard the freedom that God has entrusted to us as much as our function of personal responsibility, since, as we have already said, an absolute surrender of innate responsible freedom is in no way possible or reasonable?

Hence the argument from the Gospel in favor of religious obedience is not so simple, nor can it be proved immediately or without further examination. Our problem could be expressed succinctly in the following question: is religious obedience a concrete prolongation of obedience to the will of God, either in general, as it finds expression in the commandments of God, or in particular as it is manifested in God's direction, inspiration and providential disposition of the lives of men?

Religious obedience should by no means be considered primarily as obedience to individual commands, nor is it even the abstract notion of a general readiness to fulfill such commands. Primarily it is the permanent binding of oneself to a definite mode of life— to life with God within the framework of the Church. It involves the exclusive dedication of one's energies to those things which are the concern of the Lord and to what is pleasing to him. We accept as a form of life the expectation of God's coming kingdom of grace from on high. Obedience is concerned with the sacrifice and renunciation of the world's most precious goods; the renunciation of the right to erect a little world of our own as a field of freedom through the acquisition of wealth; the renunciation of the right to one's own hearth and the felt security to be found in the intimate love of another person through the conjugal bond. It is concerned with prayer, and with the testimony to God's grace which is to be found in what is commonly known as the care of souls and the apostolate. Beyond this we need no further description nor argument for this life of the evangelical counsels. Obedience is a permanent life-form giving man a Godward orientation. It does so ecclesiologically because by it the religious manifests the peculiar essence of the Church. It is the manifestation of God's other-worldly grace beyond the reach of earthly merit, to be accepted by faith alone in spite of all human impotence. In this manifestation the Church achieves her existential visibility and becomes historically tangible through doctrine and sacrament. This is the life to which the religious immediately and primarily pledges himself. His obedience, with reference to the individual commands which a superior may enjoin, is specified by this life-form giving it its definite religious significance. Otherwise there would be no sense to vowed obedience. It would not be a religious matter at all. It would rather be perversity to praise this kind of obedience in any other field of life; for instance, if one were to vow obedience for the better functioning of a center of chemical research in which one is employed as a research collaborator. If we suppose that a permanent vowed obligation to a religious life is of positive value in the moral order (and this is presupposed here), and if we further assume that it is proper and reasonable, though not necessary, to lead such a life in a community, then it follows that obedience to the directors of this community is justified and meaningful in the concrete pursuit of this permanent way of life.

Hence we are not trying to canonize an abstract notion of obedience as the execution of another's will as such. Such abstract obedience is due to God alone permitting no transfer to another. Beyond this case we cannot obey purely for the sake of obeying or of not doing our own will and determination. Something like this, considered abstractly in itself, would have no positive significance in the realm of morality. It would be downright absurd and perverse. The fact that this sort of thing would be "difficult" and "a perfect holocaust," hard and troublesome for him who is obedient at all times and in all things, can scarcely be itself an argument for the meaningfulness of obedience. The implied presupposition of this argument, namely that the more difficult and repugnant thing is always better and more pleasing to God, just because it is a renunciation difficult for man, cannot be the legitimate starting point of discussion.

Our concept of obedience also explains why religious obedience has its place exclusively in a religious society approved and sanctioned by the Church. The content of obedience must be guaranteed, if such obedience is to possess moral value. It is not enough that commands be morally indifferent. They must be morally good in their total context. The totality must represent for the Church and to the world the content of the evangelical counsels. One can vow only that which is better. Thus one cannot vow directly and as an end in itself to do something which under certain circumstances (even if not sinful) is less prudent, less good, less significant. Whence it immediately follows that the proper and essential object of religious obedience is an abiding way of life according to the evangelical counsels. For in accord with the teaching of the Church this is certainly the better thing, but in what this superiority consists will not be further explained here. Obedience is not at all to be conceived as the "heroic" (or almost foolhardy) concession of a *carte blanche* to a superior, so that the religious simply does not do his own will, either because this is always pleasing and hence its renunciation especially difficult, or because it is fraught with danger and hence to be avoided. Thus it is that obedience is always specified with reference to the constitutions of the given order, and the superior can only command within the framework determined by the constitutions. In seeking the real essence of obedience, the most important point is missed if only the particular command of the superior is primarily and abstractly considered according to the formula: I declare myself ready to execute the command of another, if this command be not evidently immoral. This is not the case. Obedience is the acceptance of a common mode of religious life in imitation of Christ according to a constitution, which the Church has acknowledged to be a true and practical expression of a divinely oriented existence. By virtue of this acceptance and obligation the vow explicitly or implicitly includes the carrying out of the just commands of the authority necessary in any society, when they are directed to the concrete realization of the life-form of religious commitments "according to the constitutions." Such realizations cannot be determined *a priori* once and for all. Whoever, therefore, is critical of the notion of religious obedience, is really attacking the wisdom of the life of the counsels in the church. He is attacking, moreover, the wisdom of a life that is not primarily concerned with the tangible realizations of worldly objectives, but which through faith makes the expectation of hidden grace the ground of existence, and translates this faith into act. Without such an act, faith itself would be meaningless. This act is representative of the Church and bears the Church's witness to the world. If this mode of existence is to have meaning, then it must inspire a willingness to carry out in any given instance the concrete actions, undertakings and renunciations, which in the judgment of competent authority are deemed necessary for the concrete realization of this way of life.

This is why obedience is connected with the teaching and example of Christ who was obedient even to the death of the cross. Whoever enters into a religious community, whoever perpetually and irrevocably makes this way of life his own, chooses for himself an unforeseeable destiny. For the consequences of such an election and dedication to the community and its rationale of action cannot be foreseen in detail. And these consequences can be difficult and painful. But this gamble (considered in its formal structure) is involved in every human obligation, whereby another person with his own proper will becomes an inseparable part of one's own life. We find it in marriage, acceptance of the duties of citizenship, the responsibility of office, and so forth. Hence if the religious community and its basic ideals are justified and meaningful (which in our case we legitimately assume to be true), so too is the obligation toward all its consequences which cannot be seen in advance. A human mode of life which consists in the free subordination to something higher than itself cannot exist without this element of risk. And without such a surrender the individual will remain in his own egotism behind the defenses of his own existential anxiety, which is the surest way to destruction. But the man who gives himself to what is higher and nobler, who takes the gamble, knows that he is only doing what Christ himself did in his obedience.

Under this aspect, that which in a given instance is irrational and indefensible but actually unavoidable really becomes the will of the Father. In this way the cross of Christ, a crime of the Jews and the pagans, "had" to be; it was the will of the Father who had planned it, even though it came about only as the result of the shortsightedness and guilt of men. The permanent dedication to the ideal of the counsels in imitation of Christ, who was poor and self-denying, the crucified legate of God, consecrated to prayer and atonement, is lived all but exclusively in a community professing the same ideal. Hence the obedience which it entails must be regarded as the will of God, even if a particular command appears to be senseless (just as death, failure and the other tragic circumstances of human existence appear), provided of course that what is commanded is not immoral in itself. Religious obedience is thus a real participation in the cross of Christ. Nor should one protest that the irrationality of a mistaken command frees the subject from his contract, and cannot be considered as a share in Christ's mission. We must realize that religious obedience is more than a rationally accepted agreement governing "traffic-arrangements" in a common enterprise. This, of course, is included, for life in any community demands obedience, though in our case community life is directed to God. Obedience in any other society, in the event of an unwise command, would be justified only by the rational insight that such unavoidable eventualities must also be reckoned with in the original bargain. Otherwise, obedience, which is always to some degree necessary, would end, for it would be left to the discretion of the subject to obey. But in religion the imitation of Christ is practiced. There the cross of Christ is considered not merely as something inevitable, or as the misfortune of life, by and large to be evaded, but rather as the embodiment of grace and its acceptance through faith, as something which "must" be, "so that the Scriptures might be fulfilled," since only "thus" can one enter into one's glory. There the command, judged unwise according to its immediate historical context, will be seen as something which in the framework of religious life is worthwhile, even desirable. This of course does not justify the superior in issuing such a command. Yet such an order can be understood in the same way as the saints in their imitation of Christ understood failure, shame, the shattering of cherished plans, martyrdom, and thousands of other unjustifiable contingencies. They secretly longed for them as the embodiment of their faith in God's grace now reaching its perfection.

It might here be in place to recognize that morality and spontaneous moral judgment have a greater function than is ordinarily supposed. The command of a superior may be objectively sinful, and if recognized as such by the inferior it should not be put into execution. Everyone will agree that a superior, even with the best intentions, can issue an order which is objectively wrong. If one does not consider as sins only those things which are expressly labeled as such in confessional manuals, then it will be hard to deny that that which is materially false can also very often be objectively immoral. What is more, it is not easy to explain why this is not generally so. Let us offer a fictitious example. A higher superior instructs the principal of a boarding school that he must under all circumstances make the boys go to confession once a week. Let us suppose that the subordinate, in this case the principal of the boarding school, clearly realizes what the superior in his idealistic remoteness cannot comprehend, namely, that such a demand will eventually prove very harmful to the spiritual life of his charges. Question: have we here merely an inept pedagogical practice, which must be "carried out" because commanded, or have we in fact an innocent but unjustified demand which, since it is actually a serious threat to the genuine spiritual development of these youths, should not be carried out by the subordinate? The very ineptness of the practice offends against moral principles. Must the subject now declare that he cannot square it with his conscience, and ask to be relieved of his office? Reading the older moralists one gets the impression that they were more concerned with such cases than we are today. Have we today become more moral, or has the principle "an order is an order" gained foothold even in such holy quarters as religious communities? Do we avoid talking about such possibilities out of fear of evils produced by the conscientious objector, and so act as if something of this kind practically never occurs? But is not the consequent evil caused to conscience greater than the utility of a frictionless functioning of external government requiring of subjects a literal obedience to commands? Even the subject has the duty in conscience of examining the moral admissibility of what has been commanded. The just "presumption" that the command of a superior is not only subjectively but also objectively morally unobjectionable does not constitute a simple dispensation from the essential obligation of every man to attain to moral certitude respecting the moral liceity of a free action before it is undertaken. This action is no less his own and no less one for which he will be responsible, simply because it is commanded.

As a religious grows older he asks himself with a deep and secret anxiety whether he has done anything in his life which can stand judgment in God's sight. Nothing of course can so stand, except what he has given out of pure mercy. What is worthy of God comes from God's grace alone. For this very reason what one does is not indifferent. There is an absolute difference between man's potentialities when God's grace is accepted and when it is rejected. God has told us, and he is greater than the human heart, that there are deeds of selfless devotion, obedience to God's holy will and self-forgetting dedication. Yet we always discover in ourselves, if we are not stupid, naïve or conceited, things which always make us afraid that there is nothing in us but open or disguised egotism. Are we sure that God's grace was ever operative in us? Such an event should have been life-transforming. Yet was there ever a moment when we did not seek ourselves, when success was not the fruit of egotism, when our love of God was not anxiety, when patient prudence was not really faintheartedness? The divine achievement of miraculous sanation takes different ways, giving us the right to hope that not everything in our life was open or covert self-seeking. Nor need painful anxiety about it be another manifestation of self-seeking or secret self-justification before God. Whoever is so concerned has made his life essentially simple and easy. We act on our own but the last and most important deed will be effected in us by God himself operating through the bitterness of life itself. The individual can always do one thing at least. He can give himself over to something greater than himself. He can also see to it that this greater reality be more than an ideal or a theory, which on final analysis is under his own control, and can be constructed according to his fancy, so that it can no longer be distinguished from the mere idols of the heart. The individual can strive to make this nobler reality actual. This reality must make demands on us, when we do not desire to be constrained; must act even when we do not wish it; must cause us suffering when we ourselves would rather avoid it. This happens when the greater reality to which we dedicate ourselves becomes a tangible force of incomprehensible greatness, whose word of command is directed towards us—and we obey. This means to obey silently, and in the true sense, unquestioningly; to serve, and to submit to a demand we have not ourselves invented. When this happens we have too little time and too little interest to defend or develop our personal integrity. The self has lost its importance. We might even be so fortunate as to become a true person, who exists insofar as he forgets and sacrifices self, insofar as he obeys. But we must remember that life's good fortune is God's grace. In order to become obedient, and in transcendence lose ourselves—the only way of ever really finding ourselves—we must perhaps see nothing at all extraordinary in obedience, hardly ever think of it reflexively. We should rather think of the reality which we serve as a matter of course. That being is worthy of all love and service, because ultimately it is no mere cause, but *the Person*: God. Perhaps the truly obedient man is simply the lover, for whom the sacrifice of self-surrender is sweet and a blessed delight. Perhaps we should not speak so much of obedience, for it is already threatened when we praise or defend it. Either tactic is only meaningful as an encouragement for the young in order to strengthen their wills to embrace in silence a matter-of-course service of God in the Church through a life of prayer and witness. They must learn that this is meaningful even though the heart shudders and the wisdom of this world panics at the thought of losing self in the loss of freedom. The ultimate obedience, that which demands and silently takes everything, will be exacted by God alone. It is the command to die the death which overshadows every minute of our life, and more and more detaches us from ourselves. This command, to move on and to leave all, to allow ourselves in faith to be absorbed in the great silence of God, no longer to resist the all-embracing nameless destiny which rules over us—this command comes to all men. The question, whether man obediently accepts it, is decisive for time and eternity. The whole of religious life grounded in obedience is nothing more than a rehearsal, a practical anticipation of this situation, which more and more envelops human existence. For the religious it is the participation in the death of Christ and the life concealed in him.

St. Ignatius' Intuitions
on Obedience and Their
Written Juridical
Expression

Miguel Fiorito, S.J.

The United Nations, Vatican Council II, and diocesan synods have shown, each in their own way, the importance of dialogue in the modern world. Not only do the participants seek a bond of unity among themselves, but they learn to appreciate the values and insights of others. Yet, does such dialogue have a place in an organization where each member has a vow of obedience? A purely juridical notion of obedience, set in a monarchical framework, is hardly conducive toward uniting the members in understanding and charity. When the focus in an evaluation on the nature of obedience is shifted from the subject obeying to the superior discussing, then both the subject and the superior are in a position to realize the depth and wisdom of obedience.

In the early days of any religious order, the driving charismatic spirit of the founder or founders must be put into written juridical expressions.[1] Unfortunately, this writing always entails a danger, as almost all history testifies.

Is there then, perhaps, some difference between St. Ignatius of Loyola as founder and as legislator? Or better, were those deeper spiritual intuitions and insights which he had as founder adequately transferred into the written juridical expressions or statements which

[1] See M. A. Fiorito, "Alianza bíblica y regla religiosa: Estudio historico-salvifico de las Constituciones de la Compañía de Jesús," *Stromata* 21 (1965) 291–324, esp. 318–24.

he had to use as legislator? Poets usually fall somewhat short of
their aim when they try to commit the full richness of their vision to
paper; and possibly St. Ignatius experienced similar misfortune.
Further still, with the passing of time after his death, what happened
in the evolving tradition of the Society he founded? Did some of
his juridical expressions perhaps receive from his successors such
emphasis, often unbalanced, that these later Jesuits gradually hid
the deeper spiritual intuitions which he had as founder, and thus
allowed them to be overlooked?

The present writer received a suggestion to explore this topic. He
offers the present study of St. Ignatius' concept of obedience as a
sample of what such investigation might yield.

Both in the Church and in the Society of Jesus, the juridical or
written expression of life under obedience has evolved in such a
manner that important helps to the practice of obedience have been
obscured or lost.

In St. Ignatius' deeper intuition, obedience has a threefold function. It is a help to the union of the Society's members through
charity, a means to further a sense of community among apostolic
religious through their charitable cooperation toward common ends
in their common life, and a remedy for distance when it separates
absent members from the community. In that total function and life-
giving spirit of obedience, the superior's decision is clearly only
one momentary act which ought not to be isolated from its whole
vital and spiritual context.

In the juridical expression, however, the superior's decision tends
to take on such prominence that all the other acts which government
entails seem to have only a secondary role or are even overlooked.
But for the life of union through charity they are as necessary as
the decision itself.

In Ignatius' spiritual concept of obedience, the decision is one act
which ought to be integrated into the other activities which produce
the sense of community or cooperative living, such as the manifestation of conscience, personal conversation between the superior and
subject, and the like. Ribadeneyra makes this clear in Chapter 3 of
his *De ratione quam in gubernando tenebat Ignatius*.[2] However, in
the juridical expression of obedience, the decision seems to be

[2] *Fontes Narrativi de S. Ignatio*, III, pp. 615–19, in the series "Monumenta
Historica S.J." (henceforth abbreviated MHSJ).

virtually everything, much as it is in the purely natural obedience of a pagan.

In the *Deliberation of the First Fathers* in 1539, Ignatius and his companions deliberated first about union "in one body" and then about obedience.[3] They reached agreement quickly about union but employed "many days" about obedience.[4] Among the three fundamental reasons they mention for choosing it, the second is: Obedience is a means to preserve the Society as a body.[5]

Reflection on this reveals an aspect in which Ignatian poverty and obedience are alike. If poverty is viewed as something isolated from the apostolic end, it becomes the poverty proper to other religious institutes. So too obedience, if it is isolated from its primary purpose of union into one body or religious community, is reduced to the purely natural obedience which a pagan might practice in an earthly commonwealth.

If we allow the juridical expression of obedience to occupy the chief role in our living on a supernatural plane, we create various conflicts quite like those found in purely natural types of social living. Examples are, in the Church, a conflict between the primacy of the Holy Father and the collegiality of the bishops, and in the Society, between the superior's authority to decide and his obligation to hold consultation with his subjects.

The juridical expression of obedience tends to emphasize the authority and its sufficiency, while the spiritual and Christian expression of obedience emphasizes the fact that the superior needs his subjects and they him, as St. Paul so clearly states (1 Cor. 12:2–25). The head "cannot say . . . to the feet, I have no need of you" (*ibid.*, 21).[6]

Ambiguous Consequences

The unbalanced emphasis which St. Ignatius' successors have often put upon the merely juridical expression of obedience has given rise to ambiguous consequences: for example, that of defining

---

[3] *Constitutiones Societatis Jesu* (in MHSJ), I, n. 3 on p. 3, n. 4 on p. 4 (henceforth abbreviated *Cons*MHSJ).

[4] *Ibid.*, n. 8 on p. 7.

[5] *Ibid.*; cf. *Epistolae S. Ignatii* (MSHJ), XII, pp. 331–34.

[6] Hence Paul's concept of authority, according to one exegete, entails not merely service but also need. See J. M. González Ruiz, "¿La autoridad como servicio?" *Hechos y Dichos,* n. 351 (1965) 257–60.

Ignatian government as "monarchical." This definition is correct only if there is question of affirming that there is only one head who is also a member in a kind of mystical body, in the same way as Christ is the head of the Church. But the definition is erroneous if "monarchical" is made or taken to mean that there is only one leader who imposes himself from without, much like a conqueror who imposes himself from without and remains separate from the conquered people. In the *Constitutions* of the Society, St. Ignatius calls the Father General "head" (*cabeza*) sixteen times; and nine of these instances, the majority, are in Part VIII, where he is treating explicitly about means and "Helps toward Uniting the Distant Members with Their Head and among Themselves" (*Cons.* [655]).

The juridical expression originates in the political order. There the authority often arises from force and is measured by power.[7] In Ignatius' Christian order, however, the authority originates from Christ and His "kindness, meekness, and charity"; and in exercising authority the superior ought "always to be mindful of the formula of Peter and Paul." [8]

This "formula of Peter and Paul" which a religious superior should keep always in mind is a characteristically spiritual expression. It cannot have a completely similar juridical equivalent, because it arises from the divinely inspired words of both apostles. "The priests that are among you, I exhort, . . . shepherd the flock of God that is with you, not of necessity but willingly, neither for base gain but with a ready mind, nor yet as lording it over your charges, but becoming an example to the flock" (1 Peter 5:1–3). "Become a pattern for the faithful in word, in conduct, in charity, in faith, in chastity" (1 Tim. 4:12; cf: Phil. 3:17, 2 Thess. 3:9).[9] In the juridical expression of obedience, the superior's power and the subject's obligation spring into the foremost role, but in the Christian expression the superior's spiritual obligation to be an example becomes the most prominent part. In fact, this role of the superior becomes the animating form of the whole religious body. In all his acts and in every decision, he ought to consider the whole body and his union with it.

That expression, "the formula of Peter and Paul," first appeared

---

[7] See G. Fessard, *Autorité et bien commun* (Paris, 1944), pp. 14–15.

[8] *Formula Instituti* (*Regimini*, 1540), n. 5, in *Cons* MHSJ, I, p. 28.

[9] See *Cons*MHSJ, I, p. 379, n. 17.

in the *Prima Societatis Jesu Instituti Summa* of 1539 and persisted in the *Formulae* of 1540 and 1550.[10] The ideas in "the formula of Peter and Paul" are derived from inspired Scripture just as truly as the other expression, "head" (Eph. 1:23), which has the well-known Christocentric and Christological connotations that cannot be transferred into a purely natural juridical language. For that "bringing all things to a head in Christ" (*anakephalaiosis*) takes on its full meaning only in the case of the unique mediator, Christ, even though it does have earlier but weaker analogies in the political literature of antiquity.

When one expresses religious obedience by terms which are spiritual, Christological, Petrine, and Pauline, he can readily insert into its practice such functions as dialogue, consultation, mutual information, committee discussions, and similar elements or expressions dear to modern men. But only with great difficulty do they fit into the juridical expression of obedience which makes the superior's decision the beginning and end of the matter. All these elements dear to moderns are, like the Ignatian concept of manifestation of conscience, means to developing a cooperative sense of community among those living a common life. They are means to union through fraternal charity and leadership by example. By that very fact they become a necessary means as well as an integral part in the government of a religious community.

The subject's role of obeying is a simple one and it can easily be expressed, even quite fully, in juridical language. But the superior's role contains spiritual elements which are richer, multitudinous, and very complex. They cannot easily be described in terms of black and white. And it is extremely difficult to express the necessary but delicate shadings in a written law or in terms which are exclusively juridical. This fact leads to an important consequence.

We indicated above that the juridical expression of obedience has gone through an excessive or unbalanced evolution both in the Church and in the Society. What we meant was this. The life of obedience in a religious community has been too much reduced to emphasis on the subject's role of obeying, although the superior's role is far more important for the cooperative and charitable common living.[11]

[10] In *Cons*MHSJ, I, pp. 14–21, see esp. pp. 18, 28, 379.
[11] See *Epistolae S. Ignatii* (MHSJ), XII, 335–37.

If the benefits of group dynamics are to be reaped, the superior's role cannot be reduced to the mere making of a decision.

But if the superior's role is described with all its spiritual richness, the role of the subject will be proportionally enriched, far more than has happened so far in its juridical expression.

This becomes clearer through an interesting parallel. The theology of the past, by developing somewhat excessively and unilaterally the psychological expression of the act of faith, tended to make it too similar to a mere act of assent to historical testimony; but the theology of today, by stressing the value of the word of God and its proclamation, has once again put into full light the unique character of Christian faith. Similarly, if we express the full spiritual richness of the superior's function in a religious community, we shall by that very fact gain immense benefits for the spiritual life of the subjects in that same community.

PART IV

Sources of
Christian Spirituality

Introduction

The Introduction to Part II quoted Vatican II on the renewal of religious life: the Council calls for a return to the inspiration behind the particular institute and an adjustment of the religious community to the changed conditions of the times. The ultimate inspiration of all religious institutes is the person of Jesus, whose continuing presence and action in the world appear in the life and work of religious orders; but it is the person of Jesus as seen by the special vision of the founder of the institute.

The *Spiritual Exercises* of St. Ignatius are both a record of St. Ignatius' own growth to a union of understanding and love with Christ and the chief instrument by which the Saint strove to cooperate with God's grace in bringing others to this same experience and vision. For this purpose Ignatius made abundant use of Scripture, but in a way that seems quite different from the approaches and methods of the best modern study of Scripture. Does this mean that his vision was, after all, false, or that the *Spiritual Exercises* are no longer useful as a means for renewing this Ignatian vision in our day? Fr. Fitzmyer's approach to these problems combines regard for sound exegesis with sympathy for those who, though not exegetes, must nourish themselves and others with the bread of Scripture. His conclusions are reassuring.

Fr. Stanley's essay treats the problem of the Jesuit's response to the Word of God in the liturgy. But the problem is not limited to the Jesuit who has let the Ignatian virtues promoted in the *Spiritual Exercises* grow into insensitivity and exaggerated individualism. The history of the liturgical movement suggests that the problems experienced by the Jesuits of whom Fr. Stanley writes are common to many Christians. His analysis of the tension between individual and liturgical prayer and his suggestions for resolving this tension can serve as a case study of the sort of psychological and spiritual reorientation that many of us have still to make in order to enter fully into the movement of today's Church.

ROBERT C. COLLINS, S.J.

The Spiritual Exercises
of St. Ignatius and
Recent Gospel Study

Joseph A. Fitzmyer, S.J.

The rapid development of Scripture study causes no little uneasiness with the more traditional forms of spirituality, and particularly with the *Spiritual Exercises* of St. Ignatius. Visualizing an event, which may now be considered of dubious historical character, or imitating Christ's external actions as filtered through the imagination and Easter experience of the Gospel authors, places a strain upon the docility of many retreatants. Instead of avoiding a confrontation with modern scriptural studies as if the results of scholarship concerned the mind rather than the heart, Father Fitzmyer asks the retreat master to use the new findings to enrich his understanding of St. Ignatius and his use of Scripture in the contemplations of the *Exercises*. Although the suggestions are directed mainly to retreat masters, they can provide a valuable asset to all who seek to find Christ in Gospel-centered prayer.

Recent developments in the Catholic interpretation of the gospels seem to create a problem for many preachers and retreat masters, especially for those who are accustomed to give the *Spiritual Exercises* of St. Ignatius. It is not the key meditations, like the Principle and Foundation, Sin, the Kingdom of Christ, the Two Standards, etc., which are affected by these developments, but the contemplations on the mysteries of the life of our Lord in the second, third, and fourth weeks. It seems that the new scriptural trends make the retreat master uneasy when he presents a contemplation in the more or less classic manner. Some have apparently been reproached by retreatants who complain that the manner of presentation of such contemplations

153

is not up-to-date, and corresponds neither to the questions in the minds of those who have been trained according to the "new approach" to Scripture, nor takes sufficient account of basic and fruitful biblical themes. More specifically, it is felt that the "new approach" has eliminated the historical element of the gospel episodes and has thereby swept the props from under the Ignatian contemplations themselves.

Francis J. McCool, S.J. of the Pontifical Biblical Institute in Rome, has already addressed himself to certain aspects of this problem.[1] He has rightly stressed the *type of history* which is used in the gospels and tried to allay the fears represented by the feeling expressed at the end of the preceding paragraph. There is no need to rehash this historical aspect of the problem which he has handled so competently, but there are many other aspects on which a few reflections may be permitted. These reflections will touch on the problem itself and its origin, and then concern themselves with some suggestions for a solution.

Reflections on the Problem Itself

How does the problem arise? I believe that the situation described above is created by two factors. On the one hand, there is the "new direction" in modern Catholic scriptural studies, a "new approach" which dates mainly from the time of *Divino afflante Spiritu* (1943).[2] To deny it or ignore it is to play the ostrich; it is found in countless

[1] "The Preacher and the Historical Witness of the Gospels," *TS* 21 (1960) 517–43; "The Modern Approach to the Gospels and the Spiritual Exercises," *A Cooperative Study of the Spiritual Exercises of Saint Ignatius, Held at Fordham University June 28, 29 and 30, 1961* (New York: Kohlman Hall, 1961), pp. 167–99. The reader will also consult with profit V. T. O'Keefe, "Towards Understanding the Gospels," *CBQ* 21 (1959) 171–89; D. M. Stanley, "The Conception of our Gospels as Salvation-History," *TS* 20 (1959) 561–89; J. L. McKenzie, "The Bible in Contemporary Catholicism," *Catholic World* 193 (July 1961) 225–32.

[2] This "new direction" in scripture study was well described by L. Alonso Schökel, "Dove va l'esegesi cattolica?" *Civiltà cattolica* 111, No. 2645 (September 13, 1960) 449–60; in French, "Où va l'exégèse catholique?" *L'Ami du clergé* 71 (1961) 17–22. It was this article which occasioned a violent, irresponsible and unfounded attack on the Biblical Institute; see the writer's survey, "A Recent Roman Scriptural Controversy," *TS* 22 (1961) 428–44, in which an extended summary of Alonso Schökel's article can be found (pp. 428–31). See also his *El hombre de hoy ante la bíblia* (Barcelona: J. Flors, 1959); in English: *Understanding Biblical Research*. (tr. P. J. McCord, New York: Herder and Herder, 1963).

Catholic books and articles and is used widely in Scripture courses of seminaries throughout the world. It is an approach with which all who use the Scriptures will have to reckon sooner or later. On the other hand, certain phrases or expressions in the *Spiritual Exercises* themselves seem to have been pressed more than Ignatius himself may have intended. A re-examination of some of them may well permit the retreat master to adopt the "new approach" and profit by some of the richer insights into Scripture which this approach has uncovered, and which previous generations of retreat masters may never have suspected. In other words, the problem seems to be two-faced and it will be well to approach it from both of these angles.

I

Divino afflante Spiritu, the encyclical of Pope Pius XII on the promotion of biblical studies, stimulated a new approach to the Scriptures in recommending to Catholic exegetes the serious study of the literary forms in which the ancient inspired writings had been composed.[3] This was official, papal sanction given to a method of critical, literary analysis which previous centuries of biblical exegesis had not known. But it was in accord with the assured results of the last two hundred years of intensive study of the gospels. It is well to recall briefly at this point various phases through which the study of the gospels has gone, in order to understand the position of modern Catholic exegetes with respect to them and to appreciate the background out of which the specific problem with which we are dealing has risen.

Since the time of Tatian (*ca.* A.D. 160) it was customary to harmonize the gospels (by stringing the episodes together to make

---

[3] *Rome and the Study of Scripture* (5th ed.; St. Meinrad, Ind.: Grail, 1953), pp. 97–99; Paragraphs 35–9 (NCWC Pamphlet, pp. 18–20).—Some recent pronouncements give the impression that the study of biblical literary forms is unorthodox. These pronouncements are not in harmony with the directives of Pope Pius XII. Cf., a recent article by E. Cardinal Ruffini ("Generi letterari e ipotesi di lavoro nei recenti studi biblici," *Osservatore romano,* 24 August 1961, p. 1; Engl. tr. "Literary Genres and Working Hypotheses in Recent Biblical Studies," *AER* 145 [1961] 362–5), which brands such study as an "absurdity." To appreciate the significance of this situation, see the report of H. Fesquet ("Nouvelles querelles dans les milieux romains de la critique biblique," *Le Monde,* 1 November 1961, p. 8), who juxtaposed the statements of Pope Pius XII and Cardinal Ruffini.

a sort of *Life of Christ*),[4] or to explain away discrepancies (by stressing the substantial agreement of the evangelists, as did Augustine in his *De consensu evangelistarum*),[5] or to construct *catenae* (i.e., biblical commentaries in which successive verses of the scriptural text were elucidated by "chains" of passages derived from previous commentators, especially the Fathers),[6] or finally to investigate their "four senses" (historical, allegorical, moral, and anagogical, according to Augustine of Dacia's well-known distich, *Littera gesta docet, quid credas allegoria, moralis quid agas, quo tendas anagogia*).[7] Such exegesis of the gospels was undoubtedly fruitful and provided the spiritual nourishment of untold generations of Christians; no one can deny this, and certain aspects of such study might well deserve renewed interest today. Yet for all its venerable tradition and spiritual value, such gospel study remained in many ways quite extrinsic to the text itself, and surprises, even at times shocks, the modern mind, trained to a literary and historical critique of ancient writings. In general, it can safely be said that patristic, medieval, and even renaissance exegetes were not interested in a literary analysis of the gospels which would, for instance, determine the specific purpose of Mark's gospel over against Matthew's. A comparative study of the first three gospels was beyond their interest. The reason for this attitude, in part at least, was the notion of inspiration which prevailed in those times, often equating it with a form of divine dictation. The interpretation of the gospels, consequently, concentrated on them as the *verbum Dei* and, generally speaking, little or no concern was had for the hagiographer's part in the writing.

---

[4] This method was used not too long ago by A. J. Maas, *The Life of Jesus Christ According to the Gospel History* (St. Louis: B. Herder, 1891, 12th repr., 1947). "The text is entirely framed out of the words of the gospels, in such a manner that nothing is omitted and nothing added" (p. v.). For the problems which this rather arbitrary stringing together of the various gospel texts and the labelling of it a "Life of Christ" present in the study of the gospels themselves, see the remarks of F. J. McCool, "The Modern Approach . . . ," pp. 183–4.

[5] *CSEL* 43 (ed. F. Weihrich, 1904).

[6] See, for instance, the *Catena aurea* of St. Thomas Aquinas on the Gospels. Cf. R. Devreesse, "Chaînes exégétiques grecques," *Dictionnaire de la Bible, Supplément* 1 (1928) 1084–1233.

[7] See H. de Lubac, *Exégèse médiévale: Les quatre sens de l'Ecriture* 1/1–2 (Paris: Aubier, 1959); see also R. E. McNally, "Medieval Exegesis," *TS* 22 (1961) 445–54.

The modern study of the gospels may be dated from the end of the eighteenth century with the emergence and correct formulation of the synoptic problem, that *concordia discors* of matter, order, and phraseology in the first three gospels. The nineteenth century wrestled with that problem and all sorts of solutions were proposed, chief among them being the Oral Tradition theory and the classic Two Source theory. What was characteristic of this study of the synoptic gospels was an *intrinsic analysis* of the texts themselves in their mutual relationships in an effort to detect traces of written sources which had been used by the evangelists in their composition. It has been called Source Analysis. By the end of the nineteenth century this quest for written sources had reached an impasse; even today there is no universally satisfying solution to the synoptic problem. But with the end of World War II came a new type of internal criticism of the gospels, labelled *Formgeschichte* or *Form Criticism*. This method examined the gospel texts, in an attempt to pierce back beyond the written sources and to discover the forms of the gospel stories which had been handed down during the generation between Christ's departure and the redaction of the written gospels. The chronological framework of the gospels was called in question because of the stereotyped links used by the synoptic evangelists; the gospels proved to be only collections of isolated episodes artificially linked together. The classification and comparison of the *pericopae* themselves resulted in the assignment to them of a *Sitz im Leben* (or vital context) in the early Church, which would account for the rise and development of such stories about Jesus. The result of this Form-Critical approach to the gospels posed the question of the historical value of the gospels and eventually ended in the radical skepticism of Rudolf Bultmann, for whom *der historische Jesus* could not be known, while the object of his primary concern, *der geschichtliche Christus,* was reached by faith alone.

The extreme position just described has never been accepted by Catholic exegetes, who have always emphasized the historical character of the gospel accounts, while stressing the special type of history (salvation history) which is contained in them. But a reaction against the extreme position of Bultmann soon set in among Protestant scholars as well; it was perceived that he had pushed the method beyond its legitimate limits. The reaction took several forms, but here it will suffice to mention only a few. First of all, it was noted that, even if one grants that the order of the episodes in the gospels is often quite arbitrary (compare Matthew and Luke) and the links are stereotyped formulae, there are nevertheless certain groupings of material which apparently belong to a primitive and fundamental *datum* of the gospel tradition. The studies of C. H. Dodd have shown that the scraps of the primitive kerygma which are preserved in the speeches in the first part of Acts reveal a remarkable agreement with the basic order of Mark's gospel, especially in the fourfold division of the public life of Christ: John the Baptist and the preparation for the ministry, the Galilean ministry, the journey to Jerusalem, the events of the last week in Jerusalem.[8] Such a basic framework cannot be incidental, and though it is derived from the primitive kerygma of the Church, it reflects undoubtedly the outline of the life of Christ itself. The same basic order is perceived also in the Matthaean and Lukan gospels, but in each case it is possible to show the deliberate modification of it for the purposes of each evangelist. Moreover, no matter what theory is adopted today as a solution to the synoptic problem this basic structure is acknowledged. It should, therefore, be accepted at face value and its substantial historicity acknowledged. At least to this extent it is possible, therefore, to pierce back from the *Sitz im Leben der Kirche* to the *Sitz im Leben Jesu.* The historical data of the gospels puts us at least this much in contact with *der historische Jesus.*

This may seem to leave in suspense, however, the question of the historicity of the individual episodes and even of the relative (chronological) order of the episodes within such a basic framework. The attitude of the modern Catholic exegete toward this further problem is to accept the basic historical value of the individual episodes, unless there is a *positive reason,* emerging either from the text itself or from a comparison of parallel texts in the synoptic or Johannine traditions, which may *cause* him to modify that position. Several reasons bring him to this position. First of all, although the gospel stories read in many cases like an historical narrative prima facie and are inspired accounts, it should be remembered that it has

---

[8] See C. H. Dodd, *The Apostolic Preaching and its Developments* (London: Hodder and Stoughton, 1936); "The Framework of the Gospel Narrative," *Expository Times* 43 (1932) 396–400. Also W. L. Knox, *The Acts of the Apostles* (Cambridge: University Press, 1948), p. 17; V. Taylor, *The Gospel According to St. Mark* (London: Macmillan, 1953), pp. 145–48.

never been taught by theologians that the necessary formal effect of inspiration is historicity. The mere fact that a passage is inspired does not make it historical. Pope Pius XII emphasized, "The ancient peoples of the East, in order to express their ideas, did not always employ those forms or kinds of speech, which we use today; but rather those used by the men of their times and countries. . . . No one, who has a correct idea of biblical inspiration, will be surprised to find, even in the sacred writers, as in other ancient authors, certain fixed ways of expounding and narrating, certain definite idioms, especially of a kind peculiar to the Semitic tongues, so-called approximations, and certain hyperbolical modes of expression, nay, at times, even paradoxical, which help to impress the ideas more deeply on the mind." [9] The exegete, therefore, has the obligation of determining accurately what the inspired form (history? gospel? midrash? popular tale?) really is which is being used. Though inspiration does not necessarily make a passage historical, nevertheless it may still be so for other reasons, the nature and extent of which must be determined. Secondly, even Papias long ago was aware of the fact that the gospel material had been adapted. This he frankly admits, even though he asserts the fidelity of Mark in recording accurately all that he could remember of Peter's preaching.[10] Thirdly, when parallel accounts of the same event are narrated in the gospels, there are well-known discrepancies at times, which manifest a modification of the *basic story* in the course of the tradition. If the individual text of Matthew, or of Mark, or of Luke were all we had and were accepted at its face value, the question, "What really did happen?" would probably never arise. But we do have three inspired accounts of the same event which at times differ, although it must be admitted

---

[9] *Divino afflante Spiritu,* Par. 36, 38 (NCWC Pamphlet, pp. 18–9).

[10] "And the Elder said this also: 'Mark, having become the interpreter of Peter, wrote down accurately all that he remembered of the things said and done by the Lord, but *not however in order.*' For neither did he hear the Lord, nor did he follow Him, but afterwards, as I said, Peter, who *adapted his teachings to the needs* [*of his hearers? of himself?*], but *not as though he were drawing up a connected account of the Lord's oracles.* So then Mark made no mistake in thus recording some things just as he remembered them, for he made it his one care to omit nothing that he had heard and to make no false statement therein" (quoted by Eusebius, *His. eccl.* 3.39,15; *GCS* 9/1, 290–2).—This ancient testimony, which is often so highly regarded for the authorship of the second gospel, clearly shows that Papias did not think that Mark had composed what we would call a critical biography of Christ.

that many of these discrepancies affect merely minor details.[11] And yet, some of these very modifications which have been introduced are precisely the indications given to the exegete of the deliberate theological or religious preoccupation of the compiling evangelist.[12] These modifications indicate to him that he is dealing with a religious history, with salvation history. For the gospels are not mere records of the *ipsissima verba et facta Iesu,* but often are interpretations of them compiled in order to witness to the mystery of Christ and to bring about conversion—interpretations which are explications of what Christ implicitly said or did, interpretations derived from the fuller comprehension of Christ in the early Church's post-Easter faith (cf. Jn. 2:22; 12:16; 14:26), interpretations which have arisen from the application of Christ's teaching to a new situation. It is not possible, however, to give a more specific answer here about individual episodes and their relative order of historicity within the basic structure already mentioned—more specific, that is, than the principle enunciated at the beginning of this paragraph. Individual cases would have to be examined.

In more recent times two other significant reactions to Form Criticism have taken place. First, just as Source Analysis gave way to *Formgeschichte,* so the latter has yielded to *Redaktionsgeschichte* (the analysis of the relationship of the individual gospel-units to the whole, or the attempt to sketch the "history of the redaction" of the gospel, to explain the theological import of the very framework in which the synoptic material has been arranged by the evangelist). In this type of study emphasis is put, not on the *Sitz im Leben der Kirche,* nor even on the *Sitz im Leben Jesu,* but rather on the *Sitz im Evangelium,* the gospel-context of the individual episode. What part has it in the total portrait of Christ which the evangelist is drawing? It thus acknowledges that, though the framework of the

[11] The story of the cure of the blind man at Jericho offers the classic example: in Mark (10:46) the cure takes place as Jesus and his disciples leave Jericho; in Luke (18:35) as they approach Jericho; in Mark and Luke one blind man is cured, but in Matthew (20:30) two are cured. And yet there are so many agreements in the wording of the passage that it is impossible to deny that they are parallel accounts of the same incident. See A. Huck, *Synopsis of the First Three Gospels* (9th ed., rev. by H. Lietzmann; Engl. tr. F. L. Cross; Oxford: Blackwell, 1957), pp. 150–1. Or compare Mt. 3:11 with Mk. 1:7; Lk. 3:16; or Jn. 12:3 with Mk. 14:3; Mt. 26:6.

[12] See H. Conzelmann, *The Theology of St. Luke* (tr. G. Buswell; New York: Harper, 1961).

gospel account is often quite artificial, nevertheless the evangelist must have had a reason in so ordering the individual units, and an effort is made to determine that reason and to uncover his theological purpose.

As a result of this modern approach to the gospels there are three perspectives according to which the gospels can be studied— three legitimate points of view which emerge from the *intrinsic analysis* of the texts. First is the *Sitz im Leben der Kirche,* which the original Form Critics called merely *Sitz im Leben,* meaning thereby the situation in the early Church which was responsible for the rise and development of the gospel story (sometimes even said to be the "creation" of it). Today, modern Catholic exegetes will recognize that this perspective is legitimate, because it gives an insight into the situation which was responsible, not for the creation of the story, but for the recalling and the *preservation* of the tradition about Jesus. Secondly, there is the perspective of the *Sitz im Leben Jesu,* the historical situation in the life of Jesus himself, often most difficult to ascertain because of the problems mentioned above. Finally, the *Sitz im Evangelium,* or the situation in the gospel itself. The latter is the perspective of the inspired writer, for it attempts to discern what his intention was in so using the story which he records. Of the three perspectives it is obviously the last one which is the most important, because it bears the charism of inspiration to the greatest extent. And yet, it is not the one which is most occupied with the historical question.[12a]

Still another significant reaction to Form Criticism has recently made its appearance in Scandinavia, where emphasis has always been strong on the value of oral tradition in biblical studies. Birger Ger-

[12a] Official sanction has now been given to this threefold way of viewing the gospels. It can be found in a formal, academic presentation in the Instruction of the Pontifical Biblical Commission of May 14, 1964; see *Acta apostolicae sedis* 56 (1964) 712–18; *Osservatore romano,* 14 May 1964, p. 3; see my pamphlet, *The Historical Truth of the Gospels: The 1964 Instruction of the Biblical Commission* (Paulist Press Pamphlet; Glen Rock, N.J., 1965); in article form, *Theological Studies* 25 (1964) 386–408. Both contain the text of the Instruction in English. In a more pastoral form the same threefold distinction is found in the dogmatic constitution of Vatican Council II, *Dei Verbum,* par. 19; see W. J. Abbott, *The Documents of Vatican II* (N.Y.: Herder and Herder/Association Press, 1966), p. 124. This succinct paragraph has to be read, however, in the light of the fuller treatment given in the Biblical Commission's Instruction, to which it refers.

hardsson, in a recent book entitled *Memory and Manuscript: Oral Tradition and Written Transmission in Rabbinic Judaism and Early Christianity*,[13] has shown that there existed in the early Church an institution which provided for the controlled transmission of the sayings of and narratives about Jesus. Just as in contemporary Judaism the "sayings" of the Rabbis were handed down by a group of trained "repeaters" (*tanna'im*), by a process which controlled the oral tradition from teacher to pupil, so too in the early Church there seems to have been a similar institution, for evidence of it appears in the postapostolic patristic writers, in Luke, and in Paul. The latter especially uses the Greek equivalents of the technical terms of the Jewish oral tradition (*paradosis*, "tradition", *paralambanein*, "to receive" [a teaching], *paradidonai*, "to hand down, transmit"—see Gal. 1:13–4; 2 Thess. 3:6; 1 Cor. 11:2,23; 15:1–3; etc.). This controlled transmission in the early Church was part of the *didache* and was responsible for the preservation of the traditions about Jesus' words and deeds. The evidence of this well-documented study of Gerhardsson thus heightens the historical value of the individual episodes and lends support to the perspective of the *Sitz im Leben Jesu*— although it still does not eliminate the problem which we raised earlier (especially that of the discrepancies within the synoptic and Johannine traditions). Its significance lies in the fact that it has substituted a well-documented institution of the early Church as a real *Sitz im Leben* or matrix of the gospels for the postulated and often ill-supported ones suggested by the pioneer Form Critics. If this new development is joined to the work of C. H. Dodd about the basic framework of the gospel tradition which is reflected in the primitive *kerygma*, then we see that the ministry of Christ is presented in the gospels with a certain global historicity.[14]

---

[13] Acta seminarii neotestamentici Upsaliensis 22; Lund: Gleerup, 1961. For an extended review of this important book see the writer's note, "Memory and Manuscript: The Origins and Transmission of the Gospel Tradition," *TS* 23 (Sept. 1962). —See also H. Riesenfeld, *The Gospel Tradition and its Beginnings: A Study in the Limits of 'Formgeschichte'* (London: Mowbray, 1957; also appears in a slightly abridged form, but with bibliographical references, in *Studia evangelica* [Texte und Untersuchungen 73; Berlin: Akademie Verlag, 1959], pp. 43–65; and in *The Gospels Reconsidered* [Oxford: Blackwell, 1960], pp. 131–53).

[14] This, I believe, is the reason why the recent *Monitum* on Scripture spoke about the *germana veritas historica et obiectiva Scripturae Sacrae*, in which the Holy Office by using *germana* made it clear that it was not espousing any

To conclude our remarks on the modern Catholic interpretation of the gospels, it will be well to cite a paragraph from Gerhardsson, which manifests a remarkable affinity with the position which many Catholic exegetes have been holding:

It seems to be an extremely tenaciously-held misapprehension among exegetes that an early Christian author must *either* be a purposeful theologian and writer *or* a fairly reliable historian. This misapprehension is applied to the author of Acts, to the Evangelists, and to those who preceded the Evangelists in forming the various elements of the gospel tradition. The pioneer form-critics Dibelius and Bultmann have contributed materially to the perpetuation of this error. They work on a basis of an over-simplified alternative, maintaining that the men who shaped the gospel tradition had no wish to preserve memories for posterity, but *instead* wished by their proclamation to arouse faith in Christ. This is a false alternative. To present the problem in this way fails to do justice to the deep-rooted respect for divine revelation which was felt in Antiquity (and elsewhere): to that profound reverence associated with the words which were "heard" and the things which were "seen," i.e., those events which were understood and interpreted in religious categories. Nor does it do justice even to the reverence commanded by the authoritative teacher or a received authoritative tradition. The fact of the early Christian Apostles, teachers and Evangelists having presented their material with a religious end in view does not necessarily mean *per se* that their memories ceased to function, or that their respect for historical facts vanished.[15]

The words of Gerhardsson should be pondered carefully and should not be interpreted beyond what he is really saying. It would be illegitimate to conclude from them that he is espousing the historical value of the gospels in any fundamentalistic sense. He is merely saying in other words that the gospels are a special type of history, salvation history or religious history.

To a generation of retreat masters trained on ideas about the gospels which are not in conformity with those expressed above, some of these notions may be at first a bit difficult to understand and accept. I can assure them, however, that with a little adjustment in

---

fundamentalistic reading of the gospel text, and thereby acknowledged that the evangelists, like all other writers, did not compose without employing a literary form. See further *TS* 22 (1961) 443–4.

[15] *Op. cit.*, p. 209.

their outlook it will be quite easy to see the validity of the position described above and they will in time discover that the "new approach" is often far more fruitful in its spiritual value than the older one with its preoccupation with the chronological and historical aspects. This richer and more meaningful character of the "new approach" is the real reason why the modern exegete goes out in quest of it—he is not out merely for novelty.

Be this as it may, the situation which we have been describing is certainly a major factor in the problem which is met by many retreat masters in presenting the *Spiritual Exercises* today.

II

There is, however, another factor which contributes to the retreat master's problem in handling the contemplations of the second, third, and fourth weeks of the *Exercises*. It is the understanding of Scripture which Ignatius presupposes there. In other words, the problem is not due exclusively to the modern trends in the study of the gospels. This is an obvious factor in the problem and it should be frankly recognized. For Ignatius was a child of his time and did not view the Scriptures as a modern man would. He looks on the gospel accounts as a literal and exact reproduction of what actually took place, and does not even suspect a problem of literary dependence, redactional embellishment, or transmissional modification. When faced with an obvious problem, he harmonizes the text as did the rest of his generation. Take, for instance, his first point in the contemplation on the vocation of the apostles: "St. Peter and St. Andrew seem to have been called three times. First, to some knowledge of our Lord. This is evident from the first chapter of St. John. Secondly, to a following of Christ in some way, but with the intention of returning to the possessions they had left. St. Luke tells us this in the fifth chapter. Thirdly, to follow Christ our Lord forever, St. Matthew, chapter four, and St. Mark, chapter one" (275).[16] It is of

---

[16] The translation used is that of L. J. Puhl, *The Spiritual Exercises of St. Ignatius: a New Translation Based on Studies in the Language of the Autograph* (Westminster: Newman, 1951). The numbers refer to the sections of this translation, which uses the marginal numbers of the Spanish-Latin text published by Marietti (Turin, 1928).—Ignatius' treatment of the vocation of Peter and Andrew is derived from Ludolph of Saxony; see H. Watrigant, *La genèse des Exercices de saint Ignace de Loyola* (Amiens: Yvert et Tellier, 1897), p. 83; L. M. Rigollot (ed.), *Ludolphus de Saxonia: Vita Jesu Christi ex evangelio et*

little concern to Ignatius that his added explanations of the degrees of conversion ride roughshod over statements in the gospels themselves, e. g., "And they brought the boats to land and left everything and followed him" (Lk. 5:11). This is part of Luke's account which suggests just as much as does the Markan and Matthaean accounts the everlasting commitment of Peter and Andrew to Christ. See, further, the harmonization of the text involved in the seven words of Christ on the cross (297).

For Ignatius the text of the gospels as it stands is what he means by "history" and the "facts." In the very beginning of the *Spiritual Exercises* he gives the instruction that the retreat master "should narrate accurately the facts of the contemplation or meditation (*la historia de tal contemplación o meditación*). The reason for this is that when one in meditation takes *the solid foundation of facts* (*el fundamento verdadero de la historia*), and goes over it and reflects on it for himself, he may find something that makes them a little clearer or better understood" (2). In the explanation of the first prelude of the contemplation on the incarnation he explains that it will "consist in calling to mind the history of the subject I have to contemplate (*la historia de la cosa que tengo de contemplar*) (102)" [17]

---

approbatis ab ecclesia catholica doctoribus sedule collecta (Paris: V. Palmé, 1878), I, 246–7.

[17] Just where Ignatius got the word *historia* and what he meant by it is not easily determined. It turns up in Ludolph's *Prooemium* (#16), in a paragraph which is surprisingly headed, "Evangelistae non semper rerum gestarum ordinem servaverunt." But Ludolph thinks it better to rearrange things, *ne tamen turbari possit devotio parvulorum, locis debitis, quodam ordine alio, prout res gesta, vel dicendi congruentia exigere videbatur, in sequentibus per ordinem situantur. Non tamen affirmo quod hic sit verus, ac certus et debitus rei gestae ordo descriptus quia talis vix ab aliquo reperitur expressus. In ipso autem Evangelio, reperies Verbi incarnati historiam, mandata et promissa: in quibus habes viam, veritatem, et vitam. Christi igitur exempla nosce, quia bene vivere possis, praeceptis bene vivere scias, promissis bene vivere velis* (ed. L. M. Rigollot, p. 10). By such an admission Ludolph shows some awareness of the problem which has become acute in modern times. Commentators on the *Spiritual Exercises* usually recall the fact that Ignatius has treated the sequence of gospel scenes rather freely and has not even preserved that of the gospels themselves. "Ignatius has at times changed the chronological sequence and the joining of the mysteries and made insignificant additions. Much of this is to be explained by the Saint's reading on his sickbed of the 'Life of Jesus' of Ludoph of Saxony, e.g., when he presents first the adoration of the Magi, then the presentation in the Temple, and the Flight into Egypt (## 267–9), [cf. also #161 with #280, 285–88], when the sellers of doves are 'kindly' treated (#277), when Christ speaks of the 'beloved' disciples

On at least six other occasions in the *Spiritual Exercises* Ignatius uses the word "history" in the same sense at the beginning of a contemplation. "This is the history of the mystery" (111; see also 137, 191, 201, 219). But note the significant use of the word "history" in the first prelude of the meditation on the Three Classes of Men: "This is the history of the Three Classes of Men" (150). Then he proceeds to present an imaginative, parable-like case history. It is obvious that the function of the first prelude is to give a short summary or résumé of the subject, on which the "mental representation" (*composición viendo el lugar*) of the second prelude is to be based. It is at the first prelude of the exercise that Ignatius intended the retreat master to "narrate accurately the facts of the contemplation or meditation," "the solid foundation of facts." What he means by this is not what we would call the objective, historical facts of the *event,* as a historian might try to present them, but rather the "scriptural facts," the facts of the scene as they are narrated by the sacred writer. It would be a mistake to think that he is using the word "history" in our modern, technical sense, but equally a mistake to think that he means anything less than what the Scriptures recount. Ignatius is obviously thinking of *salvation history,* those events of the past which took place "in the fulness of time" and which are recorded for our edification and spiritual profit in the gospels.

Ignatius had not the slightest concern about the historicity of an episode—whether it could be established with satisfaction or not. Like Ludolph of Saxony he was interested in other aspects of the episode. This is brought out by the way he handles the first prelude of the Kingdom of Christ: "This is a mental representation of the place. Here it will be *to see in imagination* the synagogues, villages,

---

(#278, 281, etc.). But Ignatius also departs not infrequently even from Ludolph. Fr. von Hummelauer has best explained the reasons for such departure according to the intrinsic structure of the Exercises" (E. Raitz von Frentz, *Ignatius von Loyola: Geistliche Übungen nach der Übersetzung von Alfred Feder, S.J.* [12th ed.; Freiburg im B.; Herder, 1957], p. 135, n. 1). For a résumé of the way in which Ignatius uses the word *historia* see J. Calveras, *Práctica de los Ejercicios intensivos* (2nd ed.; Barcelona: Balmes, 1952), p. 205. —For another (more traditional) view of the "solid foundation of facts" see A. López de Santa Anna, "El uso de la historia y arqueologia bíblicas en las meditaciones de los Ejercicios, según la mente de San Ignacio," *Manresa* 1 (1925) 107–17. "De esto se sigue la imperiosa necesidad de conocer los detalles bíblicos y arqueológicos para que la imaginación trabaje con provecho sobre fundamento verdadero y no sobre ficciones ridículas o al menos gratuitas" (p. 110).

and towns where Jesus preached" (91). His emphasis is above all on the retreatant's activity, on his picturing to himself what Christ did or said, in order to make it present to himself. It is true that Ignatius is not asking us to picture Christ merely walking down the pages of the New Testament, but that he wants us to picture the historical Jesus actually walking down the roads of Palestine. This is beyond doubt, but even here the emphasis is on the *mental and imaginative activity* of the retreatant. This accounts for the freedom which he takes with the sacred text itself; in the contemplation on the nativity he explains, "This is the history of the mystery. Here it will be that our Lady, being about nine months with child, set out from Nazareth, as may be piously believed, seated on an ass, and accompanied by Joseph and a maid, leading an ox. They are going to Bethlehem to pay the tribute that Caesar imposed on those lands" (111). The biblical "history" says nothing about a maid, an ass, or an ox. But who can say that Ignatius is wrong in asking the retreatant to feed his soul on such a consideration? Or again he instructs the retreatant to see with his imagination "the way from Nazareth to Bethlehem. Consider its length, its breadth; whether level or through valleys and over hills. Observe also the place or cave where Christ is born; whether big or little; whether high or low; and how it is arranged" (112). Surely he does not expect the retreatant to engage in much research to find out the length and breadth of the road, etc. By his imagination he is to make it all present to himself.[18] "For it is not much knowledge that fills and

---

[18] This approach to the Scriptures Ignatius has inherited at least from Ludolph of Saxony, if not from other spiritual writers of his time. In the *Prooemium* (#11) of his *Vita Jesu Christi* Ludolph proposed his "Methodus quo meditanda est vita Christi." It reads as follows: "Vidisti ergo ad quem excelsum gradum meditationes vitae Christi perducunt: nunc in ipsas meditationes te aliqualiter introducere tentabo, non omnia quae in Evangelio scripta sunt pertractando, sed quaedam devotiora ex his eligendo. Nec credas quod omnia, quae Christum dixisse vel fecisse meditari possumus, scripta sunt, sed ad majorem impressionem ea tibi sic narrabo prout contigerunt, vel contigisse pie credi possunt, secundum quasdam imaginativas repraesentationes, quae animus diversimode percipit. Nam circa divinam Scripturam meditari, intelligere, et exponere, multifarie possumus, prout credimus expedire, dummodo non sit contra fidem, vel bonos mores. Quicumque vero asserit de Deo aliquid quod non est tibi certum, vel per naturalem rationem, vel per synderesim, vel per fidem, vel per sacram Scripturam, praesumit et peccat. Cum ergo me narrantem invenies: Ita dixit vel fecit Dominus Jesus, seu alii qui introducuntur; si id per Scripturam probari non possit, non aliter accipias quam

satisfies the soul, but the intimate understanding and relish of the truth" (2). Finally, recall his apology for including the first apparition to Mary: "Though this is not mentioned explicitly in the Scripture, it must be considered as stated, when Scripture says that he appeared to many others. For Scripture supposes that we have understanding, as it is written, 'Are you also without understanding?' [Mt. 15:16]" (299).[19] The result of such reflections is the realization that when Ignatius speaks of the "facts" or the "history" of the mystery, he means the "scriptural facts," what is narrated by the sacred writer.[20]

Another aspect of the issue can be seen in the fact that Ignatius calls these gospel scenes of the life of Christ "mysteries." The selection of certain episodes of the life of Christ for meditation has often been traced to the period of Ignatius' convalescence.[21] It is likely

---

devota meditatio exigit, hoc est, perinde accipe ac si dicerem: Meditor quod ita dixerit vel fecerit bonus Jesus; et sic de similibus. Tu autem, si ex his fructum sumere cupis, toto mentis affectu, diligenter, delectabiliter, et morose, omnibus aliis curis et sollicitudinibus tunc omissis, ita praesentem to exhibeas his quae per Dominum Jesum dicta vel facta sunt, et ex his quae narrantur, ac si tuis auribus audires, et oculis videres, quia suavissima sunt ex desiderio cogitanti, et multo magis gustanti. Et ideo quamvis multa ex his tamquam in praeterito facta narrantur, tu tamen omnia tamquam in praesenti fierent, mediteris: quia ex hoc majorem sine dubio suavitatem gustabis. Lege ergo quae facta sunt, tamquam fiant; pone ante oculos gesta praeterita tamquam praesentia, et sic magis sapida senties et jucunda" (ed. L. M. Rigollot, p. 7). —This method of contemplation can be traced back to Bonaventure at least. "Haec et his similia de Puero Jesu meditari potes, dedi tibi occasionem. Tu vero, sicut videbitur extendas et prosequaris, sisque parvula cum parvulo Iesu, nec parvipendas talia humilia et quae puerilia videntur, meditari in ipso. Videntur enim haec dare devotionem, augere amorem, accendere fervorem, inducere compassionem" (*Meditationes vitae Christi*, c. 12 [ed. Vives, 12. 509–630]).

[19] That this is not an entirely personal idea of Ignatius is seen from the remark of Suarez: "Absque ulla dubitatione credendum est Christum post resurrectionem primum omnium Matri suae apparuisse" (*In S. Thomae*, q. 55, disp. 49, s. 1, n. 2; ed. Vives, 17. 544). But even so conservative an exegete as U. Holzmeister recognized that it was at best a pious tradition; see "Num Christus post resurrectionem benedictae Matri apparuerit," *Verbum Domini* 22 (1942) 97–102.

[20] To appreciate somewhat what the medieval historian was interested in, and what underlies Ignatius' notions of "history," one should consult the book of one of the great modern Bollandists, H. Delehaye, S.J., *The Legends of the Saints: an Introduction to Hagiography* (tr. V. M. Crawford; London: Longmans, Green, 1907), especially pp. 64–66, or in the new translation of the 4th ed., 1955 by D. Attwater (New York: Fordham, 1962), pp. 50–55.

[21] *Autobiography* #11: "He took great delight in the books he was

then that he derived this term from the spiritual books which he was reading. By the word "mystery" he may have understood nothing more than an incident in the life of our Lord, suited for commemoration or imitation or as having some spiritual significance for Christians.[22] The use of it is probably akin to the "mysteries" of the rosary. Whether the medieval mystery plays influenced the use of the word in the *Exercises* or not is not matter for discussion here, but the rendering of the scene present to the mind of the exercitant has undoubtedly some affinity with them. But, at any rate, the re-presentation of the gospel scene is what is stressed, whereby the retreatant will contemplate "the states of his sacred humanity," to use the phrase of a modern author.[23]

There is one further element in the *Spiritual Exercises* which must be considered. Throughout the second week Ignatius instructs the retreatant to pray in the third prelude "for an intimate knowledge of

reading, and the thought came to him to select some short but important passages from the Life of Christ and the Lives of the Saints. And so he began to write very carefully in a book, as he had already begun to move a little about the house. The words of Christ he wrote in red ink and those of our Lady in blue, on polished and lined paper in a good hand, for he was an excellent penman. Part of his time he spent in writing, part in prayer" (W. J. Young, *St. Ignatius' Own Story, As Told to Luis González de Cámara* [Chicago: Regnery, 1956], p. 11. Cf. H. Holstein, "Contemplation of the Mysteries of Christ," *Finding God in All Things: Essays in Ignatian Spirituality Selected from* Christus (tr. W. J. Young; Chicago: Regnery, 1958), pp. 90–103. Also H. Pinard de la Boullaye, *Les étapes de rédaction des Exercices de S. Ignace* (Paris: Beauchesne, 1945), p. 22, who maintains that the section on the "Mysteries of the Life of Our Lord" (##261–312) was probably not composed before his stay in Paris 1528–35. Similarly H. Bacht, "Der heutige Stand der Forschung über die Entstehung des Exerzitienbuches des hl. Ignatius von Loyola," *Geist und Leben* 29 (1956) 327–8, especially p. 333.

[22] The meaning of this word for Ignatius is singularly without comment in most of the standard commentaries on the *Exercises*. H. Holstein (*op. cit.*) thinks that Ignatius may have been influenced in his selection of "mysteries" by the illustrated Lives of Christ which were current. It is, furthermore, impossible to exclude the medieval meaning of *mystery* which is a synonym for the sense of Scripture "secundum allegoriam." H. de Lubac (*op. cit.*, I/2, 397) explains: "The mystical sense is the sense which refers to mystery, which is a reality, hidden at first in God, then revealed to men at the same time that it is realized in Christ. It is then the sense which contains the fulness of doctrine: 'iuxta mysticum intellectum haec omnia referuntur ad Christum' . . . A search was made in the sacred Books for 'mysticos legalium umbrarum intellectus,' i.e., they looked everywhere in them for the 'truth' of these shadows, that Truth which is Christ Himself."

[23] C. Marmion, *Christ in His Mysteries* (4th ed.; St. Louis: B. Herder, 1939), p. 24.

our Lord, who has become man for me, that I may love him more and follow him more closely" (104). Ignatius makes much of the imitation of Christ (see 109, 135, 139, 168, 175, 248). Indeed, the climax of the Three Kinds of Humility is precisely that "I desire and choose poverty with Christ poor, rather than riches, in order to imitate and be in reality more like Christ our Lord" (167). This imitation is often based on the example of Christ in the gospel scene being contemplated, but on one occasion it is even based on how the retreatant imagines Christ would conduct himself at table: "Whilst one is eating, let him imagine he sees Christ our Lord and his disciples at table, and consider how he eats and drinks, how he looks, how he speaks, and then strive to imitate him" (214). Once again, there is an obviously rich and fruitful consideration in the notion of the imitation of Christ. No one can deny that it is founded on New Testament data (Jn. 13:15; 1 Pet. 2:21; Phil. 2:5; Col. 3:13; 1 Jn. 2:6; 1 Cor. 11:1). But the problem arises from the fact that many of the events of Christ's public life are not presented by the evangelists for imitation. This is the reason why at times the retreatant senses a certain superficiality in the presentation, if, for instance, the Nativity is to be contemplated merely for the purpose of imitating Christ's poverty, or the life at Nazareth for his obedience. The modern perspective of *Redaktionsgeschichte* would rather analyze the incident in order to appreciate the reason why the story is used in the evangelist's total portrait of Christ; it tries to reckon with the final summary comment in the episode which the evangelist so frequently adds. It may be that the element of imitation is part of this perspective, but frequently it is not. John Bligh, S.J., has well stated the situation with regard to the gospels:

Did Christ during his daily life regard it as his task to set an example which should be remembered and imitated? Did he endeavor to give the moral teaching of the Sermon on the Mount concrete embodiment in a series of incidents which his followers could remember and imitate? If he did, at all events these paradigm incidents have not been remembered; the four gospels do not narrate them. . . The evidence of the gospels is that Christ regarded himself as setting a pattern not of each particular precept of his New Law but of the essentials, namely perfect obedience to his heavenly Father, willing acceptance of humiliation, and voluntary self-sacrifice for the sake of others. He set this example chiefly by taking up his cross and dying on it. He is a living law only in this sense, that he is a living embodiment of the Law of Charity, which is his "way": "I am the Way" (Jn. 14:6). If Christ's purpose during the Public Life was not to set an example of all the moral virtues required of his followers but rather to teach his hearers what the content of obedience was *for them,* still less is the purpose of the gospel accounts of the Public Life to set forth Christ's daily life as a model for our imitation. The criteria by which St. Mark selected the incidents to be incorporated in his account of the Public Life are very mysterious; but there is little to be said for the view that his choice was controlled by the aim of setting forth Christ as a model for imitation . . . the greater part of the synoptic and Johannine traditions are not concerned with Christ as a model for imitation, but Christ as lawgiver, prophet, rabbi, revealer, and worker of miracles.[24]

If this is the case, then another area of conflict may seem to arise between the modern scriptural approach and the *Exercises.*

We come finally to what is really the basic aspect of the problem. Even granting that Ignatius is a child of his time and reads the gospels like a fundamentalist Renaissance man and puts great emphasis on the imitation of Christ (in accord with the contemporary "Devotio moderna"), his handling of Scripture is completely *subordinated to the purpose of the Exercises.* His goal is ascetical; the *Exercises* have "as their purpose the conquest of self and the regulation of one's life" (21). To this end Ignatius subordinates all the Scripture which he uses, almost totally neglecting the Old Testament and ordering all that he uses of the New Testament to prepare the retreatant's soul for the key meditations. As Ignatius first conceived of and used the *Exercises,* they were calculated to produce a tremendous psychological conversion in the retreatant, an "election." This was certainly his original conception and to such a psychological goal he picked and chose those "mysteries" of the life of Christ which would be best suited for the transit from the Kingdom of Christ to the Two Standards, Three Classes of Men, Three Kinds of Humility and the Election. In the course of time the custom grew up of repeating the *Exercises,* whence has come the practice of the annual retreat today. Adaptation of the *Exercises* in such retreats has been a subject often discussed: How much has to be retained in order that the Ignatian *Exercises* be given? No one makes an election every year; with the shift of emphasis here in the repeated

[24] " 'Liturgical Mysticism'," *Heythrop Journal* 2 (1961) 333–44, esp. 341–42.

retreats greater stress was in time put on the imitation of Christ in details and the contemplations of the life of Christ were used more for this purpose. They were often used as occasions for moralizing exhortations and the question of the imitation of Christ received even greater stress. To accomplish this even more stress seemed to be needed for the historicity of the details of the scene. Now the modern biblical movement has made Catholics aware of the neglected riches in the inspired Scriptures, both of the Old and the New Testament. Recent gospel study has shifted the emphasis from the historical and chronological to the kerygmatic and theological reading of the evangelists' compilations. It seems to call once again for an adaptation of the Ignatian method—and once again the problem of the fidelity to the method of Ignatius is going to come up. Must I accept the perspective of Ignatius in the treatment of the contemplations on the life of Christ and subordinate the treatment of the gospels to it? Or can some compromise be worked out? It seems that the latter is desirable, because the retreat master will have to respect the sensibilities of retreatants, and in time more and more of them will be aware of the "new approach."

The foregoing remarks should have indicated the various aspects of the two factors which contribute to the modern problem which faces the retreat master. Part of it springs from the "new approach" in gospel study, part of it from certain Ignatian presuppositions. However, it is not a problem which is completely insoluble. In the following section we shall try to offer some suggestions for a solution.

Some Suggestions for a Solution

If we recall the three perspectives according to which the gospels can be studied, viz., the *Sitz im Leben der Kirche,* the *Sitz im Leben Jesu,* and the *Sitz im Evangelium,* it is the last named which suggests itself as the one most suited for the purposes of the retreat master. In fact, though there is a problem here, it is precisely this one among the three which best corresponds to the Ignatian view of the gospels and what we have termed his "scriptural facts." Only rarely will the *Sitz im Leben der Kirche* be of interest to the retreat master. His interest will naturally incline him toward the *Sitz im Leben Jesu,* because he would like to be sure that it really happened just so, and this perspective would seem to furnish him with the material needed to be able to "see in imagination the synagogues, villages and towns where Jesus preached" (91). But this is a complicated perspective, hard to use, and dependent on Synoptic and Form-Critical comparisons. If the retreat master happens upon a well-worked out explanation of this viewpoint for some scene or other, he can of course use it. But in the long run this perspective is somewhat removed from the purpose which Ignatius has in mind. Is it not immaterial to the retreat master whether it can be established with certainty that the event took place just as it happens to be described in the Matthaean or Lukan gospel? After all, the scene was recorded as such under the inspiration of the Holy Spirit for a very definite purpose—for the education of the people of God, for the edification of the Church, and for our spiritual instruction and nourishment. Suppose it does turn out that a certain scene as presented by the Matthaean gospel has been embellished in the light of the early Church's Easter faith, or that it can be shown that Luke has deliberately modified his account of an incident to adapt it to his theological point of view— nevertheless such embellishments and modifications are inspired. They may have to be discounted in a consideration of the episodes from the standpoint of the second perspective, but as they stand they are part of the story of Jesus intended by God for the edification of his Church. That is why the third perspective, which tries to account for the use of precisely such details as contributing factors in the whole portrait of Christ, should be preferred by the preacher and the retreat master. For it copes with the Matthaean, Markan, Lukan, and Johannine formulation and tries to perceive the pertinence of the episode to the entire message of the evangelist. Now this aspect of modern gospel study can easily be adopted by retreat masters; it fits easily into the directives of Ignatius that the "solid foundation of facts" should be exposed—the solid foundation of "scriptural facts."

In view of this I would suggest for an eight-day retreat, in which a number of episodes of the life of Christ are to be used, that they be taken entirely from one gospel. Since Mark and John lack an infancy narrative, the choice would preferably be either Matthew or Luke; and because of the contemplation on the incarnation Luke's account would probably be more suitable. However, after that initial meditation in the second week, which has, as a matter of fact, its own distinctive Ignatian cast, the Matthaean gospel could probably be used just as well. But in adopting the scenes from Luke or

Matthew, one would do well to adopt also the outlook, the theological approach, and the portrait of Christ of that evangelist. These can be found in many introductory books which explain the purpose of the gospels.[25] This solution would serve also to unify the contemplations much more than they normally are in a retreat. Ignatius is concerned that the retreatant acquire a thorough knowledge of the Christ, whose cause he is to espouse, and it is difficult to think of a better way of doing this than to follow and use as much as possible of the inspired portrait of one of the evangelists.

Of course, the Markan and Johannine gospels can also be used; the riches of the latter are always a mine for the retreat master. But the use of these would call for greater adaptation. But what should be avoided, it is suggested, is the pick-and-choose presentation of the "mysteries" derived from the different evangelists. For this might betray most quickly to retreatants who may be aware of modern scriptural developments that the retreat master is not quite *au courant* —should he really be concerned about this? If this technique is used, then it will also provide possibilities for variety, should the retreat master have to give a second or even third retreat to the same group. On one occasion, Luke's portrait could be presented, on another, Matthew's, and so on.

A number of the episodes of the life of Christ are prescribed by Ignatius and are always looked for in a Jesuit retreat. But the choice of the others is left to the discretion of the retreat master. Why should they not be so chosen from the gospel being used to build up the portrait of Christ according to the conception of one evangelist? If they are, then the problem is apparently eliminated which is caused by an extrinsic norm such as, "What scene will suit best the consideration of this or that virtue?"

What we are suggesting, then, is a slight adaptation of the *Exercises* in view of the modern development in gospel study. If one feels that this is too much of a departure from the Ignatian method, and that it is necessary to pick and choose gospel scenes arbitrarily to produce the effect intended by Ignatius, then there is little reason

[25] For example, the introduction to *La sainte Bible* (*de Jérusalem*), published by the Ecole Biblique, Jerusalem (Paris: Cerf). In this connection the recent book of H. Conzelmann, *The Theology of St Luke* (tr. G. Buswell; New York: Harper, 1961), might be used. The reader is warned, however, that it is not easy to read; see *TS* 22 (1961) 663–5. But it does highlight the Lukan theological perspective.

for the retreat master to worry about the modern Scripture movement. For such a view will not really agree with any of the perspectives of the evangelists, and is quite distinct from the modern preoccupation of *Redaktionsgeschichte*. The retreat master will then be as free and untrammeled as Ignatius in accommodating Scripture to his ascetical goal. If however, he has become aware of the neglected riches of the Scriptures now uncovered by the modern approach, then he can adopt a perspective graced with the charism of inspiration and adapt his presentation of the contemplations on the life of Christ to this perspective. For it seems to us that the adoption of the perspective, say of Luke or of John, will not change the Ignatian *Exercises* that much. After all, their fundamental drive is found in the key meditations, and the contemplations on the life of Christ are in reality psychological padding, destined to prepare the retreatant for the renovation of life (which in the normal annual retreat will find its expression much more in the deepened appreciation of "finding God in all things" of the Contemplation to Attain the Love of God), or to fortify him in a decision made in a retreat of election. But in any case a careful scrutiny of one gospel or another for scenes which will at once preserve the evangelist's perspective and stress the element of conversion to Christ would seem to be the idea—and would seem to be at most a slight modification of the Ignatian method.

As for the question of the imitation of Christ mentioned above, it should be made clear that we are not counselling the avoidance of such a theme in a retreat. There are undoubtedly gospel scenes which lend themselves to it; but the difficulty lies in the fact that many of the more important scenes for the evangelist's portrait of Christ lack precisely this element of imitation. The theme of imitation can be revitalized by presenting those aspects of Christ's *life as a whole* which are particularly apt for imitation (see the remarks of J. Bligh above). Of all the gospels it is again that according to Luke which is most suited to the aspect of imitation. Apropos of the Lukan passion narrative in particular, X. Léon-Dufour, S.J., has pointed out that Luke's presentation of the passion is that of a drama in which the reader is invited to participate, to engage himself like Simon of Cyrene, carrying his cross "behind Jesus."

The reader is invited, no longer to make a simple act of faith in God who fulfills the Scriptures and in Jesus the Son of God made manifest in his death. Unlike Mark, Luke explains, as does Matthew, the mystery which he unfolds. The reader is no longer especially invited to adore the person of Jesus who presents himself as the Son of God, the all powerful Lord (Matthew), but to recognize his own weakness with Peter and his malice with all those who have condemned Jesus, to adore the infinite mercy of Jesus, so human and so kind, and to participate especially in his patience. . . . Jesus is not simply a model, he is the type of the persecuted Upright One, resuming in his person the persecution of all times and revealing by his triumph the victory of his followers.[26]

Another comment on the imitation-theme may be permitted at this point. Ignatius instructs the retreatant often to reflect upon the matter being contemplated to draw fruit from it: "I will reflect upon this to draw profit from what I see" (106; see also 107, 108, 114, 115, 116, 122, 123, 124). In many retreats such reflection is motivated chiefly by the quest for something to imitate; the viewpoint adopted is that of exemplary causality. But (at the risk of introducing Aristotelian expressions into such a discussion as this) why could not the reflection adopt the other types of causality: material, efficient or final? Such considerations would enrich the presentation, and the last one, finality, would certainly agree with the perspective of *Redaktionsgeschichte*.

Further, though that imitation of Christ means obviously the more or less direct copying of the way in which Jesus behaved in certain situations (cf. 1 Pet. 2:21; 2 Cor. 10:1), there is more to the notion of the imitation of Christ than this simple reference to human example. Recall Paul's reference to it in 2 Cor. 8:9: "You know how gracious the Lord Jesus was. Though he was rich, he became poor for your sake, in order that by his poverty you might become rich." As C. H. Dodd has pointed out:

Clearly he does not mean that Jesus was a rich man who gave up his wealth and adopted a life of poverty, like (let us say) Francis of Assisi. No doubt he had a moderately prosperous carpenter's business at Nazareth and sacrificed it for a career which sometimes left him with nowhere to lay his head; but that could not fittingly be described as being rich and then becoming poor. No, Paul is alluding to the belief of the Church that Christ had at his disposal the power and riches of another world, and that he chose the lot of a man, and a

---

[26] *Dictionnaire de la Bible, Supplément* 6. 1476.

poor man at that, in order that he might share those riches of another world with his fellowmen.[27]

The "hard core of historical fact" here is that Jesus was crucified and went to his death in complete obedience to the will of God, like a servant whose only thought is to do what the master wants done. But Paul sees in this act of Jesus the concrete expression in history of a divine act of self-giving beyond space and time, revealing the character of God himself. He recommends to Christians the imitation of this divine and human self-giving; they should become as like Christ as possible, not by self-deification, but by walking "in love as Christ loved you" (Eph. 5:2). "It is in respect of the love which Christ showed to man that the character and action of God are to be copied." [28] This is the aspect of love which should dominate all human activity. But such a consideration, so briefly indicated here, means that the retreat master must pierce beyond the mere analysis of a gospel scene from the standpoint of exemplary causality to the other standpoints mentioned above.

When it comes to the handling of certain specific contemplations the retreat master may still feel that what has been offered as a solution above has not really come to grips with the individual problems which worry him. Perhaps a few examples may help in this regard. They are drawn mainly from questions which have been proposed to the writer from time to time; extensive illustration is impossible.

But if, for instance, the retreat master feels uneasy in suggesting that the retreatant represent to himself the Blessed Mother reciting the *Magnificat,* he can simply phrase it thus: "Picture to yourselves the Blessed Mother uttering the canticle which St. Luke puts on her lips." This much is certainly based on the "solid foundation of facts" —the inspired Lukan facts (even though the historian might hesitate to assert that the stylized Greek formulation of the hymn is precisely what the Aramaic-speaking mother of Jesus uttered on that occasion). The important thing to remember here is that it is the Lukan

---

[27] *Gospel and Law: The Relation of Faith and Ethics in Early Christianity* (New York: Columbia, 1951), p. 40. Our paragraph is largely inspired by Dodd's treatment of imitation. Perhaps also of use will be E. J. Tinsley, *The Imitation of God in Christ: An Essay on the Biblical Basis of Christian Spirituality* (Philadelphia: Westminster, 1960); see the review by J. Bligh cited in note 22.

[28] C. H. Dodd, *Gospel and Law*, p. 42.

Greek formulation which has come down to us as the inspired text, intended by God for our instruction and spiritual profit. But then let the retreat master make sure that he includes in his explanation of the canticle the part that it plays in the Lukan gospel and in the Lukan portrait of Christ (which can be found in any competently prepared commentary). This is not an introduction of extraneous matter into the Ignatian retreat, for in the long run it will give a more reliable picture of the Christ with whom the retreatant is expected to become enchanted and captivated during the course of the second, third and fourth weeks. The end-result of the incorporation of such elements into the retreat from the modern approach to the gospels can only be one of added spiritual and intellectual stimulus and nourishment.

Again, if the modern retreat master feels uneasy about the magi and their star, he is not obliged to begin the contemplation by stating, "Now there may have been no magi, but we will meditate on them anyway." Simply because individual, fallible exegetes cannot supply the retreat master with convincing reasons to assure him that the magi *de facto* did adore the infant Christ, he should not omit the meditation from the retreat. He should present it as one of the five episodes of the Matthaean infancy narrative, whose purpose is to extol the greatness of the child now born, the scion of David, the Anointed One of Israel. It is true, of course, that the scene is described with elements which appear to the modern mind as nothing more than folkloric details: astrologers following a new star on the horizon, whose vagaries across the heaven tax the imagination; their arrival with the exotic gifts of the East; their mysterious disappearance to their own land; the consternation of "Herod and all Jerusalem" at their arrival and story. Let us suppose for a moment, *dato non concesso,* that there is nothing more here than folklore. Why should not such elements be exploited for what they are intended to do: announce the birth of one of the "greats" of this world's history? Here is a child who is born, whose greatness is heralded by a "new star," similar to that said to have arisen at the birth of Abraham in Jewish legends. He is a child whom learned men from among the Gentiles were said to have come a long distance to adore. Who is this child? Why is he great? Matthew has already intimated the answer by his genealogy in chapter 1: He is the scion of David, the *Christ*—the One for whom all Israel has been waiting. Born of the ne of Abraham, a Jew of the Jews, He is heralded among the ientiles as one of the "greats" of history. All of this, of course, would erve the ulterior purpose of Matthew who implies the contrasting eception of Jesus among his own people. Even pagans acknowledge ne greatness of this Anointed One of God, who is made manifest to nem by an astrologer's star. Matthew would have recorded as part f his infancy narrative a popular tale, which for some reason divine rovidence has seen fit to endow with the charism of inspiration for ur edification and spiritual profit (but has not thereby necessarily nade out of it a piece of historical writing). By this story Matthew ; introducing into his "Little Pentateuch," which is the infancy .arrative, the theme of the rejection of the suffering messiah by the .eople of Israel. The magi, the flight to Egypt, the massacre of the nnocents, all strike the chords of this basic motif. The Jews are epresented by Herod and his consultants, who are thrown into con-ternation at the arrival of pagan astrologers seeking the king of the ews. Whether the historicity of the scene can be established or not, t has a place in the Matthaean gospel and therefore a place in Chris-ian piety and instruction.[29]

Again, the retreat master should remember that he is not an xegete as such. If Pius XII made it the duty of the exegete to "dis-ern and define clearly that sense of the biblical words which is called iteral . . . so that the mind of the author may be made abundantly lear," [30] he also stressed that the exegete was to set forth the theol-ogy of the individual books or texts so that their exposition might aid oriests in their presentation of Christian doctrine to the people and ielp all the faithful to lead a life that is holy and worthy of a Chris-ian. The exegete's study of Scripture is a restricted one, whereas the oreacher or the retreat master uses Scripture in a far wider scope. There are other uses of Scripture which are certainly legitimate—

[29] See S. Muñoz-Iglesias, "El género literario del Evangelio de la Infancia n San Mateo," *Estudios Bíblicos* 17 (1958) 243–73; J. Racette, "L'évangile le l'enfance selon saint Matthieu," *Sciences ecclésiastiques* 9 (1957) 77–85; .I. M. Bourke, "The Literary Genus of Matthew 1–2," *CBQ* 22 (1960) 160–'5; J. E. Bruns, "The Magi Episode in Matthew 2," *CBQ* 23 (1961) 51–54; A. M. Denis, "L'adoration des Mages vue par S. Matthieu," *NRT* 92 (1960) ·2–39

[30] *Divino afflante Spiritu,* Par. 23 (NCWC Pamphlet, p. 14). The whole ection here on the "Interpretation of Sacred Books" and the relation between he literal and the spiritual sense of Scripture would deserve restudy in the ight of what we have written above.

the homiletic use, the liturgical use, and even the medieval allegorical (theological) use. For the most part these are accommodated senses of Scripture,[31] and can scarcely be graced with the name of an *inspired* sense, one intended by God as the author of Scripture. However, such accommodations of Scripture have a long history in the patristic, conciliar, and theological traditions of the Church, not to mention the homiletic and liturgical traditions, where their use has been abundantly fruitful. Is not this the sort of thing to which Ignatius refers when he apologizes for the first apparition: "For Scripture supposes that we have understanding, as it is written, 'Are you also without understanding?' [Mt. 15:16]" (299)?[32] Who can deny that it is part of the divine economy of salvation to use not only the *inspired* sense (= the literal sense), but also such accommodated senses? But in so using Scripture, the retreat master is not *per se* an exegete.

Finally, it should be emphasized again that Scripture is subordinated to the goal of the *Exercises* in a retreat. The retreat master is not merely expounding a text, but he is *using* scriptural texts to an ascetical end. But he must, nevertheless, be careful. Today, modern retreatants, especially those who may have some training in modern scriptural developments (like seminarians on the theological level, certain groups of sisters or brothers, not to mention young priests) may be rather sensitive, if a very fundamentalistic interpretation of certain scriptural passages is used with them. Their sensibilities have to be respected, as the retreat master well knows. Hence, even though he is not asked to be an exegete, it is nevertheless desirable

[31] The medieval *allegorical* sense and perhaps even the *liturgical* sense might seem to some to be instances of the *sensus plenior* of Scripture. Many modern theologians debate whether or not there is such a sense in Scripture; certainly the *magisterium* of the Church has not yet come out in favor of it. Its existence is denied by many. Cf. R. E. Brown, *The Sensus Plenior of Sacred Scripture* (Baltimore: St. Mary's, 1955); Benoit, P., "La plénitude de sens des Livres Saints," *RB* 67 (1960) 161–96; synopsized in *Theology Digest* 9 (1961) 3–8. But cf. also the letters of M. M. Bourke and J. L. McKenzie on the subject, *ibid.*, pp. 66, 126.

[32] In this connection recall the words of Ludolph of Saxony cited above in note 17 ("Non tamen . . . velis") and in note 18 ("Nam circa divinam . . . mores").—By the same token, it may seem that one could legitimately extend the principle of the imitation of Christ even beyond the perspective of the evangelist. True, no one can say that it is wrong to do this, but it seems that here above all the modern retreat-master has to be careful. Let him not present it as if it were the intention of Scripture itself, for this would be the worst possible type of *eisegesis*.

that his *use* of Scripture be somewhat in line with modern exegetical principles.

But even in this regard it may be that we are talking about what is—or could be—a false problem. Just as there are poor retreat masters, who fail to comprehend the psychological build-up of the *Exercises* and never achieve in their retreats the purpose envisaged by Ignatius, so too there are retreatants who are captivated by the novelty of the modern scriptural approach and are perhaps too inclined to criticize even the good retreat master for his lack of modernity. If we have recommended above an adaptation of the *Exercises* in view of the modern scriptural developments, it is obvious that such a recommendation should aim at striking a balance or the happy medium. Consequently, it is well to reflect on the different purposes of the exegete and the retreat master and not exaggerate the problem itself. Ignatius' use of Scripture and his purpose is one thing, that of the exegete in the modern scriptural movement is another. A judicious adaptation is what is needed.

The Liturgical Word
The Spiritual Exercises
The Jesuit Response

David Stanley, S.J.

For Jesuits, trained as they are in the tradition of the *Spiritual Exercises* of St. Ignatius, prayer is an intensely private response to the call of God; a public response through liturgical prayer jars the sensibilities. The *Exercises* reflect the piety of the sixteenth century, when the stress on "fellowship" and the reading of Scripture had a certain Protestant aura about them. St. Ignatius, as a man of his time, stressed the value of the individual as opposed to the community; but the needs of our own time seem to force the pendulum over to the role of interpersonal relationship in spirituality. Fr. Stanley asks that the *Spiritual Exercises* not become a treasured and untouchable family heirloom, but rather grow with the vitalizing force of liturgy. Modern Scripture can provide the link between the *Exercises* and the liturgy by showing the gospel incidents more as public proclamation than private revelation.

That the divine revelation communicated to us in the Bible is of the nature of dialogue—a dialogue between God and man—is a commonplace in modern theology. As a consequence of this, our spiritual life may well be described as a dialogue also with Christ our Lord. And in this dialogue our Jesuit response (since we are Christians before being religious) is articulated principally by our participation in the liturgy and our practice of the *Spiritual Exercises*. And yet, if we are to be completely candid about it, we must acknowledge the presence of a certain tension, a very real tension, among us Jesuits which is keenly felt between these two expressions of our Jesuit response to the divine Word.

183

This communication is directed not so much to providing the answer or solution to this problem, as to expressing as accurately as we can the ramifications of this problem and to determining some at least of the causes of the tension. For in this way, it may be hoped, we shall be in a better position to deal with it effectively. That a solution will be found we can confidently hope in view of the imperative summons issued by the Spirit of God in the Church today through the recent *Constitution on the Sacred Liturgy*.

As a *first* approximation to a solution of this tension we may begin by reminding ourselves of the truth that both liturgy and *Spiritual Exercises* are basically proclamation. Paul describes the "breaking of the bread" to the Corinthian community in this fashion: "Every time you eat this bread and drink from the cup, you *proclaim* the death of the Lord until he comes" (1 Cor. 11:26). And Cardinal Bea observed at the Assisi Conference on the Liturgy that it is uniquely characteristic of Christian public worship to combine instruction with sacrificial offering.[1] The so-called "liturgy of the Word" in the Fore-Mass belongs in the category of proclamation, since in it the various phases of sacred history are proclaimed throughout the liturgical year.

The *Spiritual Exercises* of St. Ignatius are simply another form of gospel proclamation. The religious re-orientation of man's existence to Christ is the purpose of the *Exercises* no less than of the apostolic kerygma. The first week aims at making the exercitant experience what human existence outside the Gospel—apart from Jesus Christ—actually means. The second week reveals Jesus during his earthly life as "the way" to the Father inasmuch as the imitation of our Lord is now presented as *the* means to that goal. The third and fourth weeks reveal the very heart of the gospel proclamation: the hope-filled announcement of the definitive act of God's salvation in the death and resurrection of Christ. My former colleague, Fr. R. A. F. MacKenzie (the present rector of the Pontifical Biblical Institute of Rome) once asserted that he received a magnificent compliment for the *Exercises* when, at the conclusion of a retreat to a group of diocesan seminarians, one of his retreatants expressed his appreciation by saying, "Thank you, Father, for preaching the *simple Gospel* to us."

---

[1] A. Bea, S.J., "The Pastoral Value of the Word of God in the Sacred Liturgy," *The Assisi Papers* (Collegeville, 1957), p. 76.

We cannot afford to forget that in the liturgy, as also in the *Spiritual Exercises,* we are led by Christ's grace to a deeper awareness of the cardinal point in our Christian faith, viz., that the risen Christ is active in history in our day, that he is the dynamic force in my own personal history in the twentieth century. Indeed, he is more actively and effectively involved in this history than ever he was when he walked the hills of Galilee.[2] For the truth is that I am simply an unfinished chapter in Christian salvation history.

To come to a *second* approximation to a solution of the very real problem which concerns us in the Society today—there are three basic questions which must be proposed: (1) what do we mean by the spiritual life? (2) what is the nature of liturgical piety? (3) what is genuine Ignatian spirituality? I venture to suggest that it is only when satisfactory answers are found to such elementary questions that we shall be in a position to deal efficaciously with the tension felt on all sides in the Society between our Jesuit participation in the liturgy and our Christian way of life exhibited in the *Constitutions* and in the *Spiritual Exercises.*

The Christian Way of Life

To inquire into the meaning of the spiritual life may well seem to some an irrelevant or superfluous question. Yet there are certain indications of confused thinking on this essential point in our day. I think, for instance, of present day discussions about creating a "spirituality for the layman." Does not such an attempt to fragment or departmentalize the Christian way of life betray a misconception of the goal of all Christian spirituality? Such a proposal appears to spring from the erroneous notion that the monastic or the religious life is the Christian life par excellence, that it has ends which must be "watered down" for the Christian "in the world." This tendency would seem to imply that there is a kind of spiritual elite within the Church, which contrasts sharply with a large class of mediocre Christians. Yet on the evidence of the New Testament itself there

---

[2] We should like to recall here that the conception of heaven presented in the New Testament suggests, not detachment from this world and its history, but more active involvement in the continuing history of this world. Recall the reward promised to the two servants who acquitted themselves well by investing their master's money (Mt. 25: 14–30; Lk. 19: 11–27). They are not pensioned off, but given a greater share in the affairs of their lord.

is no such thing as "first-class" and "second-class" citizens in the kingdom of heaven—in the sense that the religious ideals of the first were not meant for the rest. Nothing in the gospels justifies any assumption that only the "professional religious" are called to perfection, while the "ordinary faithful" must content themselves with a lower level of achievement in their assimilation of the Christian reality.

Jesus made it very clear that the aim of all Christians (be they religious, clerical, or lay) is one and the same: the growth or exploitation of the baptismal grace given to all members of the Church. As the Sermon on the Mount unequivocally asserts,[3] the perfection of fraternal love constitutes an ideal of every follower of Christ. From the last to the first the various categories within the community must strive to deepen their awareness of their personal dignity as sons of the heavenly Father (and consequently, of their mutual respect and love for one another as brothers with Christ of the one Father). Is not this what Jesus meant by the command, "Be perfect as your heavenly Father is perfect" (Mt. 5:48)? There is not the slightest indication in the New Testament that our Lord ever drew a distinction, in this respect, between some kind of "inner ring" of disciples and a discipleship of truncated spiritual dimensions, of restricted ideals.

So also in the Christian Church there is no double standard by which one group is directed by one set of lofty principles while the other must aim only at a rather pedestrian level of spiritual living. For the truth is that there appears to be little, if any, grounds in the New Testament for that "classical distinction" made in ascetical theology between a "life of the evangelical counsels" and another lived on a much lower plane, geared merely to the faithful observance of the commandments. In fact, it is a mistake to regard the religious life as a "consecrated" form of existence in opposition to a "nonconsecrated" life for the laity. It may help to recall that the very term "lay" comes from the Greek word employed in the Bible to designate the People of God (*laos*)—the "plebs tua sancta."

The religious life differs from any other Christian life, not in its aims and goals (the perfection of charity incumbent upon all), but by the form of existence, in which every activity is ordered perma-

[3] For an attempt to work this out in greater detail, cf. D. M. Stanley, S.J., *The Gospel of St. Matthew* (2d ed., Collegeville, Minnesota: 1963), pp. 35–48.

nently and explicitly to the growth and perfection of the baptismal grace. For the religious this total orientation is explicit and permanent, and is effectively preserved, under grace, by the conspiracy of wills of the members of the community.

Finally, we may note in passing that it is a "spiritual" life, not in virtue of any Platonist dichotomy between "material" and "spiritual," but by reason of its governance by the Spirit of the risen Christ, whose active presence within each Christian reveals and maintains his adoptive sonship (Rom. 8:14–17).

Some Causes of the Tension

We would be less than candid if we did not admit that there is a fairly widespread opposition to liturgical participation among a not inconsiderable number of Jesuits. Can we discover some of the causes of this friction?

Fr. Gerald Ellard, whom I was privileged to have as professor of liturgical theology, used to say that the Jesuit *esprit de corps,* for which we are rightly renowned, provided us with that sense of solidarity and of security which is the principal function of the liturgy. In consequence, the Jesuit feels little or no need of the help provided to the Christian by liturgical participation. If this observation of the great American liturgist be correct, then ought we not seriously to examine this famous Jesuit solidarity of ours to see how far (or near) its source lies to the true Christian font of *koinōnia*— the Spirit of the risen Christ? In the *Proemium* to the *Constitutions,* St. Ignatius makes an act of genuine Christian faith in the presence within the Society of the Spirit of Jesus (that "interior law of charity and love which the Holy Spirit is wont to write and imprint upon men's hearts") as the principal cohesive power of our order. This Christian and supernatural *fraternitas* is surely something more than a corporate pride in Jesuit achievement, past or present.

Fr. Ellard also used to remind us that the Society had been restored at a period when the liturgical life of the Church was at a singularly low ebb. Can it be that the restorers of the Society, aware of St. Ignatius' refusal to impose the choral recitation of the divine office, actually imparted an antiliturgical bent to the spirit of the order they sought to resuscitate? I believe it may be said that in their attempts to recapture the Ignatian viewpoint, which had been lost by the break in continuity during the suppression, the Jesuits of the new Society—in their ambition to be faithful to the founder's insights—achieved in certain areas no more than a well-intentioned fidelity to *the letter* of Ignatius' directives. One of these areas was certainly that of liturgical piety.

I feel it is hard to be convincing when one attempts to cite remarks of St. Ignatius (still less, the animadversions of some of his successors in the generalate!) to show that he more or less anticipated the modern Church's attitudes towards the liturgy. He did not, and for the very good reason that he was a man of the Renaissance, not the twentieth century. Yet I daresay all will agree with the statement that, were Ignatius alive today, he would promote liturgical piety among his sons with his whole heart. The basis for such a conjecture is surely to be found in his Rules for Thinking with the Church. Father General J. B. Janssens has put it very well in his *Instruction on the Sacred Liturgy,* when he remarks: "One who does not love the liturgy of the Church does not properly love the Church herself." [4] The assertion, as will have been recognized, merely echoes a statement found in *Mediator Dei.* Since we are alive in this century, we must make necessary adaptations in certain institutions or habits of mind which belong to a bygone age. And this leads to another point.

The Counter-Reformation, it has been said, was finally concluded during the month of November, 1962, at the first session of Vatican II. Whatever be the merit of such an observation, the modern phenomenon of ecumenism surely provides a demonstration of the fact that the polemical or apologetic attitude towards Protestants is quite *passé*—and this is no less true of our devotional life than of our theology. I suggest that this now outmoded anti-Protestantism may be a contributing factor to the tension between our spirituality and liturgical piety. Certainly the sixteenth-century Counter-Reformation spirit did not promote the communal aspects of social worship. Popular participation in divine service, advocated by the hymn-singing, bible-reading reformers in order to promote Christian "fellowship" (the aim of the liturgy as we have come now to appreciate) may still strike us as rather too "Protestant."

One easy practical test of our personal attitude towards the lit-

[4] *Instruction and Ordinance of Very Reverend Father General John Baptist Janssens on the Training of Ours in the Sacred Liturgy* (Woodstock, 1960), p. 3.

urgy may be made by asking whether we truly think of confession as a liturgical action—and hence as a public act of social worship. How closely do we associate the ascetical practice of the *examen conscientiae* with the reception of the sacrament of penance, i.e., are we aware of its social dimensions, or is it merely an act of individualistic devotion? Does my reception of the eucharist signify only a fifteen-minute period of private and personal prayer, or does it involve a real social communication with all those who participate with myself in the Lord's Supper?

In the last analysis, the greatest cause of the tension between our Jesuit spirit and the liturgy is undoubtedly our ignorance about the nature of liturgy and the subsequent confusion which hobbles our attempts to reconcile liturgical prayer with those forms of prayer we have for centuries associated with our spiritual life. I believe that as a general rule our own earlier spiritual formation has—to be quite frank—left us wrongly orientated towards the divine liturgy. We are not only ignorant about the nature of liturgical prayer—we have been brought up with attitudes which run counter to its practice. One sees this occasionally in the way the problem is proposed: *viz.,* how can we fit the new liturgical life into our spirituality? how can the liturgy be used in the *Spiritual Exercises?* Surely the point of departure for any discussion on this difficult subject must be the conviction that our Jesuit spirituality, *to be genuinely Christian,* must today be liturgical. The fundamental question is *not* whether I do or do not like the liturgy. It is simply this: do I wish to be a Christian, or not?

The Nature of Liturgical Piety

We may begin the easy way, in attempting to describe the nature of liturgical piety, by saying what it is not. Interest in and devotion to the liturgy does not mean concern for rubrics. Nor is it to be characterized by an antiquarian spirit committed to archaizing for its own sake. It is not a current fad about the style or quality of altar furnishings or the cut of sacred vestments. It may be unfortunate that some promoters of the liturgical spirit have at times appeared to us somewhat frantic, or eccentric. We may as well admit that, not unlike the modern scripture movement, some of the proponents of liturgical piety have been a stone of stumbling to many.

While it obviously would require a series of lectures to describe

fully the meaning of liturgical prayer, we may attempt a brief résumé of some basic ideas about the nature of the Christian liturgy.
And here we gladly admit our indebtedness to the insights provided
by the Anglican bishop of Woolwich, Dr. John A. T. Robinson, in a
very remarkable chapter ("Worldly Piety") in his controversial book,
Honest to God.[5]

It is useful to recall that *leitourgia* originally meant "public
works," that is, it designated activities that were related to the common interest of the *polis,* the Greek city-state. "Liturgy" in its origins was concerned with the affairs of the community. The Christian
liturgy most truly deals with "real life," the life of the people of God.
To participate in the liturgy is not to turn away from "the common,"
nor to separate oneself from the realities of the world and everyday
life. The material elements requisite for the celebration of the Mass,
representing as they do the common and the communal life of the
congregation, constitute a symbolic denial of this. The everyday life
of God's people, with its common interests and needs, is not to
be ignored by, or excluded from, this holy meal which is the eucharist. All this must be gathered up and given its true significance
in the Mass. It is here that the Christian learns how Christ is to be
met: not by turning one's back upon "the world," but in and through
the common relationships of real life.

Is not this doctrine implicit in the action of Jesus himself, when,
after criticizing their human traditions, based upon the distinction
between "the clean" and "the common," as the perversion of true
religion, he abolished forever any such separation? For it is not what
comes into our lives from "the outside" that profanes a man, Jesus
had declared, "because it does not enter his heart." And one evangelist (Mk. 7:19) adds, "and thus he declared all foods clean." If
the incarnation was the initial step towards the abrogation of the
Jewish distinction between the sacred and the secular, Christ's death
and resurrection completed this sanctification of "the world." Is not
this intimated by the apocalyptic description in our gospels of the
consequences of Jesus' death, according to which "the veil of the
sanctuary was torn in two from top to bottom" (Mt. 27:51–53)?

The dramatic picture of the final judgment presented in parabolic
form in Matthew 25:31–46 is intended to teach us the one funda-

[5] John A. T. Robinson, *Honest to God* (Philadelphia, 1963), pp. 84–104.

mental lesson of the Gospel, i.e. that the glorified Son of Man is to be met and served in—and it would appear *only* in—the common human relationships of real life. The surprise elicited from those upon the right hand of the judge ("Lord, when was it that we saw you hungry and fed you . . . ?") is perhaps an indication of how hard this basically Christian attitude is to acquire. In Christianity, as Dr. Robinson points out, "the holy is the depth of the common." The fourth gospel teaches us that the world is the object of the Father's love in "his only Son" (Jn. 3:16). Only when it has through sin been alienated from its true center can it be considered ungodly and profane.

The principal purpose of the liturgy is identical with the purpose of Jesus' death and resurrection: "to gather into one the scattered children of God" (Jn. 11:52). It is not then an escape from the reality of the world to some imaginary realm of phantasy, nor a retiring from "the secular" to a "religious" sphere. The liturgy aims at making us more attentive to our Lord's presence in ourselves and in others, in the ordinary happenings of our lives. The fact is—if only we decide to demythologize the statement "the risen Christ is in heaven"—we discover that our glorified Lord exists, apart from the Blessed Sacrament, in the Church, in us, his holy people, members of his body. This is the Christian mystery which the Mass sets forth for us "in symbol and power." It is the Mass which provides us with the grace to respond with clearer insight and purified love to the Christ in ourselves and our neighbor, and to transform what is "unlovely" into Christ. The valid norm for judging the genuinesses of our participation in the liturgy is "how far it makes us more sensitive to the Christ in the hungry, the naked, the prisoner." It is not too much to say that only when we have discovered our Lord in "the common," that is in real life, can our liturgical piety pass for truly Christian devotion. Is not such a view implied in the correct understanding of the *ex opere operato*?

The Spiritual Exercise

If the *Exercises* are to have an impact upon twentieth-century man, we must succeed in bringing them out of the sixteenth century. To do this we must remove the Renaissance chrysalis and permit them to speak to the needs of the present-day Christian. In some instances, this may simply mean the recovery of a better understanding of them through scientific research and study. One simple example is the realization that most of the *Spiritual Exercises* are actually contemplations, and not—as in a tradition which appears to go back to the Roothaan interpretation—meditations. The point has some far-reaching consequences, and we shall return to it presently.

In the second place, the *Exercises* must be presented in a less individualistic, more personalist manner than the text would at times appear to indicate. Individualism was a very active element in sixteenth-century culture, which in reaction to the medieval spirit tended to set the individual over against the community. And Ignatius, who was very much a man of his times, presented his asceticism in terms of God and the individual: "ut homo vincat seipsum." Our era is more sensitive to social relationships—even to the extent of conceiving a world community. And the personalism of today demands that we respect others as persons; hence the modern concern for freedom of conscience. We have also learned to address ourselves to the problem of the Church's existence in a pluralistic society—a question scarcely perceptible in St. Ignatius' age.

To permit the *Exercises* to speak to the man of today we must be aware that they reflect to some extent a Platonist view of the human person, alien to our ways of thinking. Man is represented as a "*soul* imprisoned in this corruptible body . . . in exile among brute beasts." Modern psychology, even on the popular level, finds it impossible to consider man merely as a soul. It must of course be confessed, in fairness to their author, that the *Spiritual Exercises* do not treat the human person as a subsistent spiritual entity. But we must eschew any such images or terminology which would create such an impression in the minds of the exercitants.

We should, further, be prepared to admit that there is a certain Stoic flavor in the Ignatian formulation of some spiritual realities. The celebrated term "indifference" can very easily be construed as the Stoic *apatheia*. It is at least probable that the individualistic Stoic ideal of *autarkeia* has exercised a baleful influence upon Jesuit spirituality. The Stoic trained himself to face life on his own resources, to be self-sufficient in any situation that confronted him. He gained complete mastery of his emotions, so that no decision of his might be swayed by pleasure or pain. He became master of his own fate by cultivating heroic indifference to health and sickness, wealth or poverty, honor or dishonor, length of life, etc. He schooled himself to retreat from many of the realities of life; and his flight from the world might quite conceivably culminate in suicide.

This noblest of pagan philosophies was one of the serious obstacles to the spread of the Gospel in the apostolic age. One good reason for this was the fact that Stoic anthropology, inspired by an optimism ignorant of original sin, stood in flat contradiction to the biblical view of man. Stoic *autarkeia,* the complete reliance upon self and the human condition which for Paul was nothing but impotent human arrogance, is subsumed by the Apostle under the term "boasting." To open oneself by saving faith to the redemption in Christ Jesus, Paul declares again and again, one must rid oneself of all self-reliance.

Indeed the Bible speaks only of historical man; and historical man in the Judaeo-Christian tradition is fallen man. The sacred writers never tire of repeating that man is under condemnation by reason of his own sins and the sin of Adam. Man is "carnal, sold on the block like a slave of sin" (Rom. 7:14). He is incapable of responding even to those ideals which his better natural tendencies seek to realize in him. "The good I want to do, I fail to do; what I actually do is the evil which is against my will" (Rom. 7:19). The writers of the New Testament echo the teaching of Israel's inspired books that, while sin is a reality which man can cause, it creates an existential situation from which man is powerless to redeem himself. Paul's famous indictment of "the wisdom of this world" (cf. 1 Cor. 1:18–31) is the uncompromising Christian rejection of Stoicism, root and branch.

I do not wish to be understood as stating that the *Spiritual Exercises* promote a kind of latter-day Stoicism—much less that St. Ignatius ever intended they should do so. I believe however that it is not irrelevant to ask whether certain tendencies, rightly identifiable as Stoic, have not somehow become incorporated into a form of spirituality that passes itself off as Ignatian. At any rate, I feel that this question must be asked in our present discussion, because if the flower of Ignatian spirituality has suffered in any degree from the blight of Stoicism, this provides one very good reason for the tension between liturgical piety and Jesuit spirituality with which we are concerned. Stoic self-sufficiency and individualism with its *apatheia* towards God's creation constitute real obstacles to that

Christian fellowship which the sacred liturgy aims at creating in the community.

One feature of the division of the *Exercises* into weeks which might well need complementing or correction in the light of modern gospel studies is the separation of the passion and resurrection by the division of the third and fourth weeks. Present-day theology insists that these are but two aspects of the single Christ-event by which the world's redemption was accomplished. These twin experiences form the *transitus Domini,* and thus impart to the Christian life its essentially paschal character—a quality so strongly emphasized in the recent *Constitution on the Sacred Liturgy.*[6] To offset the danger of separating these two phases of our Lord's redemptive activity, which the New Testament assures us belong together, the giver of the *Exercises* should instill a deep appreciation of the great Johannine insight, found in the fourth gospel, that Jesus' "glorification" begins not with Easter day, but with "the Hour"—his entry into the passion.

We cannot finally afford to overlook the truth which Paul insisted upon so strongly with his Galatians, that there is but one Gospel (Gal. 1:6–9). The *Spiritual Exercises* are nothing but a reformulation, in sixteenth-century terms, of that unique proclamation, the Christian "Good News." Accordingly, if the *Exercises* are to have the impact today which we have every right to expect they shall, we must adapt the Gospel—as Ignatius did in his day—to the exigencies of twentieth-century man. For while it remains true that the Gospel is one and indivisible, still the fact that the New Testament presents it to us in a fourfold form—indeed a fifth formulation, the gospel of Paul, must also be included—reminds us to what extent a given audience determines the presentation of the basic message. If Renaissance man was intrigued by "the powers of the soul," a modern discovery in his time, we must be quick to realize that such a view of human nature may well leave a modern audience cold. The psychology which appeals to us must be rich in personalist values and in social dimensions.

However, to adapt the *Exercises,* the Ignatian gospel, to our own age, we must be acutely aware of its essential characteristics. Other-

---

[6] I have attempted to describe this recently in an article, "The Paschal Character of the Christian Life," *Catholic Messenger* (Davenport, Iowa, 1964) Vol. 82, No. 19, March 26, p. 5.

wise we run the risk of betraying instead of translating it. Hence, by way of conclusion we wish to return to a point alluded to earlier in this essay: the significance in Ignatian spirituality of the practice of contemplation.

Ignatian Contemplation, a Means to Personal Involvement

I should like to suggest here that the method of prayer in the *Spiritual Exercises* called contemplation, which a cursory examination of that little book shows to be the favored Ignatian method of prayer, is intended to produce that *contemplativus in actione* who represents, at least for Jerome Nadal, who coined the phrase, the ideal of Jesuit spirituality. And I believe it will be evident that the specifically Ignatian *acquired contemplation,* to which this exercise called contemplation leads, produces the very outlook which the liturgy seeks to instill in the Christian.

We have already seen that the proper aim of the liturgy, particularly of the eucharistic liturgy, is to produce in us a personal involvement with the contemporary plan of salvation, as it is being worked out in our day and in our lives. Through the Mass we are brought to see the holy in the common, the contemporary, and the communal. This is of course not a matter of mere intellectual insight, but is primarily the result of the increase of fraternal love, the execution of that one commandment which Jesus left us: to love one another as he has loved us. Participation in the liturgy must result in our involvement in present-day sacred history, in our collaboration with Christ's will to save that order of things of which we now form a part.

The particular Ignatian exercise of prayer, "contemplation," is in reality a piece of spiritual pedagogy which brings the exercitant into a particular mystery of Jesus' earthly life in a very personal and realistic manner. The *compositio loci* serves as an initial aid to this personal involvement. Thus for example, the contemplation on the incarnation is introduced by a "composition of place" which makes me conscious of the cosmic character of the event, embracing me and my world. It is suggested, in the contemplation on the Nativity, that I take an active part in the scene.

It would seem that Ignatius' purpose in having the exercitant repeat this kind of exercise so frequently is to enable him to make the transfer to his own contemporary situation. In this way the retreatant will be led to realize how, with the grace of Christ, he is to insert himself into that phase of salvation history which is his own Christian life in his own day.

That this is the aim of the Ignatian exercise called "contemplation" appears to be borne out by Jerome Nadal's description of the kind of *acquired* contemplation, which he considered characteristic of the prayer of the Society. In his Notes on the *Examen Generale,* Fr. Nadal makes the following observations:[7]

Ignatius we know received from God the unique grace of great facility in the contemplation of the Most Holy Trinity. . . . This type of contemplative prayer he received in a very singular manner towards the end of his years upon earth, although he had enjoyed it frequently also at other times. At that period, moreover, he possessed it to such a degree that in all things, in every action or conversation, he was aware of God's presence and felt so great a taste for spiritual things as to be lost in the contemplation of them. In a word he was "simul in actione contemplativus" . . . a habit he was accustomed to explain by remarking that God must be found in everything.

Now we believe that this same privilege, which we are aware was bestowed upon Fr. Ignatius, has been accorded to the whole Society. We feel certain that in the Society this grace of contemplative prayer awaits all of us. We declare that it has been joined to our vocation.

Fr. Nadal, as is clear, makes a distinction between the graces of mystical prayer accorded to St. Ignatius and this contemplative prayer (acquired contemplation) which he finds characteristic of Jesuit spirituality. He describes it in more detail: "The prayer characteristic of the Society favors execution. That is to say, the operative principle and the end of prayer is love. Prayer tends to the greater glory of God by proceeding from the fullness of love in such fashion that I should desire by my prayer what I ask and seek, in order to serve God more according to the vocation and Institute of the Society. Accordingly, the prayer of the Society favors execution."

By this, as Fr. Nadal indicates in the following personal anec-

[7] These references to Jerome Nadal have been taken from two articles which appeared some years ago in *Christus* 2 (1955): Maurice Giuliani, "Trouver Dieu en toutes choses," pp. 172–194; and Raymond Hostie, "Le cercle de l'action et de l'oraison d'après le Père Jérôme Nadal," p. 195–211.

dote, he means that there is a necessary continuity between our prayer and our apostolic activity. There can be no retreating from "the world," no dichotomy between our prayer and "real life."

I recall that at the time of my first entry into the Society, Ignatius suggested that I devote myself to preaching and to the service of the neighbor. I begged to be excused because of my ineptitude—the result of my sins and my spiritual poverty. The Father told me, "It is precisely in this way that you will progress, if you concern yourself with the salvation of your neighbor."

Here is the practice of the blessed Father Ignatius. Do you wish to help yourself? Do you wish to make progress? Help your neighbor. You are to preach? Pray first, and invoke God. Then study: make the subject entirely your own. Then go and carry out your assignment. You will advance and receive new graces. When you return to prayer, you will feel a greater attraction to prayer and contemplation. Thus the circle is completed. . . .

Like St. Paul, Ignatius was preoccupied with the contemporary plan of salvation and with involving himself (and his sons) in this sacred history. Ignatius adopted the contemplation as his favorite means of prayer in the *Exercises,* because he felt that through this method his Jesuit sons would best learn to discover the point of insertion into that salvation history as it unfolded itself in their day and in their world. It was there in the common that Christ was— in Ignatius' view—to be found by the Jesuit. For this reason, as Nadal points out, the prayer characteristic of the Society must "favor execution," i.e., must be related constantly to our personal involvement in "the world." For there alone is Christ to be found.

Conclusion

By way of postscript to this already lengthy communication, I might suggest that the prayerful study of the Bible is the bridge between the proper appreciation of liturgical piety in our day and our Jesuit spirituality. A profounder understanding of revealed salvation history—i.e., a new awareness, providentially provided for us in our day by modern biblical studies, of the truth that God has always chosen (and still continues) to reveal himself to us through the historical process—will serve to help us, the Jesuits, to adapt our spirituality to the new liturgical developments in the life of the

Church. For it is in this way that we shall succeed in bringing our precious heritage, the *Spiritual Exercises* of St. Ignatius, out of the sixteenth into the twentieth century—and this, not as a family heirloom valued only as a memento of another age, but as the relevant aid to modern Christians in their continuing search for God in Christ.

PART V

The
Social Apostolate

Introduction

When Pope Paul VI was Archbishop of Milan he said:

"The modern world has looked at the priest with eyes inflamed with hostile sarcasm and blinded by a utilitarian approach. The heir of the long-dead Middle Ages, the ally of selfish conservatism, the high priest of a silenced litany, the stranger in life—this is the priest. The clergy . . . has felt the repelling aversion of society in the midst of the new needs of the century.

". . . We must go out and look for the great multitudes. It is up to the priest, not the people, to take the initiative. It is useless for the priest to ring his bell. No one listens. What is necessary is that the priest be able to hear the factory sirens, to understand the temples of technology where the modern world lives and throbs. It is up to him to become a missionary anew if he wants Christianity to endure . . ." [1]

The Jesuit's attempts to listen to factory sirens and understand the temples of technology have taken various forms. Although the high schools and colleges of the Society in the United States have occasionally been criticized for not doing enough to instill a strong social consciousness in their students, individual Jesuits have fought in the front ranks of the gradual social revolution; and many of the younger men today are drawing the Society more deeply into the apostolates to the poor and underprivileged in the inner-city. When they do this, they are sharing in the great tradition of their fore-runners who established the labor schools in the late 1930's, who took risks working on the waterfronts, who have become scholars in the social sciences, and who have written on social questions in *Social Order* and *America.*

At one time the social apostolate was considered part of our defense against Communism; but, as Very Reverend Father General Janssens said in his Instruction on the Social Apostolate, October 10, 1949, "Even if Communism or some other form of materialism

[1] Quoted by Louis J. Twomey, S.J., in "The Modern World and Jesuit Relevance," Woodstock Letters 93 (1964), 308.

were not plotting against the Church and actively persecuting her, the obligation would still rest on us to come to the assistance of all our brothers in Christ, by striving for a more equitable distribution of both material possessions and goods of a higher order." Now the social apostolate embraces the whole of the Society's role in the Church's mission to the world, as well as the labor schools and the work of a handful of seminarians in Harlem. It also includes the incredibly difficult task of harmonizing the visions of different generations while speaking meaningfully to a new generation partly alienated from the faith.

The new Father General, Very Reverend Father Pedro Arrupe, spoke of the Society's new spirit in his talk at St. Ignatius Church in New York, April 3, 1966. "At the risk of startling you, let me tell you quite honestly: it is *not* this new *world* that I fear. After all, God is there—God and his Christ—however difficult it may be at times to discern his will. I would become frightened, however, if I felt that we Jesuits had become so alienated from, and foreign to, the younger generation that we had little or nothing to say to them which they found relevant to their work-a-day lives. I would be deeply concerned if I saw that we were repeating yesterday's answers to today's problems, if we talked in a way young men and women no longer understood, if we spoke in a language that did not speak to the heart of the living man."

RAYMOND A. SCHROTH, S.J.

The Modern
Concept of "Missio"

Daniel Berrigan, S.J.

The present scandal of the Church is not that men regard her as enemy (they have always done that), but that they refuse to regard her at all. In confronting secular man, the Church searches for issues to debate, errors to refute and new forms for old truths, only to find that the world no longer speaks the same tongue; man has neither the need nor the inclination to listen. Father Berrigan suggests that just as the situation determines language and role for an individual, so the needs of our day—justice, equality, hunger and peace— ought to shape the image of the Church. If the language and role of the Church are adapted to the experienced needs of mankind, the body lives, otherwise it becomes the quaint statue in the park, beautiful, but only a bronze image of a distant memory.

The suggested theme of this paper will already be familiar to you. It is the two strongest influences on the life of man. Indeed thinking men, who are also men of faith and action, have only to take a long look at their Church and their world in order to admit their Christian and human debt. And when we come more proximately to the great project that has drawn us together, it is clear that our teachers have been two; each of them living, each of them near, each of them immanent to the life of the mind and heart. I refer of course to the two teachers of man named the Church and the world.

This paper will suggest that the mission of the Church to the world implies an inevitable relationship of the world to the Church; that the mutual pressures and influences of each on each, and of both on us, modify and enrich the Church, the world, and man. And finally, an exploration of these mutual realities, Church and world, pursued in the light which each sheds upon the other, will illuminate our work, called as we are by the will of Christ to act at the center of the world today.

The recent history of the Church has not prepared us for such assertions as these; our history in fact has not prepared us either to regard the Church as immanent to the world, or indeed to act as though the immanence were a fact. From the Reformation to the late nineteenth century, believers had been foundering about in a net which is largely of their own weaving—an inability to face the world with the clearsightedness and simplicity of the Gospel eye.

To have done so would have been to admit that the mission of the world to the Church was taking a radically new form, because the world was taking a radically new form. It would have been to see that one stage of history was finished, and another was opening; and that fidelity to the new stage of things would be the most realistic proof that believers had understood their own texts.

What were some of the phenomena of this new stage of things, which was, genetically, our own situation?

Human knowledge was progressively breaking through its closed universe. The universe of knowledge, and the mind that would contain it, were potentially infinite. And the nature of the mind that dared to seek the truth was conditioned by an acceptance of an open universe as its own form. As far as the Church was concerned, all such tactics as dictation of evidence, suppression of knowledge, alienation of disciplines—these were the enemies of her best spirit. Her relationship to the new world of the mind was to be, ideally, one of friendship and encouragement. More exactly, she saw herself as a source of enlightenment which led human knowledge beyond facts to wisdom, and through multiplicity to unity.

It was clear that human knowledge, newly awakened, touchy and proud and self-conscious, would not be led by the nose. It wanted nothing to do with the Olympian Church, declaring airily that man was grass and his works a vanity. It greeted with contempt the idea of a theological astronomy or a Thomistic mathematics. It declared that such a Church, mixing fact with folly, had declared its enmity toward time and this world, and so had proven its own unworthiness of being taken seriously. The opposition between the new knowledge and the old Church proved a harsh discipline. Sometimes the discipline was brutal and violent, as when Pius IX was treated so violently by ruffians who had little sense indeed of humanity or of holiness.

Sometimes the discipline was revolutionary, in that it stung the Church to action which, apart from crisis, she probably never would have taken; as when the marxian manifesto preceded the writings of Leo, and in a certain sense, must be admitted to have provoked them. And often, the world impact on the Church was eventually salutary to her dearest beliefs, as when evolutionary or psychological findings invited a new look at biblical data, or a new look at man.

All of this is a matter of history. But what are we to say of that crucible called the twentieth century, into which the Church has been plunged, unready, as every living body is unready, for suffering and loss of foothold, and the realization, brought home to her flesh and spirit, that she, the beloved of Christ, is still the sinful, unknowing, and human body of mankind, moving in darkness, journeying far from the Father?

Truly it must be said that in comparison with this century, with this vast historic maelstrom, this bewildering amalgam of opportunity, danger, heroism, defection, realignment of loyalties, martyrdom, sudden loss and gain, every other century has been the miniscule hand of the capital design of the universe. And from the opposite point of view, these last sixty years have plucked out of the past every mode of suffering, every seed of conflict and debasement, every fury and hatred and source of division; these years have planted these phenomena in a new soil; they have flourished as never before. And all this is so true—the century is qualitatively so assaulted by oppositions and ironies of experience, by such heights and deeps of love and hatred, of murder and sacrificial altruism, of universal effort both toward peace and annihilation, toward love of knowledge and suppression of knowledge—that some feel justified in speaking, in regard to our century, of a qualitatively different experience of what it is to become human, as of what it is to be inhuman; so some reject out of hand the definitions of man as man has agreed on them through history, and insist on speaking of the altogether new man.

The Church in and to the World

All this is as may be. But more nearly to our point, we are justified in inquiring: what of the modern Church and her mission to the modern world—not to any world, not to a static Cartesian world, or an ideal world, but to the world of today—a world which in spite of our own unworthy regressive fears, is the only world, the only stage of the tears, the hope, and the victory of Christ? It perhaps will bear asserting, in an effort to approach our topic, that one does not construct a mission of the Church to the world, whole cloth, even out of so sacred a fabric as holy Scripture or the data of the councils. Neither does one construct a mission of the Church to the world that will correspond to the objective state of things without at the same time admitting that the world has a formative and purifying relationship to the Church. The relationship of the Church to the world implies understanding that the Church is subject to the world, is within the world as leaven is in dough, as the child in the mother, or the soul in the body, and that this subjection is organic, necessary, and in the strictest sense providential.

Let us speak briefly of the scriptural evidence of the mission of the Church to the world. The evidence is of massive and indeed crucial import. By way of beginning, it is clear that the early Church saw herself as sent; she was a group with an inner spirit that was simultaneously an outer urge, an inner mystery that was at the same time a summons to the nations, a self-consciousness that was, at the same time, a world-consciousness. She was to welcome all men, all that was in man. Historically, we can trace the successive steps in which the mystery of the Church undertook its self-realization. The Jerusalem community was sent to Antioch; the community of Antioch reached outward to the Mediterranean world; and to the geographical movement, an ethnic and psychological advance corresponded; by the way of crisis, resolution and revaluation, the Church welcomed the Gentile world, and the pressures exerted by this assimilation purified her of the merely residual and childish elements in her Jewish consciousness.

Among many fascinating aspects of this primitive mission, may I invite your reflection on only one? The mission of the Church was never, or only very seldom, detained by a passion for verbal or academic purity. The Church was not involved in a language laboratory, she was not seeking or experimenting with an ideal tongue or creed or set of formulas that would finally guarantee, to Greek and Hebrew alike, access to her mysteries and freedom from heresy. Rather her language was feasible and adaptable; trusting in the God of history, the God who was immanent to pagan and Jew alike, she moved into cultures and outposts of thought, with a viable, willing humility, a sense that the mystery she announced already dwelt in human life; and that all would be doctrinally well if she would hearken to the myths, the philosophic thought, or the simple human languages that in every case anticipated Christ.

This Pauline breadth of mind gave the early Church the kind of openness and breathing room which we note in the Acts of the Apostles and the early letters. And this breadth of mind, I would think, sprang from an instinctive respect for an action which preceded formulation, in the sense that the Church was always willing to listen to the heart of man before she attempted to translate the mysteries into a new language. This same good sense and humility guaranteed that when necessary formulations were finally adopted, they would not presume to exhaust the content of the Church's mystery.

The Church was in fact showing that she is exclusive and unique because she is first of all inclusive and catholic. When she announces the word of salvation among men, she does it as a speaker who is also a listener; she is catching the resonances awakened in men's hearts by the Word who already dwells there; and as in speaking she is awakening men to the mystery of Christ, so in listening she is awakening herself, in wonderment and gratitude, to a sense of the cosmic breadth of Christ. She knows that in height, breadth, depth, in every conceivable dimension, Christ inhabits mankind. So when the Church encounters man at any time or place, she recognizes the indwelling mystery already present in his culture, his thought, his passionate desires to inhabit and rule his earth.

The Church of the Councils

There came, as indeed there was bound to come, a conciliar period of intense intellectual growth in the early Church. The mission of the Church to the world was first scientifically explored at Nicaea and Chalcedon. Two points are of interest here, as we reflect on the second evidence of the Church's understanding of her mission, the great conciliar periods of the fourth and fifth centuries.

1. The councils were conceived as logical fruit of a world experience. They were preceded in every case by a world probe, an apostolic exploration. As such, the councils expressed the Church's will to hearken to the Gentiles, to legislate and define only in accord with need, to stress points of doctrine which the apostolate itself had shown as unclear or ill-defined or challenged. In a word,

the councils occurred as a profound exercise in world service and in service of "his body which is the Church." Prior to conciliar gatherings, the Church had served the body of man in corporal and spiritual works, in sympathy and prayer and martyrdom. Now, for a brief period, the work of charity yielded before the work of intelligence, as the Church sought out in the Holy Spirit the deeper implication of her being in the world. So an important historical sequence emerged: experience of the world led to some form of ecclesiastical crisis, and then to a council. From the first gathering of the brethren at Jerusalem to discuss the reception of non-Jewish converts, through the prestigious world councils of later centuries, it was clear that the men of the Church convened in the sacred matters because the Church was in the world, because she persistently took note of her responsibility to the world, because she formulated the admirable rule that "that which touches all (a law) must first be submitted to all." So vast a responsibility, so deeply realized, required that she periodically take stock of her voice and stance, her language, her ways of dealing with men, review her relevance, give her sons, both bishops and laymen, a hearing, to ponder anew that harmony of opposition in which alone, as she understood, the truth can dwell: orthodoxy and the world understanding, clarity and mystery, immanence and transcendence, Christ and mankind.

2. An example of world responsibility influencing a council is the Greek Christology hammered out at Nicaea. The reasoning, heavily influenced by the Alexandrian school, would go something like this: it was true that Christ was universal Savior; so it must be true that his life, invigorating his Church, would continue to make its entrance into the life of the nations. In rising and ascending, his life had not been taken away from us; it had been changed for the better. To the conciliar fathers, Christ was God of the Greek intelligence, as he had been rabbi and wonderworker among the Jewish peasants. And the best Greek minds had already laid down a pier upon which the daring span of Greek Christology could come to rest. Such terms as person and nature were eminently Greek contributions; they would now form the articulation of the Christian bridge, as the mystery of Christ stood forth in new clarity and strength for the sake of a new world usefulness.

The bridge was laid down by Greek builders, not for the sake of esthetics, though the bridge was also beautiful, but for the simplest of human needs: in order that humanity might pass over those stones and arches. A bridge is for passage; over danger and distance and the unknown. It links parts of a world that otherwise would remain hostile or at a distance or uncommunicative. In laying such bridge-work for such good ends, the conciliar fathers were not bringing into existence inert or useless formulas; they were really dramatizing the work of him who was the *pontifex maximus* of humanity, the builder who in Paul's phrase had made "the two to be one."

And we must continue to view conciliar action in this way; both in order to place the present council solidly in Church history, which is to say, in world history and in the history of human thought, and also to illustrate the regrettable conciliar actions of the last century, when definitions were not generally seen in this way. The earlier councils from Nicaea to Trent had acted in their deepest preoccupations and had their most lasting impact on the history of man neither from dread of heresy, nor reaction to error, nor a mean-spirited fear of the world. They proceeded from the courageous effort to span forbidding stretches of ignorance and cultural diversity, to override pockets of division, to span what we might call simply the rugged terrain of the human unknown.

We would do the great councils a great injustice, then, were we to see their doctrinal mission as an occasion for mere loyalty pledges, or as reduction of the Christian mystery to flat verbalized creeds.

The Christological formulas in fact served two great purposes, each of them entirely mission-minded. Their first purpose related more immediately to the household of believers. The formulas of Nicaea gathered into coherence the evidence of Christ: who he was, what his task was; what the Church was, what the task of the Church was. This evidence was scattered throughout the apostolic writings and a hundred oral traditions; it was now bound into creeds, easily spoken and easily memorized outlines of belief which the catechumens could master gradually and which would be of immense corporate usefulness as they were recited aloud at worship. The formulas were in fact exact without being exhaustive; they were brief without superficiality; they could allow room both for the minimal knowledge of the uninitiate and the mystical probings of the illumined. They contained in a word the whole wisdom of which Paul, John, Tertullian, Cyril, Augustine, and other early giants were to form a single linked witness.

The second purpose of the conciliar declaration is perhaps more to our point here. We could justly call them good tools of ecumenism, in the vernacular. The formulas of the councils hammered out in loud anvils could not but be overheard. And these overheard, not as murky incantations from the underground, but simply as good ideas or intriguing thought, will always invade the public ear. That ear always goes erect when religious men speak a living language. So the conciliar debates were overheard as Greek is overheard by Greeks, or English by Englishmen—in a bus, on a street, in a gathering. And if this was Greek with a difference, it remains that it was Greek cut out of whole cloth. If, in a sense, the language and thought of the Christians was new, it was not new as an import or affront; it was new because it was fresh and astute, and because it tried and stretched the mind in ways in which the Greek mind had always gloried. That mind had known a great deal about nature and per-sonality and relations and goodness and justice. Now it heard these ideas in a way which teased the mind both out of itself and more deeply into itself, which spoke of Christian mystery as though it were a Greek mystery, as indeed it was.

We would perhaps find it impossible to regain a sense of the new-ness, the dedicated complicity between the Church and the Greek world, which were implicit in these conciliar sentences. The formulas of Nicaea seem to us unexciting, cut and dried. But if we bear in mind, first of all, the primitive Jewish preaching about "the man Jesus, who . . . was crucified, and whom God has raised up," and if we bear in mind the lapidary and subtle phrasing of Cyril—the Christ of two natures and unity of person, the unbegotten, uncreated, eternal infinite One—then what breathtaking gain in understanding we witness! And more to our point of mission, what an exciting com-plement has been offered to the Greek genius, when the Church held up to it her own inmost treasury, the mystery of Christ, clothed in Greek raiment, praised, formulated in Greek thought. We are witness here to something extraordinarily important and almost unique, and a period which ranks among the very highest of the Church's history in regard to world understanding and intellectual effort; which was also an apostolate of the highest order, since within it the truth stood free, without apology or special pleading or foreign bedevilment. The Greeks were in fact invited to come to a Christ who had already come in their direction. He came toward them from the councils, speaking n Greek, ministering to Greek brethren, and in an extraordinarily adical and exciting sense, newly incarnate in the Greek islands.

The bridge-building project of the great conciliar age goes on, hrough the genius of the Protestant ecumenists and the genius of Pope John. The particular form of this radical "pontifical" work thus gains momentum from both sides; both are impatient of a history which refuses to be corrected or rewritten, as though in fact the Gospel had been amended by the passion of the sixteenth century, and living men found themselves helpless before the hatreds, polemics, and hysteria of the dead.

But the bridge-building is receiving pressures from another direction also, and it is more precisely of that direction that we speak. The pressure is not properly a Protestant pressure at all; it is a world pressure. And in comparison with the Protestant pressure the world pressure is, I would dare to say, an enormously more crushing and formative weight. The Protestant invitation to unity is only the first act in a continuing cosmic drama involving both sides, not in one or another phase of unity, a unity which looks only, or even primarily, to the reunion of world minorities in a stronger world minority, but rather to a world ecumenism. So the Protestant unity which may be thought of as the fruit of Vatican II is simply, to a long view of history, only the first light and preliminary testing of our Catholicism, the first tentative move in the direction of a vast cosmic probe—into world religions, into the world without religion, into technology and emerging world community; into world hunger and population, into the world as it is.

We are suggesting, moreover, that this Church mission to the world cannot be constructed or carried forward by Church minds alone. It must in fact go forward as contemporary life is showing us, *not only on the Church's terms, but on the world's terms as well.* The time is past, if indeed it was ever present, when the piers of the Church's mission could be staked out on unknown territory, by a colonial-minded, regressive Church, importing her workers, staking off her territories, ignoring the soul and genius of the people she comes among. Such a bridge, were it to be raised, would be more than a curse, a caricature of the Church's method. The architecture of such a bridge would be an eyesore on the landscape, it would exist only to affront and would invite to violence. Indeed such an effort, like Gothic in China and Latin in Africa and Spanish in the Near East,

would show no understanding of the architecture of Christ's missio
at all, but only of clericalism, domination, arrogance.

Moreover, the tenor and spirit of our world are not those of Nicae
or Trent or even of Vatican I. Since even the most recent of th
councils, the world has altered enormously; and I suggest that thi
world change, already in fact occurring, has already brought abou
ecclesiastical change; and I suggest further that the changes no
operating both within the world and the Church have profoundl
altered our mission.

With or without the Church

I suggest that our world has become a lay world, a secular world
This is indeed a momentous change, and a new direction which th
past five hundred years have brought to pass. Its evidence is multiple
and has been analyzed by every Catholic thinker worthy of note sinc
Leo XIII. What indeed did Leo's letters on the social situatio
recognize, if not that man had broken through the wall with his ow
naked hands, the wall on which had been written: ignorance is you
fate; poverty is inevitable; you and your children are bound to th
wheel on which your fathers were born and died? In the nineteent
century, Leo implied, man had broken through. He might have added
"with or without the Church."

"With or without the Church"—the phrase is ominous and ver
nearly universal today. With or without the Church, man's life wil
become human. With or without the Church, the chains of colonial
ism will be broken; black and yellow and red men dream of freedom
and awaken from their dream, and reach for their weapons—with o
without the Church. With or without the Church, men will stake ou
their own acre, and be masters in their own house, and sit at thei
table to break bread—a bread which will be neither a dole nor a brib
nor the refuse and crumbs from affluent nations.

With or without the Church, men will endure the journey whic
leads from slavery to freedom; they will rot in tunnels and prisons, wi
be set on by dogs and beaten with truncheons, will undertake freedon
rides and stand in kangaroo courts; and they will prevail with or with
out the Church.

There has never been a time, you will agree, when the mission c
the Church stood or fell in proportion as the Church joined or refuse
to join her mission to the hopes of men. In the past it was perhap

enough that charity on the one hand and dogmatic suppleness on the other defined the Church's mission. She was sent to an unawakened humanity, or to a humanity that had not yet put away the things of a child. So she was faithful to her mission by translating her truths into new languages and forms. Together with this, she fed the hungry and clothed the naked and ministered to the dying.

Now this history of mercy and intellectual witness wins our admiration and serves as a master image of the Christian mission. But history, even when it is endlessly inspirational, will not do for living men what they only can do for themselves: define anew the Church's mission. The needs of past times were met by a form of mission appropriate to those times; but those times are past; and so is that form of mission.

Today, in the judgment of thinking men, it is not enough that the Church minister to an adult world as though it were a world of children. It is not enough that the Church serve a viable and intelligent world as though it were a sick world, or a retarded world, or an infantile world. It is not enough that the Church have her eyes open and her mercy ready, only or primarily for the sake of those who are contributing least to the forming (or deforming) of the new world. It is not enough that the Church appoint her best men and women to care for the immature and the old, as though to minister to those were all her mission, while in the world imaginative men, the molders of life's new forms, make and break and remake human life without the Church—without her presence, her conscience, or her vision. It is not enough, in sum, that the Church conceive of the world as a vast nursery or hospital or orphanage or parish; such an idea is essentially unreal and is productive of illusion in those who accede to it.

We have said that the world has grown determinedly secular; that it has broken through the structures that formerly protected and prevented it: protected it from inner anarchy, prevented it from the discovery of its own outer world. The world believes implicitly today in its ability to define life without the Church, as it believes in its ability to run its polity without a monarchy, to shape its cultural and political future without the colonial nations—in sum, to work out its own salvation on its own terms and at its own pace.

All this is, of course, a beautifully wrong analogy; it presupposes that the Church is of a piece with dead colonialism and empty thrones. In denial of the analogy, we must continue to assert that the Church, perpetually on a mission to the world, continues to be herself—neither colonial nor monarchic, but sacred, from above, transcendent to human life. Yet we too must beware of loose language; the transcendence of the Church is not an immunity from history in the name of eternity. It is rather a transcendence which is destined to become immanent, in the image of the Word of the Father, in the image of the human soul; the Catholic mission is to act as the soul of the body of man, and in that very effort to become incarnate in mankind, again and again, according to the forms which consciousness, culture, and community are giving to man's cosmic body.

Now these forms of human life today are governed by an expanding network of structures, a complex web of socialization, so delicate, so cunningly knit, so strong, that a blow struck for or against humanity in any place in the world, sets the whole web vibrating in sympathy or anger or exultation. With or without the Church, the web is spun.

With or without the Church, the web will be spun finer, stronger, of ever increasing breadth, until its interstices include all men, all cultures, all aspirations, in a single organism of life and community. With or without the Church, man will become mankind. This is the appraisal of man today; he is simply not detained, in other words, by a sacred claim which is merely a tradition, merely transcendent, an appendage to the present; neither is he interested in any serious way in a sacred system which merely cares for his children and his old, whose mercy binds up the wounds of his brutal progress: the ill, the defeated, the broken.

The World's Point of View

The basic reason for his mere tolerance of such a Church or his positive contempt for it, lies in his growing capability of doing all these things for himself. He is increasingly well equipped to pay in works of mercy the price of his own merciless choices; his socialization systems increasingly plan for orphanages and schools and hospitals and hostels and all the other ministries of mercy, as part of his own inclusive, self-sufficient world. He plans to build these centers and staff them and maintain them. And he wants control of them. If they already exist in given underdeveloped areas, he sees them either

s part of a past now done with, or as positively tainted with colonial-
,m, as sacred monuments to secular tyranny, institutions which are
n affront to his hopes. Witness the situation in Cuba, or in parts of
.frica, or in Ceylon, where it is at least probable that the Church
ould act with more wisdom than merely to organize her political
ower to retain institutions which the new nations are determined to
ontrol. Simply, man does not need a Church that comes toward him
oday, offering to do for him what he can do as well or better for
imself. Such a concept of Church mission, unselfish and venerable
hough it be, is in fact residual. And in the eyes of the new nations it
s a luxury; it wastes personnel, it wastes money and facilities. More-
ver, it creates pockets of reaction and dissociates youth from the
nain effort of the nation, in favor of colonial or parochial loyalties.

The persistent mistaking of fringe benefits for essentials, of peace
or the will of God, of material well-being for religious vitality, comes
o its tragic term when peace and affluence are snatched from us; as
s the case in Eastern Europe, or Ceylon, or Cuba, or Mohammedan
Africa. In such a case, we find ourselves battling to preserve claims
nd institutions that time and events have declared void, but which
ve have arbitrarily and childishly identified with the will of God,
ind to which we cling with the grip, not of life, but of death itself.
Ve find ourselves in such areas fighting a rear guard action for the
ake of benefits which have nothing, or only very little, to do with the
jospel or the Church. We find Catholics in such countries, often
inder the leadership of their hierarchy, settling into a moody dream
vorld compounded of lost privilege, envy, and fear of the will of
jod. Or we find Catholics, in enormous numbers, fleeing their home-
and, to join the worst forces of reaction elsewhere. And all this
ccurs in spite of the injunction which any real sense of mission
vould give us: to imitate the heroic early Church, to stand firm under
yranny, to discover once more, under circumstances of loss, prison
ind suppression, these riches which constitute our true being: the
ont, the altar, the Word of God—one another.

The Church, like many good things which have inhabited the
:arth for a long time, has lost an old world because she was part of
hat old world. That old world was somnolent, afraid and senile. It
:ould not awaken in time; its old wits could not cope with youth,
ind fiery resolve, and the kind of hate which is a fierce new visitation
of love. Such a world, world of the right, the world of privilege that

was unearned, and of power that corrupted, could not cope with new complexity, new frenzies; its old fingers could not find the pulse of birth and death; it could not prescribe remedies or purge bad blood or give of its own blood, which was too thin and sour to restore anyone.

And in the old world, the Church had grown old too. She had traded her youth for security or peace or institutions or the super- ficial horror called, by the enemies of change, "public order." The Church grew used to a mission toward children and women, to con- ducting schools that blessed the old order and fought change to the wall. She wrapped herself in the flag of the oppressor; she grew used to being led out on state occasions, to standing in dignity among the guns and uniforms, to testifying to what we might call the colonial creed: that human liberty or human dignity were good things, but paternalism and peace and order are better things. She taught that the good Catholic will not cry aloud when liberty or dignity are in- definitely withdrawn, that the good Catholic will not take up arms in human causes until the Church has scrutinized them, that above all the Catholic will never consent to work side-by-side, fight side-by- side, with the marxian abomination, and that if he dares do so, his eternal salvation is in jeopardy.

In such a way, the Church lost her world; by such wrong reason, by such goodness grown sterile and stern and unavailing, by human concessions to evil because it was powerful and plausible, by dictating to youth and stemming its energies until youth grew too old, by turning energies that might have been her energies into envy and hatred, by shouting at man instead of listening to man, by applying the dogmatic remedy to the carnal injury, by acting clumsily or tardily or not at all, by speech when action alone would avail, by silence when only speech would avail, by sincerity which was wrong- headed and clericalism which was hard of heart. So runs the litany of our loss.

It was not that the Church was evil. It was simply that in many places she had grown old and afraid, very nearly deaf and blind to what stood before her. She was caught in a complex tangle of con- cessions and compromises, bemused by an old order posing as an only order. And she heard every clock but one; and that one must be compared to the bomb which is time itself, and whose timepiece is the human heart, whose hour is now the eleventh hour. That heart the heart of man—furious, fallible, now slowing perversely, now quickening explosively—exploded, destroyed, took command. It began a merciless purge of its enemies. And it stood at the wall those whom perverse fate had cast as enemies of the people, whom every instruction of vocation and anointing had destined as friends of man.

You note that I am attempting to approach the Church's mission from the world's point of view. This is not a popular or easy venture. It would be much more simple to concentrate on those areas of the world which still give acceptance, however superficial, to Catholic belief, which still support a mission which presumes that neither the industrial revolution, nor the Russian revolution nor the Cuban revolution, had occurred. We could speak tenderly of the past, which in so many Catholic consciousnesses is the only present. We could speak of a Church which was walking hand in hand with tyrannies of the right as though human life were a perpetual and public renewal of the vows of marriage between Church and state, as though the silence and scorn of the world meant nothing.

But life has a discomforting habit of moving on, and of drawing the Church with it, sometimes in a tumbrel, and sometimes in limousines with the great of this world, sometimes as a sweating rickshaw-boy. We are presupposing that the mission of the Church implies an openness to play all or any of these roles in the world—in any case, to move, to submit to change as the first requirement of effective change. We have said that the mission of the Church to an adult world implies a special relationship of the world to the Church, a thousand roles of the incarnation. We have further implied something that can now be stated quite openly: that the modern world, pummeling the Church with perplexing new relationships and refusals, forces the Church again and again to review her mission. Is she out of step? Is she paying court to the powerful at the price of man's hope? Is she pariah, wrapped in a colonial flag in China, drawing ruin to herself as the enemy of a culture older and more noble than that of the west? Is she touching new shores, weighed down with trinkets and possessions that will comfort the unexorcised heart but will enrage the men of thought and depth? Is her mission, finally, so badly stated, so childish, so senile, so clumsy, so disrespectful of man, so archaic as to win only smiles from the polite and contempt from all?

Such questions, induced in us by the impact of our mission meeting the realities of time and this world, are all to the good; they keep us open to human life, freed of daydreaming and idolatry of the past, of clerical arrogance and lay inertia. Such questions also help men, as only the pressures and ironies of human experiences can help us, to renew our self-understanding. They help us avoid the mortal danger to our sacred mission—the danger, that is, of identifying our mission with the past in the name of eternity, with Europe in the name of the faith, with a projected egoism in the name of true God.

The Mission of the Church

But to state our question of mission on the world's terms, what precisely can the Church do for the world which the world cannot do for itself? Or to state our question of mission on the Church's terms, in what does the immanence and transcendence of the Church consist?

Our reflections, I would suggest, invite the Church to a new understanding of her transcendence in relation to her immanence, and in this a new understanding of her mission.

She must purify herself of a transcendence which is merely an ecclesiastical will to power. This is a commonplace which in the light of the council is becoming a cliché. But it is good to reflect that the majority of thinking men in the world are unconvinced that their fate, precisely as human fate, could safely be placed in the hands of the Church.

She must purify herself of a transcendence which prevents her from taking the present times seriously. Remoteness from life, blindness to human hope are the measure of her distance from the key realities for which the best of men willingly live and die today: justice, freedom, human dignity.

She must purify herself from the transcendence which demands that human progress submit its inner being to her, that she must initiate all human movements—cultural and political and intellectual —take leadership in them, dictate their findings, or exact submission of their methods. She must, in sum, cease acting as God, which she is not, and begin acting as man, which she is.

She must purify herself of all jargon, double talk, clichés, pretension of language, curial rhetoric. She must cease talking to herself as compensation for the fact so few men listen to her. This will require facing a painful truth: that fully 70 per cent of mankind today is supremely indifferent whether she lives or dies, unconvinced of her human value, blind before her mystery, deaf before her speech. She is in fact no longer even considered an enemy or a threat; she is rather looked on as a kind of relic in a park, green with age, the statue of a child, a minstrel, an old person, a favorite beast even; the Church of Patrick's parade, *Going My Way, The Sound of Music* —but in any case, something grown more and more inconvenient to the new city, to its new architecture and layout, and therefore possibly to be melted and recast into something useful.

She must purify herself of the transcendence which has identified itself with certain institutions, whose usefulness any thinking man would bring into question. Many good men and women, by their courageous search for mission, have done just that. They bypassed a whole network of established Church life in favor of life itself. They have sought out once more the wellsprings of life, which are the person, singly or in groupings. They have avoided false and foolish effort to multiply institutions for their own sake, or to keep them going when they have lost all initial drive.

Such laymen must continue to help us see clearly and act need-fully; they help us avoid forcing the sacred to become the ape of the secular, or to compete, instead of joining ourselves to communal effort. They help us see that a sacred mediocrity is not preferable to a secular excellence.

There are lines of correction, of remedy, of rediscovery of mission here, in the effort to know what the Church is, to know what the world is. The first effort is our life-long catechumenate, and so is the second. So delicately and cunningly indeed is the membrane of our mission joined to the membrane of the world that the place of junc-ture quite disappears in an effort of mutual service: grace to the world, human richness to the Church.

We will perhaps come to realize more deeply, during those days, a truth which both the Church and the world are holding before us: that the Church can never be herself apart from the world, and that the world remains a stranger to herself apart from the Church. And such a realization has its price attached. In a Society of Jesus where the vision of men was equal to the will of Christ, such a meeting as this would undoubtedly have taken place some fifteen or twenty years ago. At such a time, our proceedings would rather have been pro-phetic than remedial. We should have been preventing and leading the times rather than reflecting and catching up with them. But the cross of believers is often constructed of their own blindness. More soberingly, it receives upon its punishing wood not the guilty but the innocent. I firmly believe that the last twenty years and our failure to act have grown the tree and fashioned the cross upon which some one-fifth of humanity now hangs in utmost deprivation, in despair, in the draining away of human and sacred life.

Still, if we are too late to claim the dignity of prophets in the Church, we can shoulder the cross and minister beneath the cross to those whose anguish we take responsibility for, whose heavy burden is our own, our brothers, flesh of our flesh, bone of our bone.

And deprived as we are of one dignity, that of the man who saw in time, spoke clearly, and acted, we find ourselves clothed in another one, pure gift. I would not presume to give our dignity a name. But it is that of men and women who seize, even out of heartache, tardiness, and unaccountably wrong measures, the largest possible hope and remedy. It is those who give, with a realism which is something close to holy despair, a larger measure of themselves than good times or normal needs could ever summon. If indeed our action is late and partial and insufficient, there still remains the kind of courage that acts most powerfully when all is very nearly lost; it does with what it can; it is not defeated by the bureaucratic absurdities, by the feverish pursuit of nonessentials, or authoritarian coldness.

It has been brought home to us that there is a healing and unifying grace in even small efforts, when these are genuine in intention, when they respond to real needs and lead in human directions. I would not suggest that the healing and unifying process stops with the students who become involved. For those priests who lend their priesthood to this service, a renascence of priestly spirit is promised. Such an effort has the simple virtue of leading us all, priests and laymen, out of the tangle and complexity of modern life into what Robert Frost called simply "the clearing."

Harlem Diary

Joseph F. Roccasalvo, S.J.

After seven years of comfortable seminary life, involvement with the desperate poor and the dedicated active Christian is a "cultural shock" every bit as unnerving as a Peace Corps worker finds overseas. The difference is the element of hope; with the Pentecost spirit of confidence in God's presence among the poor, the Christian grows in maturity and preserves the optimism of youth. Yet the optimism is tempered by reality; three wine glasses at each place on the festal table serve only to magnify the image of the brown infant first in a dirty bowl of cold rice. In his diary, Joseph Roccosalvo suggests that the liturgy, as Word and action of God, constantly replenishes the energy poured into Christ's work among the poor.

June 1

We left Shrub Oak this evening at 7:20 P.M. to begin the Harlem project. A large crowd of scholastics and fathers saw us off at the front door. Many of the fellows will be gone by the time I return on June thirteenth, and I shall miss them all. During these opening seven years of my life in the Society, I have come to realize that my roots in religious life go as deep as the individuals I have known and loved. Separation will always be difficult, but such is the price of apostolic mobility.

I was very impressed by the warm concern of all that this project go well. The ten of us are definitely on exhibition. Father Rector remarked this afternoon that the repetition of this work next summer will largely depend on our competence during the week and a half. We are beginning tomorrow at 9:00 A.M.; in the evening Fr. Dan Berrigan will come up to All Saints Church in Harlem to celebrate the liturgy for us. It is most appropriate that Dan initiate the program, for we need his mission spirit to give our own high-powered interest in this project the sensitive focusing that it requires.

At the present moment I think that we are all fundamentally at peace, knowing that a phase in our religious lives is completed, and that something new is wakening. I, for one, look to this period of twelve days as an "adventure in grace," where somehow the life of study, prayer, and preparation of seven years must harmonize with the appeal of the poor and socially deprived. All these aspects must speak through us in unison. To borrow the title of Fr. Phil Berrigan's book, we religious must be "no more strangers" to the beckoning of the poor. To begin achieving this goal in a brief week and a half, we must readily permit the grim reality of Harlem to become creative and grace us with an insight into the suffering of Christ's members and, therefore, into our own human poverty.

June 2

I am writing this entry in a state of weariness and fatigue, having been stunned by what Harlem has shown me in one short day. Nevertheless, I will do my best to reconstruct today's events.

I got up this morning at 6:00 A.M. and made meditation on the Fordham grounds. None of us attended the liturgy on campus, since Dan intended to say Mass for us in Harlem. We had an excellent breakfast in the Faber Hall dining room and ate our $1.25 full, somehow suspecting that the day would bring its heavy tolls on our stamina.

We left for Harlem by the 3rd Avenue El and sat with the indifferent crowds of morning commuters who now and again looked up to stare at us with curious eyes. After taking the Lexington Avenue Express, we got off at 125th Street and started to walk up to 130th. Don Millus and I talked of what the day might bring. One Negro man called out to the ten of us, as we swept past: "Y'all gona ma'ch on Washin'ton?" We answered: "Not today!" and walked up the remaining four blocks. I noticed that the bar and grills were alive with customers; the families of ragged children, pregnant mothers, and recuperating alcoholics had already begun to collect themselves on the stoops outside the tenements, probably to spend their day staring idly into the garbaged streets.

We arrived at the Addie Mae Collins Community Agency, which is on the corner of 130th Street and Madison Avenue, at about 9:15

A.M. We rang the bell at the center, and a Sister of Charity, Sr. Angelus, let us into a small office-room to the left. The two curates from the parish, Fr. Sugrue and Fr. Curry, Sr. Martha, a Dominican of the Sick Poor, and Sisters Mercedes and Bernard, Franciscan Handmaids of Mary, were all waiting to greet us. Soon a lively discussion began concerning what procedure we should use in our opening day's work. Five of us decided to do follow-ups on the previous contacts made by Sr. Angelus and the two curates, and also to complete all the apartments in the same tenements. The other five decided to strike out and make new contacts, and Fr. Sugrue outlined the boundaries of the parish, indicating those streets which were not yet fully canvassed. We were all given registration cards as well as cards carrying the name of the agency in order to identify ourselves. Our main purpose was to discover medical needs, food and income problems, welfare, etc., and to record these cases on our file cards. We also had a list of agencies to which we could refer these various cases.

Before we left to begin the canvassing, Sr. Mercedes gave us a few pointers on how to deal with the people, and what to expect. Sister herself is a Negro and, since she was born and raised in Harlem, she is quite able to describe the personal physiognomy of the people there. She spoke of the suspicion and fear that lay on the other side of the tenement door, which only our Christian compassion and concern would begin to unlock. After her words of advice, we left to initiate the day's work.

As I walked out into the Harlem streets, I realized that the day had grown uncomfortably muggy, and the black rabat which I wore only increased the sense of discomfort. Later I was to discover that this was a small price to pay for the sincerity and confidence of the people which our clerical garb secured.

I began my day's assignment in a tenement located on 11 East 131st Street, about two blocks from the center. I knocked on my first door and Mrs. G, a Negro woman about sixty-five years old, opened to me, first a few inches, and then, after seeing the collar, all the way. I told her why I had come, handing her the agency's card as a reminder for the future months. As I stepped into the apartment, I was introduced to both the teen-age granddaughter, Glinda, and the six-year-old grandson, Poppie; I noticed the boy had a withered hand and was anxious to hide it from my view.

As Mrs. G showed me around the three-room apartment, she complained of rats and berated the superintendent for not clearing the garbage which littered the alley. The stench was quite conspicuous. One small bedroom with a bunk-bed in it was occupied by six of the children, while the grandmother used the kitchen as a combination dining room, bedroom, and recreational area for the little boy. The back room had been emptied of all sorts of trash in order to make sleeping quarters for the oldest boy, whose sense of shame in front of his younger sisters had caused him to seek the privacy of the back room. It was still unfurnished. The bathroom was appalling, with large pieces of plaster hanging from the walls, and the toilet conditions cannot be described with discretion. The whole family was on welfare, with a pittance of extra salary being provided by the oldest boy.

Glinda shuffled around the room listlessly, only looking up once to answer my few questions. I left Mrs. G after promising that I would do my best to search for a new apartment; I also mentioned that I would call the Board of Health to provide pressure on the landlord to have the rat-holes stuffed and the garbage removed from the alley. I later discovered that apartments are as rare as white men in that area, and there are hundreds waiting for rooms in the latest projects. Most of the people who could really profit from the projects are disqualified by the twenty-two categories which exclude all families that have traces of illegitimacy or dope addiction.

I next visited the apartment of Mrs. A, and I was stunned by the living quarters which I found. As I entered the living room, I was hit by the stench of dirt and excrement which filled the air. Seven children, ranging from the ages of two to sixteen, were dressed in rags, and mostly barefooted. The mother looked no more than twenty-five. A small TV set had been placed in a corner and was blaring out some ancient war film. There was a four-foot pile of dirty laundry in another corner, which made it difficult to walk in and out of the room. The adjoining bedroom that I saw out of the corner of my eye was in shambles, and the sheets on the bed were blackened through overuse. The woman spoke slowly and with embarrassment, as if she were dazed. Gradually she began to piece together her own private tragedy: she was not on welfare since checks from her estranged husband were supposed to take care of her expenses. But she had not received a forty-dollar check in two weeks and was borrowing from neighbors in order to survive. She told me that she had very little food in the house, so I promised that I would return with a package, after doing some shopping with A&P coupons.

Shortly after I left the tenement I returned to the center. Sr. Bernard brought in a tray of sandwiches, and I hungrily downed two or three of them with a coke, before returning to Mrs. A's house. I quickly left the center and walked to 11 131st Street, where Mrs. A was waiting on the front steps. She wearily climbed the four flights of stairs as I followed behind her. I told her that I would go shopping with the oldest boy, Ernest, if she would give me a list of groceries. She went through the staples, slurring her syllables: rice, flour, bread, cereal, etc. The children began to clap their hands when I asked them whether they would like some cakes and cookies. I kept watching the youngest child out of the corner of my eye, as she dug her fingers into a dirty dish of rice, spilling it all over the floor.

Ernest put on a pair of unripped pants, and we both left the building. He was taciturn, answering me only with monosyllables, and he seemed resentful of my presence. We got to the A&P and went up and down the aisles, selecting food. I let Ernest do most of the choosing. Both our arms were filled with packages when we arrived back at the tenement, and as we entered the apartment on the fourth floor, the children began to applaud in unison. The mother smiled weakly at me. My mind translated: how long would the food last, for two days, perhaps three; and then back to the same uncertainty, the same insecurity, the familiar ache of empty bellies. I left that family with a curious feeling, compounded of elation and despair.

I left the center about a quarter to four, and arrived back at St. John's Hall on Fordham campus utterly exhausted; a quick shower helped to revive me before dinner at Faber Hall. The food was excellent, carefully selected and cooked, but all I could think of during the meal was Mrs. A and her starving brood of children. Why this stark contrast between my abundance and their penury?

After dinner I went back to St. John's to lie down for a half-hour before leaving for the evening Mass at Harlem with Father Dan. We all took the train back to 125th Street and arrived at the center about 7:15 P.M. In a brief homily during Mass, Fr. Berrigan emphasized the need for unity among ourselves in order to accomplish the work of the two weeks. He reminded us that we needed the challenge of the poor to tell us of our own spiritual poverty, and that it was among the desperate and discarded of humanity that we could truly become Christian.

After liturgy, we went up to Fr. Sugrue's room, and entertained each other with freedom songs from the Peter, Paul, and Mary repertoire. We stayed till about 9:30 P.M., said good-bye to Dan (who promised to visit us on campus during our stay), and then proceeded to the various subway stations, where we regaled the commuters with more folk songs, much to their delight and bewilderment. I arrived home at 10:30 P.M., but didn't get to sleep till quite late.

June 3

We got up at 6:30 A.M. and had Mass with Fr. Mooney at Dealy Hall. He said the votive mass of the Ascension, which we accompanied with hymns and guitar. After breakfast, I took advantage of the train ride to write this diary out in longhand. I arrived at the center at 9:05 A.M. and quickly made out a list of the names of the various welfare agencies. I had to hurry, because I had an appointment with Mrs. Roark, the Guidance Counselor at P.S. 133. I had a very nice chat there with two Negro teachers at the school, the Reverend Roberts and Mr. Jackson. The Reverend Roberts invited me back to see him some time this week, and I shall certainly take advantage of the invitation, to find out the type of rehabilitation work he is doing in the area.

On my way back to the center, Glinda G stopped me, but didn't know what to say when I paused to speak with her. Evidently, she remembered me clearly from my brief visit the other day. As I looked into that bewildered face, I kept thinking: another dazed victim of the jungle!

I also stopped to talk with Mrs. Blanche Tucker, a convert to Catholicism. She rhapsodized about her new-found faith, even inviting me to come to her baptism in three weeks. I told her that it wouldn't be possible (I'll be in Philadelphia, studying) but that I would come around to see her on Monday.

I arrived back at St. John's around 4:15 P.M. and at about 9:15 P.M. we had a group discussion in the lounge downstairs in St. John's Hall. Fr. Phil Hurley, Dick Kane, and one other father asked to sit in on the meeting. I thought the whole discussion deeply moving. There is a reinforcement of commitment in such discussions, as was clear this evening. In general, I think we all felt rather overwhelmed, almost in a state of shock from the little that Harlem disclosed of itself. It is very difficult to think the passion and *resurrection* together in Harlem, especially when one sees Calvary everywhere, and when it seems that no one can rise out of the tombs of those filthy tenements.

I went to bed at about 11:15 P.M. very tired. I hope our stamina keeps up.

June 4

We got up at 6:30 this morning. It's getting increasingly difficult to rise early each day. We had Mass once again with Fr. Mooney at Dealy Hall, and then breakfast at Faber. We took the usual two trains to get to the center, and there were the same crowds of Negro and Puerto Rican workers on their way to work, showing the same curiosity at seeing "priests" riding with them at such an early hour.

We arrived at the center at 9:05 and had coffee with Sr. Angelus. She began to talk about her previous assignment as a Sister of Charity. She was working formerly as a nurse in Nassau and the Bahamas, where she opened up two prenatal clinics. When she came back to the States, she found life here a little too comfortable, a little too snug, so she asked to be transferred to Harlem, where she felt she could be of use to the people. She is a most dedicated and self-effacing woman!

Sister suggested that we wait until ten o'clock before we start knocking on doors. Many of the women sleep till mid-morning, because they have been out on the stoops late to avoid the infernal heat of the tenements. It's rather distressing to get them out of bed in the morning; they are not exactly anxious to speak with anyone, even with a Roman collar.

I went to 54–56 East 129th Street and managed to contact about five families. I visited with Mr. and Mrs. F who are both great-grandparents, not much older than sixty years. The Harlem residents have their children early, most of them born out of wedlock.

They are very unassuming about this, and I don't think that the word "illegitimate" is found in their vocabulary. Mr. and Mrs. F needed food and clothing, so I promised I would return in the afternoon, as I handed the great grandmother the card of the agency. I have usually left one at each house where I've stopped.

Since I had promised to buy clothes for Mrs. F, I went shopping with Mike Duffy at the Salvation Army Shop, located on 125th Street and Madison. I bought two pairs of pants, some shirts, and a few other assorted articles, all of which cost me a dollar; the woman behind the counter, noticing my collar, assured me that she would ask for no more since it was for charity.

Mike and I returned to the center, passing as we walked the shop where the kids buy dope and goof-balls, the house where the prostitutes display their wares on the stoops, where the men casually walk past, eying them up and down. I stopped in at Mr. and Mrs. F's apartment on 129th Street and brought the food and clothing which I had promised that morning. I also left a large stuffed doll for the little great-grandchild, Lynette. The girl was overjoyed, as were her great-grandparents.

I came back to the center and had a cup of coffee with Sr. Angelus; it really hit the spot. Since I had completed most of my assignments early, Jim Heff and I decided to leave early. As the two of us walked down the street, the children waved and their parents came up and greeted us. All the suspicion which had been the atmosphere of our first arrival in Harlem now dispersed into a general aura of friendliness and gratitude. Even the old men and women greeted us as we walked to the train trestle.

There has been the possibility of some publicity for the group of us, probably in the *Daily News* or the *Tablet*. However, Fr. Sugrue has been adamant in not allowing such coverage; and I heartily agree with him. Why assuage the consciences of so many indifferent Catholics by giving them the impression that "we are in the field"? Our numbers are the proverbial drop in the bucket.

I returned to Fordham and for my first time in the past couple of tedious days I slept early and soundly.

June 6

I spent a quiet day here on the Fordham campus; I just wanted to rest, to be by myself, mostly to distance the whole Harlem experience of the past week. After breakfast, I made my meditation on the people I had met in Harlem, the remarks of Fr. Sugrue and Sr. Angelus. I came back to the hall about 9:30 A.M. and did some typing in this diary, but found I couldn't get very far. So I lay down and read a section from Fr. Phil Berrigan's book, *No More Strangers*.

I kept my attention on the chapter for an hour or so, and then dozed off to sleep. I awoke in about an hour, and Jim Heffernen came in to talk about the project and our own reactions to it. The Mass of the morning came up in the course of conversation. The Pentecost liturgy had moved us all. For one thing the Mass was at 10:15 A.M. so that we were all fully awake and deeply intent on getting as much out of the liturgy as possible. The singing, too, was superb, as Raoul and Dick alternated on the guitar for parts of the Rivers' Mass. Each of us included special remembrances of Harlem residents at the Memento of the living and dead. Fr. Frank Winters' homily was also a high point during the Mass. He compared our being present together in Harlem, helping to renew the image of the Church there, to the apostles in the upper room; having been touched by the Spirit of Love that warmed their minds and hearts, they flung open the doors and rushed out, restless to communicate the "good news."

I have learned one lesson thus far from the people of Harlem: tragedy wears the same humanly distorted face. Pain and desperation are redundant in those tenements, defeatism the atmosphere, where nothing is expected, and what is given in charity is received with no hope of repetition.

The dinner at Faber Hall was replete with three different kinds of wine and numerous entrées. I had to laugh at the contrast between this feast and the beggar's supper of nothing at all, which I had witnessed in Harlem. In spite of myself I felt awkward and ashamed, as the champagne sparkled in my glass. I don't write this to reproach our manner of eating on big occasions. After all, one can legitimately exteriorize certain feasts, like the birthday of the Church, with special celebration. But it is hard to enjoy the festivities when so many, whom you have come to love, are excluded: the poor, the destitute, the homeless. The wedding garments have been distributed without equity.

June 7

I spent the morning working with one family on East 129th Street. I use the word "family" in a very broad sense, for only Miss G was living at home; her husband had abandoned her, leaving her with one son, Michael. Miss G impressed me as a very courageous woman, and she insisted that I address her as Winnie. She told me that her son Michael was a premature baby, and developed early a case of bronchitis and hernia. She is also raising her sister's two children; for, as Winnie suggested, either they stay with her, or they go out on the street.

When I had entered her apartment and asked her about finances, Winnie told me that she only had seven dollars to care for herself and the three children for a period of two weeks. She receives sixty-six dollars every two weeks from Welfare, and fifty-nine dollars go for paying the rent.

I gave her five dollars to tide her over and promised to come back with food and clothing. Her awareness of the center just two short blocks away was rather vague; she preferred, she said, to be independent for as long as she was able, and let the poorer people profit from the center's resources.

I went shopping at the A&P to get her some meat and then came back to the center to make her up a box of canned goods. I also packed some blouses and dresses for her niece and herself, as well as some baby clothes for her son Michael. When I delivered the food and clothing, she was simply overjoyed; and as she unpacked the bags and box, she announced each article out loud, like some contestant who had won a jackpot on a quiz show.

I asked Winnie whether the children were still attending religious instructions at All Saints Church and discovered that two of them were not even baptized. Without apologizing, she explained that the half-day jobs of sewing and washing left her little time to bring the children over for baptism, and so she never bothered to make an appointment. I talked to her about the sacrament, assuring her that God would remain with her children by making them his own, and that he would help them to achieve a moral strength of which she would some day be proud. Winnie listened intently, her big eyes fastened on my face, and I think my little homily moved her. She immediately responded by asking that I make an appointment with Fr. Sugrue for their christening.

I went back to the center and had lunch till 1:15 P.M. When I went up to the office afterwards, there was a man about twenty-seven years old waiting to see me. His name was Jonathan W. He told me that he had been in a serious fire accident earlier in the year and had suffered third-degree burns which made it impossible for him to hold a job. His wife had left him and taken the children with her, so that he was now completely alone. Sr. Angelus had been most kind to him by her visits at the hospital where he was recuperating, but, as she later suggested to me in private, he was becoming too dependent on her and on the center's resources.

Jonathan asked me for some food and clothing. I told him that I would go shopping and meet him on 129th Street where I would deliver the goods. After shopping at the A&P, I packed everything in a box and then walked down to 129th Street in the blazing heat. I waited a half-hour for Jonathan, but he never came. I walked back to the center, with cans slipping out from a ripped corner of the box, and nearly stopped the traffic on 129th Street and Fifth Avenue. I just about made it back to the center, my arms crippled with the weight of the canned goods, but I didn't notice because I was too busy being angry at the tardiness of Mr. Jonathan. I was exhausted when I got back to the center; it must have been close to ninety-five degrees in Harlem that day. "A modern inferno," I kept musing, "with the people on the outer circle and the landlords in the middle."

As I sat there mopping my brow, a woman with her young daughter Jerrie came in for some food and clothing; so I gave her the box of goods which I had packed for Jonathan. Who should walk in about ten minutes after but Jonathan, with ready apologies falling from his mouth? I packed another box of the groceries that remained and told him I would shop for clothes the next day at the Salvation Army shop.

After dinner I sat and talked with Ty about what we were aiming for in this whole project. I think he hit it when he suggested, at one point, that we were trying to leave in Harlem a little "fundamental hope," without the rashness of thinking that we could achieve a full-scale victory. I thought later: even Christ predicted that the poor we will have always with us, a by-product, no doubt, of man's greed and misuse of freedom. It is good for the Church to show its face in these tenements through the medium of our own faces . . . to leave there some fundamental hope!

June 8

I got down to the center this morning about 9:50 A.M. and immediately went to the Salvation Army Family Center at 125th Street to get some clothing for Jonathan. The Negro women there were most kind and helped me to find a pair of pants and some shirts for him. I kept thinking of Jonathan as I walked back to the center. His case, involving that fire accident, won't come up for another year and a half; how will he get along during that period without any compensation?

The streets were very hot and muggy with that thick haziness which acts as a magnifying glass, intensifying the unpleasantness. All Harlem needs, I thought, is some rain to clear the air—rain and grace. By the time I reached the center, my rabat and tee shirt were soaked again; so I removed my jacket to cool off.

I then called Family Court to find out whether Mrs. A, the woman I had met earlier in the week, had received her check for forty dollars. Much to my satisfaction (and, I bet, to hers) the check had been sent out, showing that a little clerical pressure, even by telephone, produces results.

Sr. Angelus wasn't at the center today, because she had gone for X-rays on her leg. It has been bothering her for days, but she has said nothing—typical of her devotion. I sat with Sr. Martha and Sr. Bernard and we discussed the problems of the area: dope addiction, prostitution, and all the other muck, singly or in combination, that dirties Harlem. Later, Fr. Sugrue joined us and made it a point to mention again that he did not want any newspaper publicity for the center, unless the *complete* story was printed. He did not want the ten of us to be thought of as clerical "white daddies" who are part of the patronizing program of black Harlem. During that afternoon, I learned more than I ever have about the politics, housing, and Catholic indifference that dates back to 1945 in that area.

June 9

I left the center about 10:15 A.M. to visit P.S. 133. While I was at the school, I decided to have an informal conversation with one of the teachers there, the Reverend Roberts. I had met him earlier in the week, and he had invited me back for a chat to discuss his work at the Liberal Catholic Church and his activities within the

Harlem area. I rang for him and he came down to the reception desk rather quickly. We both decided to use one of the adjoining classrooms for our conversation. He was in a particularly good frame of mind, because a group of the fellows from the school had won a swimming meet and the coveted trophy that went along with the victory. I asked him why he had chosen to teach in a grade school, especially when his pastoral duties were a sufficient responsibility. He answered that his main reason and purpose was to provide the young Negro boys of the school with a male image with which they could identify. Many of them, he continued, have either no father, or too many. He was certainly loved and admired by the youngsters. Throughout the conversation, many would enter the classroom and ask whether they could do something for him.

The Reverend Roberts went on to discuss the problems of housing and education which he feels are the two main areas for renewal in Harlem. He talked of the rent strikes, the newest weapon of the poor to force landlords to improve a dilapidated tenement building. I asked him whether he worked with any of the local Churches in the area, and he replied that there is a tremendous spirit of ecumenism developing, particularly in central Harlem. He himself has been most active in achieving rapport with the various denominations in the immediate area.

I went back to the center after thanking the Reverend Roberts for his time and enlightening comments. While I was having lunch with the other scholastics, Fr. Sugrue stopped in to suggest that we visit some of the other parishes adjoining All Saints and thus get a broader picture of what the various curates are accomplishing.

I called up Fr. Meehan at Resurrection parish and made arrangements to come over and speak with him. Heff and I took the train to 151st Street. Fr. Meehan talked with us for about an hour and then suggested that we take a walk around the parish area. We saw many of the low-priced projects which are being raised in the vicinity; the slums we saw are certainly as poor, if not poorer, than those in All Saints, but I think there is a larger proportion of middle class in Resurrection parish. At around 3:30 P.M. we saw our last project in housing development, located on 153rd Street and Eighth Avenue.

Jim and I took the D train to Fordham and walked down the hill to the campus. The area around 151st Street was still flashing in my mind: the alcoholics in the street, the prostitutes sitting on cars soliciting, some of them badly scarred by knives or razors, the heat of the tenements forcing swarms of families out on the stoops . . . the same redundant portrait of the poor.

After dinner we met. Fr. John McCarthy was present and, since he is head of the Social Service School in downtown Fordham, we asked him to direct the discussion. From the comments made by each of us, we were agreed on the complexity and, often, the insolubility of each case we discovered. We also discussed the problem of "manipulation," how difficult it was to obtain the complete history in any one case, so dense were the defense mechanisms which the people unconsciously set up. Fr. McCarthy went on to comment that, technically, we had done very little to relieve the suffering and misery within the radius of the few blocks which we covered. But what we had left in Harlem was a deep love for its people, something so subtle, so qualitatively transforming that it could not be measured. I thought to myself: we are the links in the chain of Christ's victory, forged by each minor contribution of love. In this time and place we must let him be; difficult though it is in the face of the vast indifference to the poor, yet *we* religious cannot be oblivious to his words: what you do to the least, you do to me. Otherwise, we have squandered his death and his rising. Fr. Berrigan was also at the meeting and had occasion to comment on an article that was published in *Atlantic Monthly* about the overwhelming shock of the Peace Corps workers who witness the cheapness of human life in the teeming suburbs of India; how thousands die in the street each day; how death becomes the constant companion of the young. In Harlem it is dying rather than the final repose of death which confronts its victims, the dazed eyes of the helpless. Here is Calvary, as it were, without resurrection. It is only the vision of faith that would dare compel us to look further.

June 10

All of us got up late this morning (7:30); we thought it would be good to have a late sleep, since we have been racing around without thought to expenditure of energy. I was beat from yesterday's activity, including the evening discussion, which was quite draining despite its richness: just to relive a whole day in Harlem, even in reflection, is to challenge one's resources.

We had to go to Mass at Loyola Hall, in a basement that is parti-
tioned by curtains in order to make available space for all the visiting fathers. Consequently, the Masses are said silently (mutely
would be a better word) with back to server. After the engaging
liturgies which I have been accustomed to, the whole Mass, said
in the old manner, struck me as a meaningless pantomime, a kind
of "closet drama" with no participation except inert presence. I
began to wonder how the people, for so many years, were able to
accept this taciturn liturgy, cut off from its interior richness. Thank
God for the liturgical changes, which so readily admit the people
into the mystery of Christ's sacrifice. There have been days in
Harlem when only because I was able to retrieve the offering of
the morning Mass was I capable then of continuing my work with
the people.

As I walked over to Faber Hall for breakfast, I watched the
ordinandi moving rhythmically in double line with Cardinal Spell-
man following behind. The Mass of Ordination was soon to begin.
The procession itself was moving: so many years of preparation, of
waiting, were now coming to term in this one ceremony.

I thought I would go to another parish church in Harlem during
the afternoon, to see what other activities the local curates are engaged in. I called up Fr. Lucas, one of the few Negro Catholic
priests in the United States; he is presently stationed at St. Charles
Borromeo. He answered the telephone, and when I asked whether
he would be in that afternoon, he said that he wouldn't be back to
the rectory until late. He suggested that I come over anyhow and
speak with a Mr. John Grady, a young layman working with pre-
school Negro children. Having recently secured a Drew Foundation grant, he has managed to enroll thirty-one Negro children in
Montessori schools. John wasn't there when I telephoned, but I
spoke with his secretary, Miss Thornberry, who invited me to visit
some free afternoon.

June 11

Today was the last day of the project. Since I had completed all
my canvassing, I thought I would leave St. John's later than usual.
So after breakfast and Mass I went back to sleep—the past week
has taken its toll in energy. After an hour's nap I began work on
this journal, which I have been trying to bring up to date by typing

out each day's notes. I wrote for an hour and then left for the center with Jim and John. We arrived at about 10:45 A.M. and waited for Sr. Angelus to come. When she finally walked in, she insisted that we have an early lunch with her down in the cafeteria. The hot pizza and orangeade served their purpose, quieting those stomach gurgles which were due to an early and scanty breakfast.

After lunch I went over to say good-bye to Rose, Lilo and Madeleine. I am especially fond of Madeleine, our two-hundred-pound Negro cook, and while I clasped her hands, she announced: "You has been so easy ta tawk wit, Jozeph; dat's how ah knows you is goina be a pries'."

I decided to leave the center in order to have time to bring this chronicle up to date. The hardest hour of the two weeks lay just ahead: saying good-bye to Sr. Angelus and Fathers Sugrue and Curry. Sister is a real soldier, strong yet so uncompromisingly gentle in her devotion to the poor. The courage of Fr. Sugrue, and Fr. Curry's patience, their combined and unyielding Irish fight, are qualities I shall miss immeasurably. How easily, I thought, does the heart attach itself to what is truly good. Yet it seems so unfair that these three should be battling in Harlem relatively alone with so few Christians in the field with them.

When I got into the Harlem streets, a feeling of nostalgia welled up. This would probably be the last time that I would be in Harlem for a long while. Some of us, however, do intend to drop in and see Fr. Sugrue toward the end of the summer. We are thinking of buying him a liturgical medal and chain with the following inscription on the back: "Beatus spiritu pauper. June, 1965. The Scholastics."

June 12

We all got up around 8:30 A.M. and shortly after had breakfast at Faber Hall. Frank Winters decided to have a late liturgy and we readily complied. The Mass and participation this morning were particularly gratifying. There was somehow that unison of mind and heart in our worship which I would point to more as an atmosphere than a describable sentiment. John Cunningham gave a homily that was quite beautiful in its thought and articulation. For his text he used a remark which Fr. Horace McKenna made during one conversation we had with him at haustus. Father has labored in the Negro missions for over forty years, yet, even in his seventies, he has maintained an infectious vivacity that is most attractive. When humorously asked how he had remained a "new breeder" despite his "old" age, he remarked: "I've never had much chance to grow old, because I've spent my life with the poor." John developed Father's statement in terms of that Christian love which keeps one perennially young: it was Fr. McKenna's compassion and love for the poor that had left his heart and mind vibrant.

Well, the project has come to a close with this Mass, and there is a certain sense in which we can all be justly proud: first, of one another, that we closely cooperated with God to dispose us to a challenging task; secondly, that our "community within a community" (Frank's phrase) remained one in mutual support of our goal. There was union of suffering for the plight of Harlem's people as well as union of joy for all the times we laughed together and managed to boost each other's morale during the difficult hours. Perhaps what is more amazing is how delicate nuances of personality, lost to our eyes at Shrub Oak because of its vastness, came to presence in the morning light of close companionship.

The epistle of the morning's Mass was the grace I have been awaiting, one which helps me to understand a little better how Christ's death and resurrection are inextricably present in Harlem. The words are from Saint Paul's Letter to the Romans: ". . . we rejoice in our sufferings also, knowing that suffering produces endurance, endurance produces virtue, and virtue produces hope. *And hope does not disappoint,* because God's love is poured forth in our hearts by the Holy Spirit who dwells in us." This text came as an answer to a question that is a subtle threat to faith; for all apparent absence of God amid pain, whether in Harlem or Vietnam, challenges one's faith. But now I see that in Harlem we were being asked to become messengers of his hope, "and hope does not disappoint." Because we loved Harlem's people, we therefore brought God where he had been obscured, leaving his light to shine a little less dimly than before.

My prayer now is one of continual gratitude for these two weeks; during this season of the Spirit, this experience, too, was pentecostal.

Revolt and Reform

Joseph F. MacFarlane, S.J.

Conflicts between the generations take a variety of disguises; the issues are as numerous as they are insoluble. Joseph MacFarlane isolates one: the attitude toward structure. While the "younger generation" or "New Breed" see structure as inhibiting growth and reform, a wastebasket filled with bureaucratic forms in triplicate, their elders clasp it in the hope of finding some stability in these chaotic days. The conflict has two faces, both with an expression of truth. Youth has not experienced change; it measures the present against the possible, while traditional thinkers, looking at past and present through the vision of one lifetime, see danger and pain in abandoning long sought and proved procedures which provide some shape and direction to action. To concretize the struggle and ambiguity of instincts in the Church, statements of Pope Paul VI demonstrate that painful uncertainty in the matter of progress has reached even to the nerve center of Christianity. This article appeared first in *Direction,* Summer, 1965.

One of the most serious sources of conflict today between the older generation and the new generation is structure.

The two generations are not easy to define. They cannot be identified by age, education, or class. But there is one fairly reliable guide for grouping them: their reaction to this thing called structure. The older generation generally accepts it and the new generation questions it.

From the start, let me restrict discussion of the two groups to those who are genuinely concerned about Christianity. There are irresponsible ones among the new generation, I know, just as there are obstinate authoritarians among the older generation. But there is a serious lack of understanding and communication today between the genuine people on both sides. Both must find a way to work together if Christianity's problems are to be solved. It seems to me that the biggest block to this necessary, mutual understanding is the different way each looks at structure.

To the new generation, structure is "the set-up." It is the fixed approach to any situation. It is an attitude of mind and an elaborate set of procedures presented as the established way of doing things.

As an attitude, structure is coming to a discussion with the final decision already made; approaching a new situation with a preestablished plan; replying to an objection with an appeal to authority; attempting to solve today's needs from past experience only; and being reluctant to admit that the new generation might be able to discover some better ways to meet their needs.

As a set of procedures, structure is many things. The new generation can sense structure immediately; the older generation finds it hard to pin down, because they take structure so completely for granted that rarely is it considered anything but common sense. It is codes of conduct ranging in scope from basic morality to talking too loud. It is laws covering everything from murder to stop signs. It is rules as divergent as country club regulations and how to run a Sodality meeting. It is the chain of command; the remote control; the unbending, remote, impersonal, omnipresent establishment that seems more concerned with enforcing old laws than with meeting new needs.

The structure the new generation objects to is not revealed truth, or divine law, or the authority given to the Church by Christ. Nor are they questioning authority as such, or the right of authorities to formulate laws and administer them. What they do object to is a misuse of authority by treating all aspects of structure as immutable and backing this stand with authority. They insist that even if tradition, or eternal truth, can be invoked to support some methods of procedure in the past, adaptations or totally new procedures must be devised to meet genuine new needs.

It is important to realize that this new generation really has something to say. I am convinced they are the forerunners of what is coming. What the relatively few articulate ones are now saying, the majority coming along behind them will be taking for granted. Furthermore, Vatican II marks a turning point in history. There will be no turning back. Vatican II did not create the new mood. It had been developing underneath for some time. With or without the Council, it would have come. What Vatican II did was to open the way for discussion *within* the Church and *throughout* it, not at the *top only,* or *outside* it. Thirdly, the new generation must not be thought of as a few ex-seminarians or journalists. It already includes a wide spectrum of lay people as well as clergy and religious, who have been reading books and attending institutes and lectures by outstanding scholars. The ferment among the collegians is almost entirely in this direction.

It is only a start, admittedly, but the roots are spread wide and deep. This new generation is feeding its mind on the brightest and most challenging scholars of our day or any day. Few spokesmen for the older generation can match the appeal of modern scholars or their research into the latest sources. Almost none of the scholars of the coming generation are taking up the thinking of the older generation. The book publishers know only too well that the intellectual trend is all in one direction. In this country, the defense in print of the older generation is being left more and more to a few clerical magazines, pathetic independent efforts like *The Wanderer,* and some diocesan weeklies.

The new generation has some worthwhile things to say which those who have accepted a structured society look upon as daring and upsetting. There is a parallel between the upsurge of the outspoken new generation today and the rise of representative government in the late eighteenth and early nineteenth centuries. "The common people demanding a voice! Telling kings and rulers how to govern! Unheard of!" The demand to be heard may be upsetting to those who defend structure, as happened in the dying days of kingdoms, but the genuine spokesmen for the new generation within the Church had better be heard, or another great popular and permanent movement in history will pass the Church by and force on her, a century later, a struggle to catch up with the times, as has happened so often before.

The new generation holds that those whose consciences are to be bound by laws and codes should have some say in discussing their revision. They don't think it should be left entirely to those in authority, especially those with vested interests in the structure, to decide whether structure should be adapted to their needs or not. They maintain that all available knowledge should animate lawmaking and they do not admit that all wisdom is limited to those in authority and their staffs. (The older generation would add, "or limited to the new generation, either.")

They also object to the structured position as one that is too pre-occupied with impersonal norms and goals rather than with personal feelings and fulfillment and—to meet today's needs—one that is too dependent on conclusions derived from traditional theories rather than from present-day experience.

The claim of the oldsters that their structured positions are drawn from actual and long experience only brings the reply that today's world is too different from other generations for earlier experiences to provide all the answers for today's needs.

To the new generation, it seems as if the older generation ignores too many of the faults of the past and fails to see how relatively few of the whole human race lived as really authentic Christians under the structured society of the past; gives too much credit to structure for whatever was good in the past; and expects structure to solve the problems of today.

Pope Paul VI

A striking example of what the new generation would call the structured approach is the recent address on sanctity by Pope Paul VI to an audience group in Rome. As reported in the press, and in translations so varied that they must be inexact, the pope contrasts the attitudes of some of the new generation with the traditional Church view. The pope is rightly disturbed about the extreme re-belliousness, immorality, resistance to law and order which must be reported to him from all over the world. To him, the established order of Christianity is stabilized by the body of laws and teachings of the Church and is exemplified in the holy lives of dutiful followers of Christ. To him, this order is "sacrosanct."

As he looks at the world, he sees widespread "indocility and re-bellion" to this "tempered moral code" and to "those moral precepts *the Church* prescribes for the sanctification and moral dignity of *her children*."

"The aggiornamento . . . is not to be thought of as blunting the tempered moral code of the modern Catholic but . . . makes him more aware of his duties."

". . . We are living in a period of profound transformation of thought and custom which explains how certain traditional standards are often being called into question, standards which induce those who observe them to live good, orderly, and saintly lives. A spirit of criticism and even of indocility and rebellion is calling into question norms of Christian life, of ecclesiastical comportment and religious perfection that are sacrosanct."

". . . The notion of obedience . . . is challenged and its constitutional function in the order of the ecclesiastical community is contested."

To the new generation, this is the structured approach in classical language, however imperfect the translation may be. Those among the new generation who are genuinely concerned about authentic Christian living—there are many, and it is of them that I am speaking, not the beatnik rebels who wish to throw off all moral restraint—do not question for a minute that the pope had a right to oppose the views of the extremists among their generation, or that, to the older generation, this approach of dealing with a whole movement by singling out the extremist's position for refutation in sweeping general statements may have made some sense.

But the sad fact is that the new generation doesn't respond to this approach at all. It doesn't reach them. It doesn't strike that responsive chord in them which must be touched if it is to spark the inner process of motivation. To them, the exclusive concern with the structured position fails to acknowledge real needs of people who are not in authority. Nothing so far reported in the statement recognizes any good in any of the new generation's thinking, or admits there are any standards that call for rethinking, or that the sincere ones in the new generation might have some worthwhile criticisms to make that should be listened to. The world that might once have been influenced by such a sermon is dying. It says nothing that is relevant to the new world. This is the way they see it.

If you explain to the new generation that the pope was not handling all the problems of the new generation, that he was addressing pilgrims from many parts of the world during a mid-week audience on real errors held by extremists, they reply with insistent objections, "But even if he didn't mean us, others will apply his words to us. This is the way structure operates. We don't repudiate all authority. We do criticize things. We call some traditional standards into question. We don't think everything that is called a norm of Christian conduct or of ecclesiastical comportment (whatever that is), is sacrosanct. We think the notion of obedience, as we have often seen it enforced, should be contested. But the pope will be quoted against us. This is structure."

You point out to them that the pope has a right on such occasion to discuss only general themes. You show them that the same pope quoted in the same diocesan paper, in an address sent to another group, assembled at the famous Semaine Sociale (Social Week) in France, said, "The reorganization of cities calls for bold decisions." "In humanizing great cities," he said, "Christians must act without fear of offending traditional patterns of behavior." Later he repeated the need for "bold decisions" to save the cities' people, and said that planners must stand up against "claims of tradition when these are simply brought forth as an excuse to hinder solutions." He also said "It is useless weeping over the past. We must face the current situation and find the solutions to the various problems that have arisen."

The new generation retorts, "The pope in the second address is not referring to churchmen, but to laymen, politicians, and property owners. The laymen's traditions don't get treated as sacrosanct by churchmen, but don't ask the churchmen to question their own codes. They are sacrosanct. Obedience, not bold decisions, must greet the traditional formulas of churchmen."

Then you begin to wonder if the two generations are ever going to understand each other. The new generation wishes the pope had given a different talk on the tension between authority and criticism because they know full well that his talk is just the type of thing that many of the older generation will pick up eagerly to use against them quoting the pope out of context.

Actually, the pope gave another address two weeks later in which he did show genuine concern about the right use and abuse of authority in the Church. In it he cautioned, "But remember that it is difficult to form an exact concept of authority and particularly of ecclesiastical authority. Experience and history offer us images of this which are not always faithful and are not always happy ones. It is necessary to deepen the idea of the authority of the Church, to purify it of forms which are not essential to it . . . and to return it to its original and Christian principle."

Even on a subject as old and basic as authority, we still have a long way to go, it seems. But it is the problem of structure, rather than authority directly, which bothers the new generation.

The authoritarianism of structure is very often paternal, which makes its visage less forbidding and its motives seem purer. Yet in almost any confrontation with structure the new generation finds structure defended by an appeal to authority without critical self-examination as to whether authority might not be more effectively applied to a different approach to problems. Whenever structure is questioned, the authority behind it tends to defend authority itself rather than to examine the reasonableness of the questions. Authority gives structure, in all its subtle ramifications, a protection of prestige and power, and a guarantee of immunity from criticism which it doesn't always deserve on its own merits.

This is, as I see it, what is meant to the new generation by "structure." In civil life something like it is known as "the establishment," or the "power bloc." It exists in all walks of life. But there is one important difference: directly behind the ecclesiastical establishment there is somewhere, truly, and inescapably—God. But precisely where?

The Holy Spirit

This is the problem. Is the Holy Spirit only behind static structure? Only behind movement and change? Only on the side of the older generation? Only behind the new?

Putting the problem this way makes the state of the question obviously absurd. The evil word, the misleading word, the paralyzing and confusing word is "only."

Somehow we must find a place for the word "also," and work out the proper proportions in practice between *only* and *also*. The good on both sides should be developed. The limitations of each side should be recognized in dynamic perspective.

There is an old saying that there are two sides to every story. This is not quite true. There are at least four sides to every story: the good and the bad on each side. Each side usually knows best its own virtues and the other's faults.

Can we not get together and see all four sides for the sake of the genuine good on both sides?

The defenders of structure know, love, and respect the infallible Church, divine revelation, the apostolic traditions, the unerring guide, the solicitous mother of all, the sublime truths, the unshakable rock, the light of truth, the commission from Christ, the constant support

of so many good things and the fearless opposition to so many evils
the spiritual supremacy of eternal truth, the voice of the Holy Spirit
the authority of God, and the record of the Church—on the good
side. To them, these are sacred. They know their value. They have
seen the good they have accomplished.

To the older generation, it seems that the new generation does not
give enough attention to the substantial achievements of the Church
in its actual historical situations; it exaggerates the power bloc of
structure; and unduly emphasizes failures and blunders which it attributes solely to *structure* within the Church.

The new generation replies that structure is blind to its own shortcomings and, because it doesn't face them honestly, resists reform.
It points to the record: corrupt Italian and Spanish control of the
medieval papacy; the Galileo case; the Inquisition; Tetzel; church
benefices to powerful families; the illiteracy of the lower clergy until
Trent (and after); the luxurious living of popes and the wealth of
religious orders and bishops in the midst of widespread squalor of
the people for centuries; papal armies in battle; the passivity toward
slavery until late in the nineteenth century; the resistance to the Bible
in the vernacular; the historic opposition to all democratic government; the sycophancy toward the wealthy even to this day; the
twenty centuries of subservience to the clergy demanded of the laity;
the second-rate citizenship accorded to women in the Church; the
catastrophic decay of the clergy and hierarchy before the Reformation; the unconscionable delays of the Roman marriage tribunal in
handling appeals for nullity; the centuries of all but silence, until
Leo XIII, on the full *rights* of laboring men, women, and children;
the colonialism accompanying so many missionary efforts until the
twentieth century; the destitute, religious illiteracy of ninety percent
of the Latin Americans for three centuries, along with its inexplicably
high ratio of bishops; the feeble impact on intellectuals, scientists, and
artists made by the Church in America; the liturgical vacuum in
Catholic lives almost everywhere until recently; the failure of systematic Catholic theology and philosophy to make any impact on the
non-Catholic intellectual community of East or West for centuries;
the progressive defection from even basic Christianity of large numbers of Germans, French, English, North and South Americans,
Belgians, Italians, including Romans, not to mention others, for over
a hundred years.

The new generation may be too sharply critical of others and too little critical of themselves, but they are realistic enough to see that structure, somehow, for all its backing by authority, permitted these abuses and defects and was mighty slow to admit them and to reform. They question seriously the permanent, immutable value of a structure system which has in its possession the good news of the Gospel, the channels of grace, and the presence of the Holy Spirit and has failed to touch interiorly the vast majority of mankind in twenty centuries, as it was commissioned to do.

And the new generation asks, if the defects of the Church in the past can be partially explained away by appealing to historic conditions, why can't a new approach be defended in the light of new historic conditions?

This is the structured Church of the older generation as seen by both sides, and if the position of the older generation is too briefly stated here, it is because it has been voluminously presented before, whereas, until recently, much too little of the new generation's thinking was given a hearing.

The New Generation

Now let's look at the new generation from both sides.

The new generation looks on itself as one that has grown up in a world of insecurity amid plenty and uncertainty amid unlimited power of production and destruction. It doesn't know the solution to all problems, but it also knows that the older generation doesn't know all the answers either.

It sees the UN in constant debate. Labor and management are in constant debate. The Vatican Council was in almost constant debate. Educators, politicians, economists, military strategists, art critics, religious leaders, etc., are in constant debate. The new generation has seen almost every value in human life, from the most sublime theological concepts to the latest method of warfare, submitted to reexamination within one generation. If the older generation concludes from this that too much criticism causes all this unrest, the new generation concludes that too many things need criticism.

The new generation has heard that America is the greatest land of freedom and of prosperity and has learned that one third is helplessly impoverished. They have been lectured on the common good and have witnessed all too common hardships of individuals for whom nobody cared. They know that half the world goes to bed hungry every night and that overweight is a problem to the other half. They hear sermons on what faith can do for men, and they know that much of the human race couldn't care less.

They are unmoved by generalizations about society, common good, eternal truths which they know have left individuals helpless in tragedy. So they are *existentialists* and *personalists*. They are not selfish individualists. To them person means the human center of a complex of relationships. They know they are not fully persons until they fulfill the potential of their entire personality. This does not mean abstract duties to the abstract human race. It is literally love of one's neighbor, black, white, rich, poor, privileged, or destitute. It is sharing. It is experiencing as a person the life and love of other persons at Mass, in work, at play, in conversation, at prayer, in love, in poverty, at every level—now!

They do not want to start with conclusions and outlines the older generation inherited, accepted, tried, and couldn't make work too well. They want to work out many things for themselves. They do not trust formulas of wisdom handed down to them; they want to acquire their own wisdom through the only way it can be acquired— personal experience.

The older generation shudders at this "immature" approach to the complexities of life. It would like to shield them from the mistakes of the past as far as possible. It would like to prepare them for the responsibilities of the future, but at the same time it would deprive them of the risks and hardships which are necessary to produce wisdom.

In the eyes of the best and most discerning of the older generation, the new generation doesn't seem to realize that one day they, too, will need order, obedience, continuity, sacrifice of individuals for the common good, moral laws, clear dogmatic truths, and a stable society based on laws and the acceptance of laws by the community. The new generation appears too impatient, too inexperienced to appreciate the necessity of these values.

The new generation gives the impression of wanting to be allowed to think and act as though nothing that has ever been learned from experience or history is applicable to them; as though nothing of the past is valid for the present; as though each generation must begin over from scratch because life wasn't perfect before.

To many, some of the new generation are not willing to start so completely over that they will go back to frontier log cabins, home-spun clothes, cold water, and wagon trains. Lots of them like scholar-ships, allowances, universities all set up for them, government sub-sidies, credit cards, libraries, automobiles, places to go for which someone else pays taxes, etc. They are willing to join the Peace Corps and the service groups, but they are apt to forget that millions of dollars and years of work by other people, who accepted structure, had to be enlisted to make these programs possible.

The older generation has to admit that many of the new genera-tion, to their credit, are willing to live in slums, give up their vaca-tions, live on next to nothing, suffer with the poor they serve, and strive heroically to equip themselves to be of service to the under-privileged.

But far too many of the new generation seem to want to experi-ment with life and learn for themselves within the framework of an established society whose values they reject. They are willing to face now the possibility that their present ideas may not work out. They are not quite willing to see that, if their generation fails, at least one more generation after them will fail, too, through their fault.

The new generation runs the danger of putting *too much hope* in untried experimentation. It prefers person-to-person relationships and small group association, because they are not complex and need no structure, but it fails to see that society cannot survive or progress if it remains as just so many cells, disconnected, unrelated, unorganized toward the good of the whole body. It fails to realize sufficiently that, by demanding only its own approach, it may be seriously jeopardiz-ing *continuity* in human life.

Among the things certainly to be recognized as worthwhile and necessary in human life, two should be emphasized here: the right of a person to develop in his own world, and the right of the next generation to start out with a measure of security in life. Overin-sistence on structure can prevent the first. Total denial of any struc-ture can destroy the second. Order and freedom; structure and ex-perimentation; continuity and personal fulfillment;—these are the values that must be balanced in any intelligent human growth.

The rigidity of structure has got to go, but some structure is neces-sary. The older generation wants to start with structure and yield as little and as slowly as possible to change. The new generation wants to start with free discussion and concede as slowly as possible to a minimum of structure in the end.

Can there ever be a meeting of minds between these two generations? I honestly don't know, but I think it is tragic if both sides don't try, for mankind needs very much what both are trying to achieve from opposite points of view. Great harm can be done by those within the structured system who want to extend authority and restrict freedom in defense of an immutable historic structure. Equally great harm and great loss can come to this new generation and to their successors, no matter how exhilarating the present adventuresome atmosphere of revolt is, if they leave to posterity no progress, no conclusions of their own or anyone else's, and can only say to their children and their descendants, "Well, we tried. We have nothing to tell you from our experience except that we enjoyed it. Anything else would be to revert to structure. You'll have to find out everything for yourselves. We have had our own experience. It is your turn to have yours. Nothing can be handed on. Start over and live life your way."

There is no easy answer, but we *must* strive toward one. There are four sides to this problem and all four must be heard. As it is now, each generation exaggerates the faults of the other's position and tends to idealize its own virtues. Each side wants to preserve certain values and to eliminate certain dangers. The older generation wishes the new generation would be more concerned about law and order; the new generation wishes the older generation cared more for freedom and personal fulfillment.

As long as we stand apart this way, there will never be a meeting of minds. I recommend that representatives of both sides come together, but not until a considerable amount of homework is done. Try stating the position of the other generation as you see it. State explicitly its values and its weaknesses. Then do the same for your own generation. After this is done, exchange your statements with representatives of the other generation and let each edit the other's copy. Point out what they have misrepresented, but face up to their criticisms, if they have validity.

Then try to come together. There will be disagreement for a while and much discussion, but we must narrow the gap. Each side can learn from the other only if we come together in charity and in truth.